KU-307-271

THE CHEESE AND THE WORMS

THE CHEESE AND THE WORMS

THE COSMOS OF A SIXTEENTH-CENTURY MILLER

CARLO GINZBURG

Translated by John and Anne Tedeschi

ROUTLEDGE & KEGAN PAUL
London and Henley

Originally published in Italy as *Il formaggio e i vermi: Il cosmo di un mugnaio del '500,* copyright © 1976 by Giulio Einaudi editore

First published in Great Britain in 1980
by Routledge & Kegan Paul Ltd
39 Store Street,
London WCIE 7DD and
Broadway House,
Newtown Road,
Henley-on-Thames,
Oxon RG9 1EN
Printed in the United States of America by Universal Lithographers, Inc.

English translation copyright © 1980 by The Johns Hopkins University Press and Routledge & Kegan Paul Ltd

No part of this book may be reproduced in any form without permission from the publisher, except for the quotation of brief passages in criticism

ISBN 0 7100 05911

Illustrations on pp. iii, viii, xi, xiii, xxvii, 1, and 179 are from the emblem book collection of the Newberry Library.

Illustrations on p. xxv are from *Il sogno dil Caravia.*

Tout ce qui est intéressant se passe dans l'ombre.
On ne sait rien de la véritable histoire des hommes.

—Céline

CONTENTS

TRANSLATORS' NOTE

We take great pleasure in presenting in English translation Carlo Ginzburg's *Il formaggio e i vermi,* a lively and ingenious attempt to reconstruct the intellectual world of a sixteenth-century miller who lived out his days in a remote Friulian village. The book has been rightly hailed as one of the most significant recent contributions to a burgeoning field of study, the popular culture of early-modern Europe. We are hopeful that the present endeavor will help to draw attention to the need of making other distinguished Italian works of history available to a larger public through translation.

The Cheese and the Worms differs slightly from the original Einaudi edition published in 1976. New are a second preface especially written for this version, the insertion of a date in the first page of the text, and the reply to a critic at pp. 154–55 n. No systematic attempt has been made to bring the references up to date. However, the appearance of recent contributions by Elizabeth Eisenstein, Emmanuel Le Roy Ladurie, and a handful of others could not be ignored and have been noted at appropriate points in the book. English titles of works in other languages used by the author have been supplied whenever they were known to us.

On the organization and procedures of the Roman Holy Office—the institution whose insistence on a full recording of all events transpiring before its tribunal made the present study possible—there is unfortunately no modern comprehensive study available in any language. A few observations, however, are in order. The Roman Inquisition, founded in 1542 by Pope Paul III as a direct response to the Protestant challenge in Italy, should not be confused with the Inquisition in Spain or other areas of Europe nor with the Inquisition of the Middle Ages, which was the subject of Henry Charles Lea's history. The Inquisition, far from being a monolithic structure, was an institution that experienced development and change, in terms of organization, procedures, and definitions of the law, throughout its long history. The two stages, medieval and modern, must not be understood as a single phenomenon. Furthermore, while *moral* justice was impossible in a context where the Catholic Church felt, together with virtually all other secular and religious authorities on both sides of the Alps, that it had the right, even the duty, to persecute those who differed in their religious beliefs, *legal* justice in sixteenth-century terms was dispensed by the Roman Inquisition. It was not a drumhead court, a chamber of horrors, or a judicial labyrinth from which escape was impossible. Capricious and arbitrary decisions, misuse of authority, and wanton abuse of human rights were not tolerated. Rome watched over the provincial tribunals, enforced the observance of what was, for the times, an essentially moderate code of law, and maintained, to the extent that a consensus existed, uniformity of practice.

A word of explanation should be given on the subject of inquisitorial record keeping. A permanent and indispensable member of every inquisitorial court was the notary (or a cleric deputized to assume this function), who transcribed in writing as the legal manuals required "not only all the defendant's responses and any statements he might make, but also what he might utter during the torture, even his sighs, his cries, his laments and tears" (E. Masini, *Sacro Arsenale* [Genoa, 1621], p. 123). Since most trial records were generally reviewed by the supreme tribunal in Rome before the pronouncement of sentence, the practice of recording legal proceedings in their entirety was designed to discourage irregularities, including the tendency of some examiners to ask leading or suggestive questions. The notary's charge was to transcribe everything that transpired verbatim. On occasion, however, as portions of the present book indicate, both questions and answers were reported in the third person. The author naturally is obliged to place such passages within quotation marks because they are part of the trial record even if they are not direct quotes. An example of this occurs in section 20 where a question by the inquisitor is transformed by the notary into an indirect form of discourse: the defendant is exhorted to name "all his accomplices, or else more rigorous measures would be taken against him. . . . "

Further brief introductory remarks on the subject are provided in John Tedeschi, "Preliminary Observations on Writing a History of the Roman Inquisition," in *Continuity and Discontinuity in Church History*, ed. F.

F. Church and T. George (Leiden, 1979), pp. 232–49. Readers wishing to learn more about the productive career of Carlo Ginzburg, the brilliant young scholar who is the author of this book, are invited to turn to the profile by Anne J. Schutte, "Carlo Ginzburg," *Journal of Modern History* 48 (1976): 296–315.

Our translation benefited greatly from the many constructive criticisms and suggestions received from the author and from the staff and consultants of The Johns Hopkins University Press, especially Henry Y. K. Tom, Mary Lou Kenney, and Eduardo Saccone. Professors Paolo Cherchi of The University of Chicago and Ronnie Terpening of Loyola University, Chicago, struggled with us patiently over a number of mystifying terms of sixteenth-century Friulian dialect. Bernard E. Wilson of The Newberry Library read the entire manuscript of the text and left his mark on almost every page. We are extremely grateful to him as well as to all others named and unnamed whose advice and support helped to bring *The Cheese and the Worms* into being.

With mixed sentiments of sadness and relief we take leave of this book and its quixotic protagonist, Menocchio. We feel confident that both will capture the reader's esteem and affection, as they did ours.

J. T.
A. C. T.

PREFACE TO THE ENGLISH EDITION

As frequently happens, this research, too, came about by chance. In 1962 I spent part of the summer in Udine. In the extremely rich (and at that time still unexplored) deposit of inquisitorial papers preserved in the Archivio della Curia Arcivescovile of that city I was searching for trials against a strange Friulian sect whose members were identified with witches and witchdoctors by the judges. Later I wrote a book about them (*I benandanti: Stregoneria e culti agrari tra Cinquecento e Seicento* [1966; reprint-ed., Turin, 1979]). Leafing through one of these manuscript volumes of trials I came upon an extremely long sentence. One of the accusations against the defendant was that he maintained the world had its origin in putrefaction. This phrase instantly captured my curiosity; but I was looking for other things: witches, witchdoctors, *benandanti*. I wrote down the number of the trial. In the next few years that notation periodically leaped out from among my papers and from my memory. In 1970 I resolved to try to understand what that statement could have meant for the person by whom it had been uttered. At that time what I knew about him was only his name: Domenico Scandella, called Menocchio.

This book tells his story. Thanks to an abundant documentation we are able to learn about his readings and his discussions, his thoughts and his sentiments—fears, hopes, ironies, rages, despairs. Every now and then the directness of the sources brings him very close to us: a man like ourselves, one of us.

But he is also a man very different from us. The analytical reconstruction of this difference was necessary, in order to reconstruct the physiognomy, partly obscured, of his culture, and of the social context in which it had taken shape. It has been possible to trace Menocchio's complicated relationship with written culture: the books (or, more precisely, some of the books) that he read and the manner in which he read them. In this way there emerged a filter, a grill that Menocchio interposed unconsciously between himself and the texts, whether obscure or illustrious, which came into his hands. This filter, on the other hand, presupposed an oral culture that was the patrimony not only of Menocchio but also of a vast segment of sixteenth-century society. Consequently, an investigation initially pivoting on an individual, moreover an apparently unusual one, ended by developing into a general hypothesis on the popular culture (more precisely, peasant culture) of preindustrial Europe, in the age marked by the spread of printing and the Protestant Reformation—and by the repression of the latter in Catholic countries. This hypothesis can be linked to what has already been proposed, in very similar terms, by Mikhail Bakhtin, and can be summed up by the term "circularity": between the culture of the dominant classes and that of the subordinate classes there existed, in preindustrial Europe, a circular relationship composed of reciprocal influences, which traveled from low to high as well as from high to low. (Exactly the opposite, therefore, of "the concept of the absolute autonomy and continuity of peasant culture" that has been attributed to me by one critic—see notes pp. 154–55.)

The Cheese and the Worms is intended to be a story as well as a piece of historical writing. Thus, it is addressed to the general reader as well as to the specialist. Probably only the latter will read the notes—which have been deliberately placed at the end of the book, without numerical references, so as not to encumber the narrative. But I hope that both will recognize in this episode an unnoticed but extraordinary fragment of a reality, half obliterated, which implicitly poses a series of questions for our own culture and for us.

I should like to express my warmest thanks to my friends John and Anne Tedeschi for the patience and intelligence with which they have translated this book.

PREFACE TO THE ITALIAN EDITION

1

In the past historians could be accused of wanting to know only about "the great deeds of kings," but today this is certainly no longer true. More and more they are turning toward what their predecessors passed over in silence, discarded, or simply ignored. "Who built Thebes of the seven gates?" Bertold Brecht's "literate worker" was already asking. The sources tell us nothing about these anonymous masons, but the question retains all its significance.

2

The scarcity of evidence about the behavior and attitudes of the subordinate classes of the past is certainly the major, though not the only, obstacle faced by research of this type. But there are exceptions. This book relates the story of a miller of the Friuli, Domenico Scandella, called Menocchio, who was burned at the stake by order of the Holy Office after a life passed in almost complete obscurity. The records of his two trials, held fifteen years apart, offer a rich picture of his thoughts and feelings, of his imaginings and aspirations. Other documents give us information about his economic activities and the lives of his children. We even have pages in his own hand and a partial list of what he read (he was, in fact, able to read and write). Though we would like to know much more about Menocchio, what we do know permits us to reconstruct a fragment of what is usually called "the culture of the lower classes" or even "popular culture."

3

The existence of different cultural levels within so-called civilized societies is the premise of the discipline that has come to be defined variously as folklore, social anthropology, history of popular traditions, and European ethnology. But the use of the term "culture" to define the complex of attitudes, beliefs, codes of behavior, etc., of the subordinate classes in a given historical period is relatively recent and was borrowed from cultural anthropology. Only through the concept of "primitive culture" have we come to recognize that those who were once paternalistically described as "the common people in civilized society" in fact possessed a culture of their own. In this way the bad conscience of colonialism joined itself to the bad conscience of class oppression; if only verbally we have now gone beyond not only the antiquated conception of folklore as the mere collecting of curious facts but also the attitude that saw in the ideas, beliefs, and world views of the lower classes nothing but an incoherent fragmentary mass of theories that had been originally worked out by the dominant classes perhaps many centuries before. At this point a dialogue began concerning the relationship between the culture of the subordinate classes and that of the dominant classes. To what degree is the first, in fact, subordinate to the second? And, in what measure does lower class culture express a partially independent content? Is it possible to speak of reciprocal movement between the two levels of culture?

Historians have approached questions such as these only recently and with a certain diffidence. Undoubtedly, this is due in part to the widespread persistence of an aristocratic conception of culture. Too often, original ideas or beliefs have been considered by definition to be a product of the upper classes, and their diffusion among the subordinate classes a mechanical fact of little or no interest. At best, what is noted is the "decay" and the "distortion" experienced by those ideas or beliefs in the course of their transmission. But the diffidence of historians has another, more understandable, reason of a methodological rather than an ideological order. In contrast to anthropologists and students of popular traditions, historians obviously begin at a great disadvantage. Even today the culture of the subordinate class is largely *oral,* and it was even more so in centuries past. Since historians are unable to converse with the peasants of the sixteenth century (and, in any case, there is no guarantee that they would understand them), they must depend almost entirely on written sources (and possibly archeological evidence). These are doubly indirect for they are *written,* and written in general by individuals who were more or less openly attached to the dominant culture. This means that the thoughts, the beliefs, and the aspirations of the peasants and artisans of the past reach us (if and when they do) almost always through distorting viewpoints and intermediaries. At the very outset this is enough to discourage attempts at such research.

But the terms of the problem are drastically altered when we propose to study, not "culture *produced by* the popular classes," but rather "culture *imposed on* the popular classes." This is what Robert Mandrou attempted to do more than a decade ago on the basis of sources that had been exploited only slightly up to that time: the literature of *colportage,* those inexpensive, crudely printed booklets, (almanacs, songsters, recipes, tales of miracles or saints' lives), which were sold at fairs or in the countryside by itinerant vendors. An inventory of the principal recurring themes led Mandrou to formulate a somewhat hasty conclusion. He defined this literature as "escapist," suggesting that it had nourished for centuries a view of the world permeated by fatalism and determinism, the miraculous and the occult, thereby preventing those whom it affected from becoming aware of their own social and political conditions, and playing, perhaps intentionally, a reactionary role.

Mandrou did not limit himself to the evaluation of almanacs and songsters as documents of a literature deliberately intended for the masses. With a hasty and unjustified transition he defined them as instruments of a victorious process of acculturation, "the reflection . . . of the world view" of the popular classes of the *Ancien Régime,* tacitly attributing complete cultural passivity to the latter and giving a disproportionately large influence to the literature of *colportage.* The peasants who were able to read, in a society that was three-quarters illiterate, were certainly a very small minority. Even if press runs were apparently very high and each one of those booklets was probably read aloud, thus reaching large segments of the illiterate population, it is absurd to equate "the culture produced by the popular classes" with "the culture imposed on the masses," and to identify the features of popular culture exclusively by means of the maxims, the precepts, and the fables of the *Bibliothèque bleue.* The shortcut taken by Mandrou to circumvent the difficulties inherent in the reconstruction of an oral culture actually only takes us back to the starting point.

A similar shortcut (but starting with a very different set of presuppositions) was used with notable naiveté by Geneviève Bollème. In the literature of *colportage* this scholar has seen, instead of Mandrou's instrument of an (improbable) victorious acculturation, the spontaneous expression (which is even more improbable) of an original and autonomous popular culture permeated by religious values. In this popular religion based on Christ's humanity and poverty, the natural and the supernatural, fear of death and the drive for life, endurance of injustice and revolt against oppression were seen as being harmoniously fused. With this method we substitute for "popular literature" a "literature destined for the people" and thus remain, without realizing it, in the sphere of a culture produced by the dominant classes. It is true that Bollème suggested incidentally the existence of a gap between the pamphlet literature and the way in which it was in all probability read by the popular classes. But even this valuable idea remains unfruitful since it leads to the postulate of a "popular creativity," which can't be defined and is apparently unattainable, having been part of a vanished oral tradition.

4

The stereotyped and saccharine image of popular culture that results from this research is very different from what is outlined by Mikhail Bakhtin in a lively and fundamental book on the relations between Rabelais and the popular culture of his day. Here it is suggested that *Gargantua* or *Pantagruel,* books that perhaps no peasant ever read, teach us more about peasant culture than the *Almanach des bergers,* which must have circulated widely in the French countryside. The center of the culture portrayed by Bakhtin is the carnival: myth and ritual in which converge the celebration of fertility and abundance, the jesting inversion of all values and established orders, the cosmic sense of the destructive and regenerative passing of time. According to Bakhtin, this vision of the world, which had evolved through popular culture over the course of centuries, was in marked contrast to the dogmatism and conservatism of the culture of the dominant classes, especially in the Middle Ages. By keeping this disparity in mind, the work of Rabelais becomes comprehensible, its comic quality linked directly to the carnival themes of popular culture: cultural dichotomy, then—but also a circular, reciprocal influence between the cultures of subordinate and ruling classes that was especially intense in the first half of the sixteenth century.

These are hypotheses to a certain extent, and not all of them equally well documented. But the principal failing in Bakhtin's fine book is probably something else. The protagonists of popular culture whom he has tried to describe, the peasants and the artisans, speak to us almost exclusively through the words of Rabelais. The very wealth of research possibilities indicated by Bakhtin makes us wish for a direct study of lower-class society free of intermediaries. But for reasons already mentioned, it is extremely difficult in this area of scholarship to find a direct rather than an indirect method of approach.

5

Certainly there is no need to exaggerate when we talk about distortions. The fact that a source is not "objective" (for that matter, neither is an inventory) does not mean that it is useless. A hostile chronicle can furnish precious testimony about a peasant community in revolt. The analysis of the "carnival at Romans" by Emmanuel Le Roy Ladurie is outstanding in this sense. And, on the whole, in comparison with the methodological uncertainty and the poor results of the majority of studies devoted explicitly to the definition of popular culture in preindustrial Europe, the research of Natalie Zemon Davis and Edward P. Thompson on the "Charivari," which throws light on particular aspects of that culture, is of an exceptionally high level. In short, even meager, scattered, and obscure documentation can be put to good use.

But the fear of falling into a notorious, naive positivism, combined with the exasperated awareness of the ideological distortion that may lurk behind the most normal and seemingly innocent process of perception, prompts many historians today to discard popular culture together with the sources that provide a more or less distorted picture of it. After having criticized (and not without reason) the studies mentioned above on the literature of *colportage,* a number of scholars have begun to ask themselves whether "popular culture exists outside the act that suppresses it." The question is rhetorical, and the reply is obviously negative. This type of skepticism seems paradoxical at first glance since behind it stand the studies of Michel Foucault, the scholar who, with his *Histoire de la folie,* has most authoritatively drawn attention to the exclusions, prohibitions, and limits through which our culture came into being historically. But on second glance, it is a paradox only in appearance. What interests Foucault primarily are the act and the criteria of the exclusion, the excluded a little less so. The attitude that led him to write *Les mots et les choses* and *L'archéologie du savoir* was already at least partly implicit in the *Histoire de la folie,* probably stimulated by Jacques Derrida's facile, nihilistic objections to the *Histoire.* Derrida contended that it is not possible to speak of madness in a language historically grounded in western reason and hence in the process that has led to the repression of madness itself. Basically, he maintained that the Archimidean point from which Foucault embarked on his research neither can nor does exist. At this point Foucault's ambitious project of an *archéologie du silence* becomes transformed into silence pure and simple—perhaps accompanied by mute contemplation of an aesthetic kind.

Evidence of this regression can be found in a recent volume containing essays by Foucault and some of his associates plus various documents concerned with the early-nineteenth-century case of a young peasant who killed his mother, his sister, and a brother. The analysis is based principally on the interaction of two languages of exclusion, the judicial and the psychiatric, which tend to cancel each other out. The person of the assassin, Pierre Rivière, is relegated to secondary importance—and precisely at the time when the testimony he had written at the request of his judges to explain how he had come to commit the triple murder is finally being published. The possibility of interpreting this text is specifically ruled out because it is held to be impossible to do so without distortion or without subjecting it to an extraneous system of reasoning. The only legitimate reactions that remain are "astonishment" and "silence."

Irrationalism of an aesthetic nature is what emerges from this course of research. The obscure and contradictory relationship of Pierre Rivière with the dominant culture is barely mentioned: his reading (almanacs, books of piety, but also *Le bon sens du curé Meslier)* is simply ignored. Instead he is described wandering in the forest after the crime, as "a man without culture . . . an animal without instinct . . . a mythical being, a monster whom it is impossible to define because he is outside any recognizable order." We are dazzled by an absolute extraneousness that, in reality, results from the refusal to analyze and interpret. The only discourse that constitutes a radical alternative to the lies of constituted society is represented by these victims of social exclusion—a discourse that passes over the crime and the cannibalism and becomes embodied indifferently either in the memoir written by Rivière or in his matricide. It is a populism with its symbols reversed. A "black" populism—but populism just the same.

6

Enough has been said to demonstrate the confusion in the concept of "popular culture." First there is attributed to the subordinate classes of preindustrial society a passive accommodation to the cultural sub-products proffered by the dominant classes (Mandrou), then an implied suggestion of at least partly autonomous values in respect to the culture of the latter (Bollème), and finally an absolute extraneousness that places the subordinate class actually beyond or, better yet, in a state prior to *culture* (Foucault). To be sure, Bakhtin's hypothesis of a reciprocal influence between lower class and dominant cultures is much more fruitful. But to specify the methods and the periods of this influence (Jacques Le Goff has begun to do so with excellent results) means running into the problem caused by a documentation, which, in the case of popular culture, is almost always indirect. To what extent are the possible elements of the dominant culture found in popular culture the result of a more or less deliberate acculturation, or of a more or less spontaneous convergence, rather than of an unconscious distortion of the source, inclined obviously to lead what is unknown back to the known and the familiar?

I faced a similar problem years ago in the midst of research on witchcraft trials of the late sixteenth and early seventeenth centuries. I wanted to understand what witchcraft really meant to its protagonists, the witches and sorcerers. But the available documentation (trials and especially treatises of demonology) served only as a barrier, hopelessly preventing a true grasp of popular witchcraft. Everywhere I ran up against inquisitorial concepts of witchcraft derived from sources of learned origin. Only the discovery of a current of previously ignored beliefs connected with the *benandanti* opened a breach in that wall. A deeply-rooted stratum of basically autonomous popular beliefs began to emerge by way of the discrepancies between the questions of the judges and the replies of the accused—discrepancies unattributable to either suggestive questioning or to torture.

The disclosures made by Menocchio, the miller of the Friuli who is the protagonist of this book, in some ways constitute a case similar to that of the *benandanti.* Here, too, the fact that many of Menocchio's utterances cannot be reduced to familiar themes permits us to perceive a previously untapped level of popular beliefs, of obscure peasant mythologies. But what renders Menocchio's case that much more complicated is the fact that these obscure popular elements are grafted onto an extremely clear and logical complex of ideas, from religious radicalism, to a naturalism tending toward the scientific, to utopian aspirations of social reform. The astonishing convergence between the ideas of an unknown miller of the Friuli and those of the most refined and informed intellectual groups of his day forcefully raises the question of cultural diffusion formulated by Bakhtin.

7

Before examining the degree to which Menocchio's confessions assist us in understanding this problem, it is only proper to ask what relevance the ideas and beliefs of a single individual of his social level can have. At a time when virtual teams of scholars have embarked on vast projects in the *quantitative* history of ideas or *serialized* religious history, to undertake a narrow investigation on a solitary miller may seem paradoxical or absurd, practically a return to handweaving in an age of power looms. It is significant that the very possibility of research of this kind has been ruled out *a priori* by those who, like François Furet, have maintained that the reintegration of the subordinate classes into general history can only be accomplished through "number and anonymity," by means of demography and sociology, "the quantitative study of past societies." Although the lower classes are no longer ignored by historians, they seem condemned, nevertheless, to remain "silent."

But if the sources offer us the possibility of reconstructing not only indistinct masses but also individual personalities, it would be absurd to ignore it. To extend the historic concept of "individual" in the direction of the lower classes is a worthwhile objective. Certainly, there is the risk of succumbing to the anecdote, to the notorious *Histoire événementielle* (which is not only, nor necessarily, political history). But it is not an inevitable risk. A number of biographical studies have shown that in a modest individual who is himself lacking in significance and for this very reason representative, it is still possible to trace, as in a microcosm, the characteristics of an entire social stratum in a specific historical period, whether it be the Austrian nobility or the lower clergy in seventeenth-century England.

Is this, then, also the case with Menocchio? Not in the least. He cannot be considered a "typical" peasant (in the sense of "average," or "in the statistical majority") of his age: this is clear from his relative isolation in the town. In the eyes of his fellows, Menocchio was a man somewhat different from others. But this distinctiveness had very definite limits. As with language, culture offers to the individual a horizon of latent possibilities—a flexible and invisible cage in which he can exercise his own conditional liberty. With rare clarity and understanding, Menocchio articulated the language that history put at his disposal. Thus, it becomes possible to trace in his disclosures in a particularly distinct, almost exaggerated form, a series of convergent elements, which, in a similar group of sources that are contemporary or slightly later, appear lost or are barely mentioned. A few soundings confirm the existence of traits reduceable to a common peasant culture. In conclusion, even a limited case (and Menocchio certainly is this) can be representative: in a negative sense, because it helps to explain what should be understood, in a given situation, as being "in the statistical majority"; or, positively, because it permits us to define the latent possibilities of something (popular culture) otherwise known to us only through fragmentary and distorted documents, almost all of which originate in the "archives of the repression."

With this, it is not my intention to pass judgment on qualitative versus quantitative research; quite simply, it must be emphasized that, as far as the history of the subordinate classes is concerned, the precision of the latter cannot do without (cannot *yet* do without, that is) the notorious impressionism of the former. E. P. Thompson's telling remark about "the gross reiterative impressionism of a computer, which repeats one conformity *ad nauseam* while obliterating all evidence for which it has not been programmed" is literally true in the sense that the computer, obviously, executes but does not think. On the other hand, only a series of specific in-depth investigations may permit the development of an articulate program to submit to the computer.

Let us take a concrete example. In recent years several quantitative studies have been made on the production and diffusion of French books in the eighteenth century. This research grew out of the legitimate desire to broaden the traditional framework of the history of ideas through a census of a vast array of titles (almost forty-five thousand), which previously had been systematically ignored by scholars. Only in this way, it was said, would it be possible to weigh the incidence of the inert and static element in the book trade and at the same time grasp the significance of a breakthrough in the truly innovative works. An Italian scholar, Furio Diaz, has objected that, on the one hand, this approach almost always succeeds only in laboriously discovering the obvious; on the other, it risks dwelling upon what is historically misleading, and he underscored this with the following example. Late-eighteenth-century French peasants certainly did not assault the castles of the nobility because they had read *L'Ange conducteur.* They did so because "the new ideas that were more or less implicit in the reports received from Paris" coincided with "interests and . . . old animosities." Clearly, this second objection (the other is more solidly founded) denies the very existence of a popular culture as well as the usefulness of research on the ideas and beliefs of the subordinate classes, thereby reinforcing the older history of ideas of an exclusively hierarchical type. Actually, the criticism that should be directed to the quantitative history of ideas is quite another: namely, not that it is too little hierarchically inclined, but rather, too much. It starts from the premise that not just the texts alone but even the titles themselves furnish unequivocal data. Instead, this is probably less and less the case the lower the social level of the readers. The almanacs, the songsters, the books of piety, the lives of the saints, the entire pamphlet literature that constituted the bulk of the book trade, today appear static, inert, and unchanging to us. But how were they read by the public of the day? To what extent did the prevalently oral culture of those readers interject itself in the use of the text, modifying it, reworking it, perhaps to the point of changing its very essence? Menocchio's accounts of his readings provide us with a striking example of a relationship to the text that is totally different from that of today's educated reader. They permit us to measure, at last, the discrepancy that Bollème quite properly suggested existed between the texts of "popular" literature and the light in which they appeared to peasants and artisans. In Menocchio's case the discrepancy seems to be extremely profound and probably uncommon. But again, it is precisely this peculiarity that furnishes precious indications for future research. As far as the quantitative history of ideas is concerned, only knowledge of the historical and social variability of the person of the reader will really lay the foundations for a history of ideas that is also *qualitatively* different.

8

The gulf between the texts read by Menocchio and the way in which he understood them and reported them to the inquisitors indicates that his ideas cannot be reduced or traced back to any particular book. On the one hand, they are derived from a seemingly ancient oral tradition. On the other, they recall a series of motifs worked out by humanistically educated heretical groups: tolerance, tendential reduction of religion to morality, and so forth. This is a dichotomy in appearance only. In reality it reflects a unified culture within which it is impossible to make clear-cut distinctions. Even if Menocchio had been in more or less indirect contact with educated circles, his statements in favor of religious tolerance and his desire for a radical renewal of society have an original stamp to them and do not appear to be the results of passively received outside influences. The roots of his utterances and of his aspirations were sunk in an obscure, almost unfathomable, layer of remote peasant traditions.

Here we could ask ouselves if what emerges from Menocchio's speeches is not a "mentality" rather than a "culture." Appearances to the contrary, this is not an idle distinction. That which has characterized studies of the history of mentalities has been their insistence on the inert, obscure, unconscious elements in a given world view. Survivals, archaisms, the emotional, the irrational: all these are included in the specific field of the history of mentalities, setting it off from such related and established disciplines as the history of ideas or the history of culture (which, however, for some scholars encompasses both of the preceding). To discuss Menocchio's case only within the limits of the history of mentalities would mean downgrading the strong rational element (which is not necessarily identifiable with our own rationality) in his vision of the world. But an even more crucial argument against following the methods of the history of mentalities is its decidedly classless character. It probes what there is in common between "Caesar and the least of his legionnaires, Saint Louis and the peasant who tilled his fields, Christopher Columbus and one of his mariners." In this sense the adjective "collective" added to "mentality" is in most cases redundant. One should not deny the legitimacy of this kind of research, but the risk of reaching unwarranted conclusions with it is very real. Even Lucien Febvre, one of the greatest historians of this century, fell into a trap of this sort. In a fascinating but mistaken book he attempted to distinguish the mental coordinates of an entire age on the basis of studying a single individual, albeit a very exceptional one—Rabelais. There is no problem as long as Febvre limits himself to the question of demonstrating the nonexistence of Rabelais's supposed "atheism." But the argument becomes unacceptable when Febvre turns to "collective mentality (or psychology)" and to the insistence that religion exercised an influence on "sixteenth-century men" that was both restrictive and oppressive and also inescapable, as it was for Rabelais. Who, in fact, were these poorly identified "sixteenth-century men"? Were they humanists, merchants, artisans, peasants? Because of this notion of a classless "collective mentality," the results of research on a narrow stratum of French society composed of cultivated individuals are extended by implication, with no one excepted, to encompass an entire century. There is a return to the traditional history of ideas in this theorizing about collective mentalities. The peasants, the overwhelming majority of the population of the time, barely emerge in

Febvre's book to be hastily dispatched as a "mass . . . half savage, a prey to superstitions"; while the statement that it was not possible in that age to formulate a critically coherent irreligious position leads to the obvious. The seventeenth century was not the sixteenth and Descartes was not Rabelais's contemporary.

Despite these limitations, the manner in which Febvre succeeded in identifying the complex of motifs that connect an individual to an historically determinate environment and society is exemplary. The methods he used in examining the religion of Rabelais can also serve to analyze the quite different religion of Menocchio. Nevertheless, it should be clear at this point why the term "popular culture," which is unsatisfactory in some cases, is preferable to "collective mentality." A concept of class structure, even if conceived in general terms, is still a big advance over classlessness.

This is not to assert the existence of a homogeneous culture common to both peasants and urban artisans (not to mention such marginal groups as vagabonds) in preindustrial Europe. The intention here is simply to suggest an area of research within which specific analyses similar to the present one will have to be conducted. Only in this way will it be possible in the future to build on the conclusions reached in the present study.

9

A case such as Menocchio's was made possible by two great historical events: the invention of printing and the Reformation. Printing enabled him to confront books with the oral tradition in which he had grown up and fed him the words to release that tangle of ideas and fantasies he had within him. The Reformation gave him the courage to express his feelings to the parish priest, to his fellow villagers, to the inquisitors—even if he could not, as he wished, say them in person to the pope, to cardinals, and princes. The enormous rupture resulting from the end of the monopoly on written culture by the educated and on religion by the clergy had created a new and potentially explosive situation. But the possibility of finding a common ground between the aspirations of a segment of upper-class culture and those of popular culture had already been definitively crushed more than a half century before Menocchio's trial when Luther scathingly condemned the Peasants' War and the claims that underlay it. By Menocchio's time only a very small minority among the persecuted, such as the Anabaptists, continued to be inspired by that ideal. With the Counter-Reformation (and simultaneously with the consolidation of the Protestant churches) an age opened marked by the increasing rigidity of authority, the paternalistic indoctrination of the masses, and the extinction of popular culture by the more or less violent shunting aside of minorities and dissident groups. And even Menocchio finished at the stake.

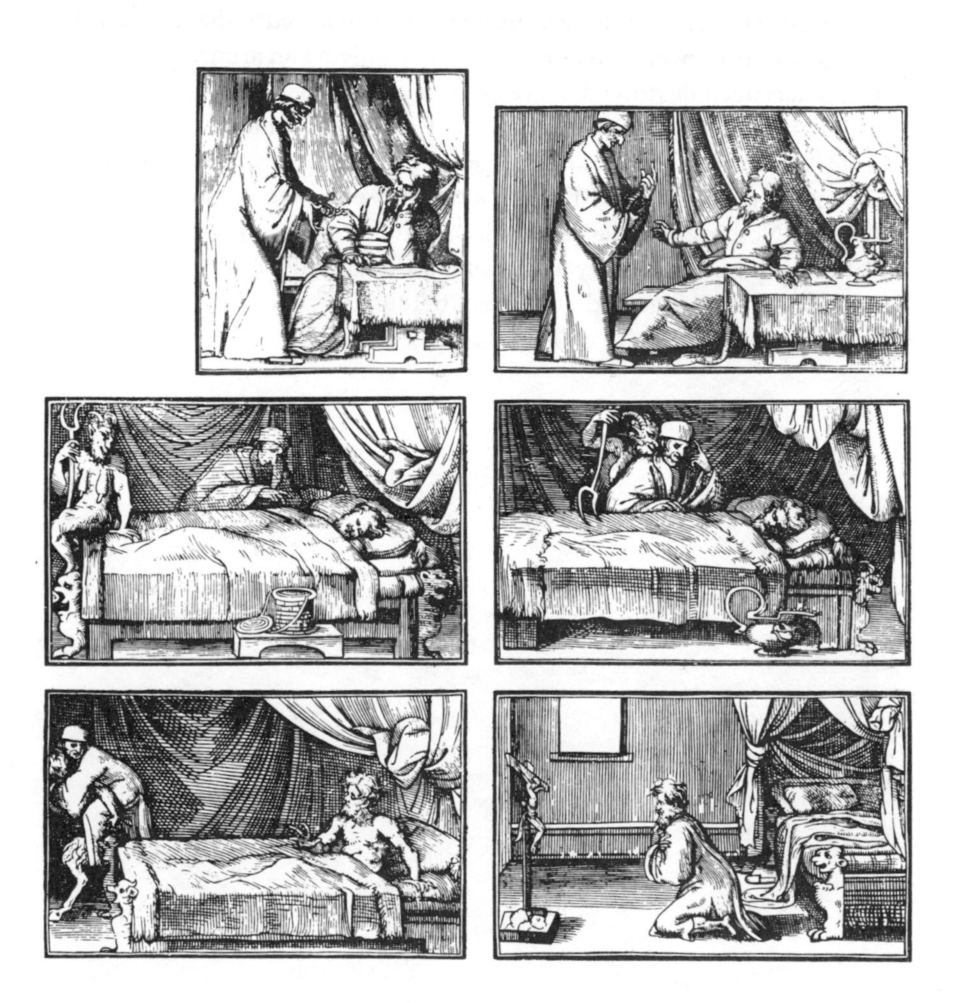

10

We have said that it is impossible to make clear-cut distinctions within Menocchio's cultural world. Only hindsight permits us to isolate those themes, already beginning to coincide with motifs shared by a segment of the upper levels of sixteenth-century culture, which became the patrimony of the "progressive" circles of later centuries: aspirations for a radical reform of society, the eating away at religion from within, tolerance. Menocchio falls within a fine, tortuous, but clearly distinguishable, line of development that can be followed directly to the present. In a sense he is one of our forerunners. But Menocchio is also a dispersed fragment, reaching us by chance, of an obscure shadowy world that can be reconnected to our own history only by an arbitrary act. That culture has been destroyed. To respect its residue of unintelligibility that resists any attempt at analysis does not mean succumbing to a foolish fascination for the exotic and incomprehensible. It is simply taking note of a historical mutilation of which, in a certain sense, we ourselves are the victims. "Nothing that has taken place should be lost to history," wrote Walter Benjamin. "But only to redeemed humanity does the past belong in its entirety." Redeemed and thus liberated.

ACKNOWLEDGMENTS

An earlier version of this book was first discussed in a seminar on popular religion held in the fall of 1973 at the Davis Center for Historical Studies at Princeton University and later in a seminar directed by the author at the University of Bologna. I am deeply grateful to Lawrence Stone, director of the Davis Center, and to all those who have helped me to improve this work with their criticisms and suggestions: especially, Piero Camporesi, Jay Dolan, John Elliott, Felix Gilbert, Robert Muchembled, Ottavia Niccoli, Jim Obelkevich, Adriano Prosperi, Lionel Rothkrug, Jerry Seigel, Eileen Yeo, Stephen Yeo, and my students in Bologna. I should also like to thank don Guglielmo Biasutti, librarian of the Archiepiscopal Curia of Udine; Aldo Colonnello; Angelo Marin, secretary of the town of Montereale Valcellina, and the staffs of the archives and libraries mentioned below. Other debts are acknowledged in the course of the book.

1

His name was Domenico Scandella, but he was called Menocchio. He was born in 1532 (at his first trial he claimed he was fifty-two years old) in Montereale, a small hill town of the Friuli twenty-five kilometers north of Pordenone at the foot of the mountains. Here he had always lived, except for two years when he was banished following a brawl (1564–65). These years he spent at the neighboring village of Arba and in an unspecified place in the Carnia. He was married and had eleven children; four of whom had died. He declared to the canon Giambattista Maro, vicar general to the inquisitor of Aquileia and Concordia, that he earned his living as a "miller, carpenter, sawyer, mason, and other things." But mostly he worked as a miller; he also wore the traditional miller's costume, a jacket, cloak, and a cap of white wool. Thus dressed in white he presented himself at his trial in 1584.

A couple of years later he told the inquisitors that he was "very poor": "I do not have anything but two rented mills and two fields in perpetual lease, and with these I have supported and continue to support my poor family." But certainly he must have been exaggerating. Even if a good part of the income went to pay the rent (probably in produce) on the two mills, in addition to the ground rent on the land, there must have been enough left over to live on and to scrape by on even in difficult times. When he had found himself banished to Arba, he had immediately rented another mill. When his daughter Giovanna married (Menocchio had died about a month before), she received a dowry equal to 256 lire and 9 soldi: she wasn't rich but she was not that poor either, considering the practices of the area in those years.

On the whole, it seems that Menocchio's place in the small world of Montereale wasn't the most negligible. In 1581 he had been mayor of the village and surrounding hamlets (Gaio, Grizzo, San Lonardo, San Martino) as well as, at an unspecified date, "*camararo*" or administrator of the parish church of Montereale. We don't know if here, as in other localities of the Friuli, the old system of rotating offices had been replaced by elections. If the latter were true, the fact that he knew how to "read, write, and add" might have given Menocchio an advantage. Administrators, in fact, were almost always selected from among persons who had attended an elementary public school, even learning perhaps a little Latin. Schools of this type existed at Aviano and at Pordenone; Menocchio may have attended one of these.

On 28 September 1583 Menocchio was denounced to the Holy Office. He was accused of having uttered "heretical and most impious words" about Christ. It wasn't a matter of an occasional blasphemy. Menocchio had actually tried to disseminate his opinions, bolstering them up by "preaching and dogmatizing shamelessly," a fact that seriously aggravated his situation.

His attempts at proselytization were attested to abundantly at the preliminary inquest, which opened a month later at Portogruaro and was continued at Concordia and in Montereale itself. "He is always arguing with somebody about the faith just for the sake of arguing—even with the priest," Francesco Fasseta testified to the vicar general. And another witness, Domenico Melchiori added: "He will argue with anyone, and when he started to debate with me I said to him: 'I am a shoemaker, and you a miller, and you are not an educated man, so what's the use of talking about it?' " Such questions concerning the faith are supposed to be exalted and difficult, out of reach of millers and cobblers. To talk about them one needed knowledge, and the repositories of knowledge were, above all, the priests. But Menocchio liked to say that he didn't believe the Holy Spirit governed the church, adding, "Priests want us under their thumb, just to keep us quiet, while they have a good time"; as for him, *he* knew God better than they did. So when the village priest took him to the vicar general in Concordia so that he might be set straight, the priest warned him, "these fancies of yours are heresies," and Menocchio promised not to meddle in such matters again—only to begin anew soon afterward. In the public square, at the inn, on his way to Grizzo or Daviano, returning from the mountains, "no matter who his companion might be," stated Giuliano Stefanut, "he usually turns the conversation to matters concerning God, and always introduces some sort of heresy. And then he argues and shouts in defense of his opinion."

2

It isn't easy to understand, from the records of the inquiry, what the villagers' reaction was to Menocchio's words. It's clear that no one was willing to admit to having listened approvingly to the talk of a suspected heretic. In fact, one of them went so far as to tell the vicar general who was conducting the inquest of his own indignant reaction: "Menocchio, please, for the love of God, do not say such things!" Domenico Melchiori claimed to have exclaimed. And Giuliano Stefanut testified: "I told him many times, and especially on our way to Grizo, that I am fond of him but I cannot stand his talking about things that concern the faith, because I would always fight with him, and if he killed me a hundred times and I returned to life, I should die for the faith again." The priest Andrea Bionima even uttered a veiled threat: "Be still, Domenego, do not say such things, because one day you may regret it." Another witness, Giovanni Povoledo, addressing the vicar general, ventured to pin a label on Menocchio, however vague: "He has a bad reputation; he has evil ideas like those of the sect of Luther." But this chorus of voices shouldn't mislead us. Almost all those interrogated declared that they had known Menocchio for a long time, some for thirty or forty years, some for twenty-five, some for twenty. One, Daniele Fasseta, said that he knew him "from childhood because we were in the same parish." Apparently, some of Menocchio's assertions went back not just a few days but "many years," as much as thirty years before. In all that time no one in the village had denounced him, yet his talk was known to everyone: people repeated it—perhaps out of curiosity, perhaps shaking their heads. In the testimony gathered by the vicar general one doesn't discern real hostility toward Menocchio, at most disapproval. True, some of the testimony came from his relatives, for example, Francesco Fasseta or Bartolomeo d'Andrea, his wife's cousin, who called him "an honorable man." But even Giuliano Stefanut who had stood up to Menocchio and had declared himself ready to "die for the faith," added "I like him very much." This miller who had been mayor of the village and administrator of the parish church certainly wasn't living on the fringes of the community of Montereale. Many years later at the time of the second trial a witness asserted, "I see him having dealings with many, and I think he is everybody's friend." And yet at a certain point someone had denounced him, a denunciation that paved the way for the inquest.

Menocchio's children, as we shall see, immediately suspected that the anonymous accuser was the priest of Montereale, don Odorico Vorai, and they weren't mistaken. The two had a long-standing disagreement. For four years Menocchio actually had been going outside the town for confession. Granted, Vorai's testimony, which closed the preliminary inquest, was singularly vague: "I don't remember specifically what things he said. I have a bad memory and had other things on my mind." Apparently, no one was in a better position to inform the Holy Office on this matter than he was, but the vicar general didn't press him. He had no need to; it had been Vorai himself, instigated by another priest, don Ottavio Montereale, a member of the local seigneurial family, who had furnished the circumstantial evidence on which the vicar general based the specific questions he addressed to the witnesses.

The hostility of the local clergy can be easily explained. As we saw, Menocchio didn't recognize any special authority in the ecclesiastical hierarchy when it came to questions of the faith: "What popes! What prelates! What priests! These words were spoken with contempt. He just did not believe in these people," Domenico Melchiori testified. By haranguing and arguing in the streets and inns, Menocchio must have ended by practically setting himself up against the authority of the priest. But what was Menocchio saying, in fact?

To begin with, not only did he blaspheme "beyond measure" but he also insisted that to blaspheme is not a sin (according to another witness, he had said that to blaspheme against the saints wasn't sinful, but to blaspheme against God was). He added sarcastically, "Everybody has his calling, some to plow, some to hoe, and I have mine, which is to blaspheme." He also said strange things, which the villagers reported in a more or less fragmentary and disconnected way to the vicar general: "The air is God . . . the earth is our mother"; "Who do you imagine God to be? God is nothing but a little breath, and whatever else man imagines him to be"; "Everything that we see is God, and we are gods"; "The sky, earth, sea, air, abyss, and hell, all is God"; "What did you think, that Jesus Christ was born of the Virgin Mary? It's impossible that she gave birth to him and remained a virgin. It might very well have been this, that he was a good man, or the son of a good man." Finally, it was said that Menocchio possessed prohibited books, particularly the Bible in the vernacular: "He is always arguing with one person or another, and he has the vernacular Bible and imagines that he bases his reasoning on it, and he remains obstinate in these arguments of his."

While the evidence was accumulating, Menocchio sensed that something was shaping up against him. So he had gone to the vicar of Polcenigo, Giovanni Daniele Melchiori, a childhood friend who urged him to present himself voluntarily to the Holy Office, or at least to obey immediately if he should be called. He warned Menocchio: "Tell them what they want to know, and try not to talk too much; do not go out of your way to discuss these things. Answer only their questions." Even Alessandro Policreto, an ex-lawyer who Menocchio had met casually in the home of a friend, a lumber merchant, had advised him to present himself before the judges and admit his guilt, but also to declare that he had never believed his own heretical statements. And so Menocchio went to Maniago in response to the summons of the ecclesiastical court. But the next day, 4 February, the inquisitor himself, the Franciscan Fra Felice da Montefalco, who had followed the course of the inquest, ordered him arrested and "conducted in handcuffs" to the prison of the Holy Office in Concordia. On 7 February 1584 Menocchio faced his first interrogation.

3

Despite the advice he had received, Menocchio immediately proved quite ready to talk, although he tried to put himself in a more favorable light than suggested by the testimony of the witnesses. While admitting that two or three years earlier he had had some doubts on the virginity of Mary and had expressed these doubts to several individuals, including a priest at Barcis, he observed: "It is true that I said these things to various people, but I was not telling them they should believe all this. On the contrary, I urged many of them: 'Would you like me to teach you the true way? Try to do good and walk in the path of my ancestors and follow what Holy Mother Church commands.' But I uttered those other words because I was tempted to believe them and teach them to others. It was the evil spirit who made me believe those things and who also persuaded me to say them to others." With these very words, Menocchio unwittingly confirmed the suspicion that in the town he had taken upon himself the role of teacher of doctrine and behavior ("Would you like me to teach you the true way?"). It was impossible to doubt the heretical nature of this kind of preaching—especially when Menocchio explained his singular cosmogony. A confused echo of it had reached the Holy Office: "I have said that, in my opinion, all was chaos, that is, earth, air, water, and fire were mixed together; and out of that bulk a mass formed—just as cheese is made out of milk—and worms appeared in it, and these were the angels. The most holy majesty decreed that these should be God and the angels, and among that number of angels, there was also God, he too having been created out of that mass at the same time, and he was made lord, with four captains, Lucifer, Michael, Gabriel, and Raphael. That Lucifer sought to make himself lord equal to the king, who was the majesty of God, and for this arrogance God ordered him driven out of heaven with all his host and his company; and this God later created Adam and Eve and people in great number to take the places of the angels who had been expelled. And as this multitude did not follow God's commandments, he sent his Son, whom the Jews seized, and he was crucified." But, Menocchio added, "I never said that he allowed himself to be hung up like a beast." (It was one of the accusations that had been made against him: later, he did admit that yes, perhaps, he might have said something of the kind.) "Indeed, I really said that he let himself be crucified, and he who was crucified was one of the children of God, because we are all God's children, and of the same nature as the one who was crucified and he was a man like the rest of us, but with more dignity just as the pope is a man like us, but of greater rank, because he has power, and he who was crucified was born of St. Joseph and Mary, the Virgin."

4

During the preliminary inquest, because of the strange tales reported by witnesses, the vicar general had first asked them if Menocchio spoke "in earnest or in jest" and later, if he was of sound mind. The answer to both questions had been clear: Menocchio spoke "in earnest" and "he was sane, not mad." Actually, after the beginning of the trial it had been one of his children, Ziannuto, at the suggestion of some of his father's friends (Sebastiano Sebenico and an unidentified "pre Lunardo"), who spread the word that Menocchio was "mad" or "possessed." But the vicar put no worth in this, and the trial continued. There had been the temptation to dismiss Menocchio's opinions, and especially his cosmogony—the cheese, the milk, the worm-angels, God, the angel created out of chaos—as a mass of impious but innocuous fantasies, but it was discarded. A century or so later Menocchio probably would have been committed to an insane asylum, as someone affected by "religious delirium." But while the Counter-Reformation was in full sway, methods of exclusion were different, the most prevalent being that of identifying and prosecuting one as a heretic.

5

Let's put aside Menocchio's conception of the universe for the time being and follow instead the progress of the trial. Immediately after Menocchio's arrest, one of his sons, Ziannuto, had tried to assist him in a number of ways: he hired a lawyer, a certain Trappola of Portogruaro, he went to Serravalle to confer with the inquisitor, he obtained a statement from Montereale in favor of the prisoner and sent it to the lawyer, offering to obtain additional character references if they were required: "and if evidence is needed from Montereale that the prisoner went to confession and took communion every year, the priests will provide it; if there is need of proof from the village that he had been mayor and warden *(retor)* in the five hamlets, it will be provided; and if necessary, confirmation can also be given that he had been administrator of the parish church of Montereale and performed his duty honorably, and also that he had served as collector of tithes *(scodador)* of the parish church of Montereale. . . . " Also, with his brothers, Ziannuto (who was illiterate) pressured the parish priest of Montereale, who in his eyes was responsible for the whole affair, into writing a letter to Menocchio, then confined in the prison of the Holy Office. The priest urged Menocchio to promise "complete obedience to the holy Church and say that you do not believe and are not about to believe anything except what is commanded by God our Lord and the holy Church, and that you intend to live and die in the Christian faith as commanded by the holy, Roman, Catholic, and apostolic Church; in fact, that you would be ready, if need be, to give up your life and a thousand more lives, if you had so many to give, for love of the Lord God and of the holy Christian faith, since you know that you have your life and every good thing from Holy Mother Church . . . " Apparently, Menocchio didn't recognize the hand of his enemy, the parish priest, behind these words. Instead he attributed them to a Domenego Femenussa, a wool and lumber merchant who came to his mill and occasionally lent him money. But, in any case, Menocchio found it difficult to follow the advice given in the letter. At the end of the first interrogation (7 February) he said to the vicar general with evident reluctance: "Sir, I can't tell you whether what I said, either through the inspiration of God or the devil, is the truth or a lie, but I ask for mercy and will follow what is taught me." He was seeking to be forgiven but was not retracting anything. During four long examinations (7, 16, 22 February and 8 March), he stood his ground against the vicar's objections—he denied, he explained, he reaffirmed. "It would appear from the trial records," Vicar Maro stated, "that you have said you do not believe in the pope, nor in the laws of the Church, and that everyone has as much authority as the pope." To which Menocchio replied, "I beg Almighty God to strike me dead this instant if I am aware that I said what your Lordship charges." But, he was asked, was it true he had said that Masses for the dead were useless? (According to Giuliano Stefanut, the words spoken by Menocchio one day when they were returning from Mass had been precisely these: "What are you doing giving alms in memory of these few ashes?") "I meant," Menocchio explained, "that we should be concerned about helping each other while we are still in this world, because afterwards God is the one who governs over souls; the prayers and alms and Masses offered for the dead are done, as I understand it, for love of God, who then does as he pleases, because souls do not come to take those prayers and alms, and it belongs to the majesty of God to receive these good works either for the benefit of the living or the dead." It was intended to be a clever explanation, but actually it contradicted the teachings of the Church on purgatory. "Do not try to talk too much," the priest of Polcenigo, a friend who had known Menocchio well from infancy, had advised. But, obviously, the latter couldn't restrain himself.

Suddenly, toward the end of April, a new element entered the picture. The provincial Venetian governors *(rettori)* requested that Fra Felice da Montefalco, the inquisitor of Aquileia and Concordia, comply with the Venetian regulations requiring the presence of a secular official along with ecclesiastical judges in all Holy Office cases. The conflict between the two jurisdictions was of long standing. We don't know if the defense lawyer, Trappola, hoping to advance his client's interests, was behind this particular move. At any rate, Menocchio was conducted to the mayor's residence in Portogruaro, where, in the presence of the mayor, he had to certify the interrogations that had already taken place. After this the trial resumed.

Many times in the past, Menocchio had told his fellow townsmen that he was ready to and, in fact, desirous of stating his own "opinions" on matters of the faith before religious and secular authorities. "He said to me," Francesco Fasseta related, "that if he ever ended up in the hands of the law for this, he would like to go peacefully, but that if he were treated poorly, he would speak out against superiors about their evil deeds." And Daniele Fasseta asserted: "Domenego said that if he did not fear for his life he would say enough to astonish everyone; I think he meant talking about the faith." Menocchio verified this testimony before the mayor of Portogruaro and the inquisitor of Aquileia and Concordia: "It's true I said that if I did not have to fear the sword of justice I would amaze everyone with my talk; and I said that if I had permission to go before the pope, or a king, or a prince who would listen to me, I would have a lot of things to say; and if he had me killed afterwards, I would not care." Then they urged him to talk, and Menocchio threw caution to the wind. It was the 28th of April.

6

He began by denouncing the way the rich tyrannized the poor in the courts by using such an incomprehensible language as Latin: "I think speaking Latin is a betrayal of the poor because in lawsuits the poor do not know what is being said and are crushed; and if they want to say four words they need a lawyer." But this was only one instance of a prevailing exploitation in which the Church was an accomplice and participant: "And it seems to me that under our law, the pope, cardinals, and bishops are so great and rich that everything belongs to the church and to the priests, and they oppress the poor, who, if they work two rented fields, these will be fields that belong to the Church, to some bishop or cardinal." It should be remembered that Menocchio leased two fields whose owners are never identified; as for his Latin, apparently it was nothing more than the Credo and the Pater Noster learned while serving Mass; and his son Ziannuto had hastened to find him a lawyer as soon as he had been arrested by the Holy Office. But these coincidences, or possible coincidences, shouldn't mislead us. Even if Menocchio's opinions grew out of his own predicament, they ended by becoming much broader in scope. His call for a church that would abandon its privileges and reduce itself to poverty alongside the poor was tied to a different religious concept, rooted in the Gospels, free of dogmatic requirements, and reduced to a core of practical precepts: "I would want us to believe in the majesty of God, to be good, and to do as Jesus Christ commanded when he replied to those Jews who questioned him about what law was to be kept: 'Love God and your neighbor.' " For Menocchio this simplified religion didn't call for confessional restrictions. His impassioned exaltation of the equality of all religions was based on the idea that illumination was granted to all men in equal measure—"the majesty of God has given the Holy Spirit to all, to Christians, to heretics, to

Turks, and to Jews; and he considers them all dear, and they are all saved in the same manner." And he concluded with a violent outburst against his judges and their doctrinal arrogance: "You priests and monks, you too want to know more than God, and you are like the devil, and you want to become gods on earth, and know as much as God, following in the footsteps of the devil. In fact, the more one thinks he knows, the less he knows." And casting restraint and prudence aside, Menocchio declared that he rejected all the sacraments, including baptism, as human inventions, as "merchandise," instruments of exploitation and oppression in the hands of the clergy: "I believe that the law and commandments of the Church are all a matter of business, and they make their living from this." About baptism he said: "I believe that as soon as we are born we are baptized, because God who has blessed all things, has baptized us; but this other baptism is an invention, and priests begin to consume souls even before they are born and continue to devour them even after their death." On the subject of confirmation: "I believe it is a business, an invention of men, all of whom have the Holy Spirit; they seek to know and they know nothing." About marriage: "God did not establish it, men did. Formerly a man and a woman would exchange vows, and this sufficed; later these human inventions followed." About ordination: "I believe the spirit of God dwells in all of us . . . and I also believe that anyone who has studied can become a priest without being ordained, because it is all a business." About extreme unction: "I believe it is nothing, and is worth nothing, because it is the body that is anointed; the soul cannot be anointed." About confession he used to declare: "You might as well go and confess to a tree as to priests and monks." When the inquisitor questioned these words, Menocchio explained with a trace of complacency: "If that tree could give the knowledge of penance, it would be good enough; and if some men seek out priests because they do not know what penance has to be made for their sins in order that the priests may teach it to them, if they had understood this matter, there would be no need to go to them; and for those who already know it, it is useless." The latter should instead confess "to the majesty of God in their hearts, and beseech him to forgive their sins."

Only the sacrament of the altar escaped Menocchio's censure, but even that was reinterpreted in a heretical sense. The words reported by the witnesses sounded like blasphemies or disdainful condemnation. On a visit to the vicar of Polcenigo one day when the wafers were being made, Menocchio had exclaimed: "By the Virgin Mary, these are great beasts." And, on another occasion, while arguing with a priest, Andrea Bionima, he had said: "I do not see anything there but a piece of dough, how can this be our Lord God? And what is God anyway? Nothing but earth, water, and air." But to the vicar general he explained: "I did say that the host is a piece of dough, but I also said that the Holy Spirit descends into it from heaven, and I really believe this." And the vicar, incredulous, asked, "What do you believe the Holy Spirit to be?" Menocchio replied, "I believe it is God." But did he know how many persons were in the Trinity? "Yes sir, there are the Father, the Son, and the Holy Spirit." "Into which of these three persons do you think the host is changed?" "Into the Holy Spirit." "Precisely which person of the Holy Trinity do you believe to be in the host?" "I believe it is the Holy Spirit." Such ignorance seemed incredible to the vicar. "What did your parish priest say was in the most holy host when he preached about that most holy sacrament?" But it wasn't a matter of ignorance on Menocchio's part: "He said that it is the body of Christ, but I believed nevertheless it was the Holy Spirit, because I believe the Holy Spirit is greater than Christ, who was a man, whereas the Holy Spirit came from the hand of God." We can see that whenever he got the chance, Menocchio showed himself ready, almost insolently, to exercise his freedom of judgment, and his right to assume an independent stand. To the inquisitor he stated: "I like this about the sacrament, that after one has confessed, one goes to take communion, and receives the Holy Spirit, and one's spirit is joyful . . . ; as for the sacrament of the Eucharist, its function is to control men, made up by men through the Holy Spirit; and the celebration of the Mass is a device of the Holy Spirit, and similarly the adoration of the host, so that men will not be like beasts." Thus, the Mass and the sacrament of the altar were being justified from a point of view that was almost political, as civilizing instruments— in a sentence, however, that echoed involuntarily, but with the figures reversed, the remark made to the priest of Polcenigo ("hosts . . . beasts").

But on what did this radical criticism of the sacraments really rest? Certainly not on Scripture, which itself was subjected by Menocchio to a pitiless scrutiny and reduced to "four words" that constituted its essence: "I believe that sacred Scripture was given by God, but was afterward added to by men; only four words would suffice in this holy Scripture, but it is like the books about battles that grew and grew." For Menocchio even the Gospels, with their discrepancies, had lost touch with the brevity and simplicity of God's word: "As for the things in the Gospels, I believe that parts of them are true and parts were made up by the Evangelists out of their heads, as we see in the passages that one tells in one way and one in another way." Thus, we can understand how Menocchio could have said to his townsmen (and again in the course of the trial) that "Holy Scripture has been invented to deceive men." It was a refutation of doctrine, a refutation even of the scriptural writings, a unilateral insistence on the practical aspect of religion. "[Menocchio] also told me that he only believed in good works," Francesco Fasseta had testified. On another occasion, still addressing himself to Francesco, Menocchio had exclaimed, "I do not want anything else but to do good." Sanctity for him was a way of life, practical behavior, nothing more: "I believe that saints were upright men who did good works, and because of this God made them saints and I think that they pray for us." Neither relics nor images should be venerated. "As for their relics, such as an arm, a body, a head, a hand, or a leg, I believe that they are like ours when they are dead, and we should not adore or revere them . . . we should not adore their images, but God alone who created heaven and earth; don't you see," exclaimed Menocchio to the judges, "that Abraham cast down all idols and images and adored only God?" Christ also, by his passion, had given men a model to live by: "He has been beneficial . . . for us Christians, serving as a mirror, and just as he was patient, suffering for love of us, we should die and suffer for love of him; let us not wonder that we also die, since God decreed that his son should die." But Christ was only a man, and all men are children of God, "of the very same nature as he who was crucified." Consequently, Menocchio refused to believe that Christ had died to redeem humanity: "If a person has sinned, it is he who must do penance."

Menocchio said most of these things in the course of a single, lengthy interrogation. "I would say enough to astonish everyone," he had promised the townsmen. And indeed, the inquisitor, the vicar general, and the mayor of Portogruaro must have been astonished at a miller who could expound his views with such assurance and force. Menocchio was convinced of their originality: "I have never associated with anyone who was a heretic," he said, responding to a specific question from the judges, "but I have an artful mind, and I have wanted to seek out higher things about which I did not know. But I do not believe that what I have said is the truth, and I want to be obedient to the Holy Church. And I have held opinions that were wicked, but the Holy Spirit has enlightened me, and I beg mercy of almighty God, of our Lord Jesus Christ, and of the Holy Spirit, and may he strike me dead if I am not telling the truth." At last, he had decided to follow the course advised by his son, but first he had wanted, as he had been promising himself for such a long time, "to speak out against his superiors for their evil deeds." Certainly he knew the risk he was taking. Before being conducted back to his cell he begged the inquisitors for mercy: "My lords, I beg you, by the passion of our Lord Jesus Christ, to settle my case; and if I deserve death, send me to it; and if I deserve mercy, exercise it, because I want to live as a good Christian." But the trial was far from over. A few days later (1 May) the interrogations resumed. The mayor had to be absent from Portogruaro, but the judges were impatient to hear Menocchio again. "In the previous examination," the inquisitor said, "we told you that it appeared from the trial that your mind was filled with these humors and pernicious doctrines. Therefore, this holy tribunal desires that you finish opening your mind to us fully." And Menocchio: "My mind was lofty and wished for a new world and way of life, because the Church did not act properly, and because there should not be so much pomp."

7

We'll return later to the significance of the reference to "new world," and to a new "way of life." First we must try to understand how this miller of the Friuli could have expressed ideas of this kind.

The Friuli in the second half of the sixteenth century was a society with pronounced archaic features. The great families of the feudal nobility continued to exercise a dominant role in the region. Such institutions as the *masnada* form of serfdom had persisted until just the previous century, much longer than in neighboring areas. The ancient medieval parliament had preserved its proper legislative functions, even if actual power had been for some time in the hands of Venetian officials. In reality, Venetian rule, which had begun in 1420, had left things as they were as much as possible. The only concern of the Venetians had been to create a balance of power that would neutralize the subversive tendencies existing among some of the feudal nobility of the Friuli.

At the beginning of the sixteenth century, conflicts within the nobility had intensified. Two parties had formed, the *Zamberlani,* who were favorable to Venice and had rallied around the powerful Antonio Savorgnan (who was later to die in exile in the imperial camp) and the *Strumieri,* who were hostile to Venice and were led by the family of the Torreggiani. An extremely violent class struggle added itself to the political conflict between the noble factions. As early as 1508 the nobleman Francesco di Strassoldo had warned in a speech in the *Parlamento* that in several areas of the Friuli the peasants had banded into "conventicles," some of them numbering as many as two thousand people. There, among other things, they uttered "certain nefarious and diabolical words, particularly about cutting to pieces priests, gentlemen, feudal lords, and citizens, and even of holding a Sicilian Vesper and many other filthy words." And this wasn't idle talk. On Maundy Thursday 1511, shortly after the crisis ensuing from the Venetian defeat at Agnadello and coinciding with an outbreak of the plague, the peasants loyal to Savorgnan rebelled, first at Udine and later in other localities, slaughtering nobility of both parties and burning their castles. The immediate restoration of class solidarity among the nobles was followed by a ferocious repression of the revolt. But the violence of the peasants had on the one hand thrown fear into the Venetian oligarchy and on the other suggested the possibility of a daring policy of containment of the Friulian nobility. In the decades following the ephemeral uprising of 1511, the Venetian inclination to support the peasants of the Friuli (and those of the *Terraferma* in general) against the local nobility, grew stronger. As part of this system of counterweights, an extraordinary institution, the *Contadinanza,* came into being in the Venetian dominions themselves. This organ had both fiscal and military functions. It collected a series of tributes based on a so-called "list of hearths," and by means of "lots" organized local peasant militias. This second provision, in particular, was a real affront to the nobility of the Friuli when one recalls that the statutes of the *Patria,* so imbued with feudalistic spirit (among other things it threatened penalties for peasants who dared to obstruct the noble exercise of the hunt by snaring hares or hunting pheasants at night), contained a provision entitled *De prohibitione armorum rusticis.* But the Venetian authorities, while maintaining the peculiar characteristics of the *Contadinanza,* were also determined to make it the official representative of the interests of the rural population. Thus, the legal fiction that the *Parlamento* was the body representing the entire population was eventually dropped, even as a formality.

The list of measures taken by Venice in support of the peasants of the Friuli is a long one. Already in 1533, in response to a petition presented by the *decani* of Udine and other places in the Friuli and the Carnia who complained that they were "very oppressed by several types of rents paid to various noble citizens and others in the *Patria,* and to other lay persons, due to excessive prices prevailing on crops for several years," it was allowed that rents could be paid on the perpetual leases (excluding those held in emphyteusis) in cash rather than in kind—on the basis of unit prices established once and for all, which, at a time of severe inflation, obviously favored the peasants. In 1551 "in response to a plea from the peasantry of the *Patria,*" all perpetual leases dating from 1520 on were reduced 7 percent by an edict that was confirmed and amplified eight years later. Again, in 1574, the Venetian authorities attempted to restrain usury in the countryside by enjoining that "from the peasants of that *Patria* no large or small animals suitable for working the land are to be taken as security, nor any kind of farm implement, at the insistence of any creditor, except when offered by the owners themselves." In addition, "to alleviate the condition of the poor peasants, from whom, due to the greediness of the creditors who give them various things on credit, crops are snatched away almost before they are reaped, at a moment when the price is at the lowest point of the entire year," it was decreed that creditors could only make their claims after the 15th of August.

These concessions, which were intended primarily to keep latent tensions under control in the countryside of the Friuli, at the same time created a real sense of solidarity between the peasants and Venice against the local nobility. As a response to the continuing reduction of rents, the latter attempted to transform the long-term leases into simple rents, a type of contract that clearly made conditions worse for the peasants. This trend, which was widespread in this period, met heavy obstacles, especially of a demographic kind, in the Friuli. When manpower is short, it's difficult to make agricultural arrangements that favor the landlords. Within the space of a hundred years, between the mid-sixteenth and mid-seventeenth centuries, due to the effect of recurring plagues and to an increase in emigration, especially toward Venice, the total population of the Friuli declined. The reports of the Venetian officials of this period emphasize the miserable conditions of the peasants: "I have suspended all collections of private debts until the harvest," Daniele Priuli wrote in 1573, describing how, "everything is being taken, from clothing off women's backs, though they might be clutching their little ones, to the locks on the doors, things that are impious and inhuman." In 1587 Carlo Corner stressed the natural poverty of the *Patria:* "[It is] very barren since it is mountainous in part, gravelly in the lowlands, and prone to flooding from many streams and to damage from storms, which generally prevail in the area." And he concluded, "therefore since the nobles do not have great wealth, so also the people, especially the peasants, are very poor." At the end of the century (1599) Stefano Viaro painted a picture of decay and desolation: "For several years the *Patria* has been so devastated that there is scarcely a village where two-thirds, or even three-fourths, of its houses are not in ruins and uninhabited, and a little less than half its fields are uncultivated, really a very pitiful thing since, if this situation continues, every day the inhabitants are being forced out of necessity into leaving, only the poorest and most miserable will remain." At a time when the decline of Venice was beginning to become apparent, the economy of the Friuli was already in an advanced state of decay.

8

But what did a miller like Menocchio know of this tangle of political, social, and economic contradictions? What conception did he have of that enormous play of forces that was silently conditioning his existence?

His was a rudimentary and simplified image, but a very clear one just the same. Many grades of "rank" existed in the world. There were the pope, cardinals and bishops, and the parish priest of Montereale; there was the emperor, there were kings and princes. But beyond hierarchical gradations, there was a fundamental distinction between "superiors" and "poor people," and Menocchio knew that he was one of the poor. It was a totally dichotomous view of the class structure, typical of a peasant society. Nevertheless, in Menocchio's statements there's an indication of a more discriminating attitude concerning "superiors." The violence of his attack against the highest religious authorities—"and it seems to me that under this law of ours the pope, cardinals, and bishops are so great and rich that everything belongs to the Church and to the priests, and they oppress the poor . . . "—contrasts with the much milder criticism of political authorities that follows immediately after: "It also seems to me that these Venetian lords harbor thieves in that city, so that when a person goes there to buy something, and asks 'How much do you want for these things?' they reply a ducat, even if they are only worth three *marcelli;* and I wish that they would do their duty. . . . " These words testify, first of all, to the reaction of the peasant who has suddenly come into contact with the distant reality of the city. The jump from Montereale or Aviano to a great city like Venice was a big one. But the fact remains that while the pope, cardinals, and bishops are directly accused of "oppressing" the poor, he says simply of the "Venetian lords" that "they harbor thieves in that city." This difference in tone certainly can't be attributed to prudence, for when he spoke these words Menocchio was standing before both the mayor of Portogruaro and the inquisitor of Aquileia and his vicar. In his eyes the ecclesiastical hierarchy was the principal embodiment of oppression. Why?

Menocchio himself seems to provide the first clue: "Everything belongs to the Church and to the priests, and they oppress the poor, who, if they work two rented fields, these will be fields that belong to the Church, to some bishop or cardinal." As we've said, we don't know if this was also the case with Menocchio himself. From an assessment made in 1596—twelve years after these statements—it appears that one of the fields presumably leased to Menocchio bordered a tract of land that a member of the local seigneurial family, Orazio di Montereale, had allocated to a ser Giacomo Margnano. The document also lists several pieces of land owned by local or neighboring churches and let out on lease: eight belonged to Santa Maria, one to San Rocco (both of Montereale), and one to Santa Maria of Pordenone. Montereale certainly wasn't an isolated case. At the end of the sixteenth century, the amount of property held by the Church in the Friuli, as in the entire Veneto, was still extensive. And where it had decreased quantitatively, it had increased and improved in quality. All this suffices to explain Menocchio's words, even if he had not personally experienced the oppressive effects of Church ownership of land (which had always been explicitly exempted from the reduction in rents introduced by the Venetian authorities). He had only to open his eyes and look around.

The extent of ecclesiastical property in Montereale and vicinity explains the bitterness of Menocchio's accusations but not their implications, nor their application on a more general level. The pope, cardinals, and bishops "oppress" the poor. But in whose name? With what right? The pope "is a man like us" except for the fact that he has power ("puo' far") and thus has greater "rank." No difference existed between clergy and laity. The sacrament of ordination was "a business." All the sacraments and laws of the Church, for that matter, were "merchandise," "inventions" upon which the priests grew fat. Against this enormous edifice built on the exploitation of the poor, Menocchio set forth a very different religion, where all members were equal because the spirit of God was in all of them.

Menocchio's awareness of his own rights, then, had specifically religious origins. A miller may claim to be able to expound the truths of the faith to the pope, to a king, to a prince, because he has within himself that spirit which God has imparted to all men. For the same reason he may dare "to speak out against his superiors about their evil deeds." What led Menocchio to denouce the existing hierarchies so impetuously in his speeches wasn't only his perception of the oppression, but also a religiosity that affirmed the presence in every man of a "spirit" that he sometimes called "Holy Spirit," sometimes "spirit of God."

9

It would seem, even at first glance, that all this can be explained by the great blow dealt to the principle of authority by the Protestant Reformation, not only in the area of religion but also in the political and social realms. But what was Menocchio's connection with Reformation groups and their ideas?

"I believe a Lutheran is one who goes about teaching bad things, and eats meat on Friday and Saturday," Menocchio at one point told the judges who were interrogating him. But this was certainly an intentionally simplified and distorted definition. Many years later, at the time of the second trial (1599), it came out that Menocchio had said to a converted Jew named Simon, that at his own death "some Lutherans will learn of it, and will come to collect the ashes." At first glance this would seem to be solid evidence. Actually, it's just the opposite. Apart from the difficulty of evaluating the grounds for Menocchio's expectations (to which we shall return), the term "Lutheran" is in a context that confirms the general way with which it was used in this period. According to Simon, in fact, Menocchio had denied all value to the Gospel, had rejected the divinity of Christ, and had praised a book that may have been the Koran. We would appear to be very far from Luther and his doctrines. All this compels us to return to the point of departure and begin again, proceeding cautiously one step at a time.

What may be called Menocchio's ecclesiology, which we can reconstruct on the basis of statements he made during the interrogations in Portogruaro, has relatively precise features. In the complex religious picture of sixteenth-century Europe, in several respects it resembles chiefly the teachings of the Anabaptists. Insistence on the simplicity of the word of God, rejection of sacred images, ceremonies, and the sacraments, the denial of Christ's divinity, the adherence to a practical religion based on works, the polemic with the stamp of pauperism against ecclesiastical "pomp," the exaltation of tolerance, are all elements that can be traced to the religious radicalism of the Anabaptists. Granted, Menocchio doesn't appear to have been a supporter of adult baptism. But we know that it wasn't long before Italian Anabaptist groups reached the point of refusing baptism as well as the other sacraments, accepting at the very most a spiritual baptism based on the inner regeneration of the individual. For his part, Menocchio considered baptism totally useless: "I believe that as soon as we are born, we are baptized, because God who has blessed all things has baptized us. . . . "

After having spread through a large part of northern and central Italy, especially the Veneto, the Anabaptist movement was broken in mid-sixteenth century by the religious and political persecution unleashed after the defection of one of its leaders. But a few dispersed conventicles survived clandestinely for some time even in the Friuli. For example, those artisans of Porcía imprisoned by the Holy Office in 1557, who had been accustomed to meeting in the houses of a tanner and of a weaver to read Scripture and to discuss "the renewal of life, . . . the purity of the Gospel, and abstention from sins," could have been Anabaptists. As we'll see, Menocchio, whose heretical beliefs, according to a witness, went back thirty years, may have been in contact with this very group.

Nevertheless, despite the similarities that have been noted, it doesn't seem possible to label Menocchio an Anabaptist. His favorable opinion of the Mass, the Eucharist, and, within limits, confession, would have been unthinkable in an Anabaptist. Above all, an Anabaptist who viewed the pope as the incarnation of the Antichrist could never have spoken about indulgences as did Menocchio: "I believe that they are good, because if God has put a man in his place as pope to grant a pardon, that is good, because it is as if we are receiving it from God since these indulgences are given by one who is acting as his steward." All this emerged during the first interrogation at Portogruaro (28 April). The proud, sometimes haughty, posture assumed by Menocchio on that occasion again suggests that we can discard straightaway the hypothesis that such statements were dictated either by caution or by calculation. Moreover, the variety of texts that Menocchio later identified as the "sources" of his religious beliefs is as far removed as one can imagine from the rigid sectarian exclusiveness of the Anabaptists. For the latter, the only source of truth was Scripture, or even simply the Gospels. For example, the weaver who was a leader of the above-mentioned Porcía group declared, "aside from this no other writing is to be believed, and in no other writing but the Gospels is there anything that pertains to salvation." For Menocchio, instead, inspiration could come from the most disparate books: as much from the *Fioretto della Bibbia* as from the *Decameron.* In conclusion, there were real similarities between the views of Menocchio and those of the Anabaptists, but they were set in clearly different contexts.

If Anabaptism alone doesn't explain the case of Menocchio, wouldn't it be advisable to fall back on a more general definition? Apparently Menocchio declared that he was in contact with "Lutheran" groups (a term that at the time included an extremely broad area of heterodoxy). Why not settle for this vague kinship that we earlier recognized as possibly having existed between Menocchio and the Reformation?

Actually, even this hardly seems possible. At one point a typical exchange took place between the inquisitor and Menocchio. The former asked, "What do you understand by justification?" Menocchio, who was always so ready to expound his "opinions" at length, this time didn't understand. The monk had to explain to him *"quid sit iustificatio,"* and Menocchio replied, as we've seen, denying that Christ had died to save mankind since, "if a person has sinned, it is he who must do penance." It was the same with predestination. Menocchio didn't know the meaning of this word, and only after the inquisitor's explanation did he reply, "I do not believe that God has predestined anyone to eternal life." Justification and predestination, the two themes around which religious debate revolved in Italy in the age of the Reformation, literally meant nothing to this miller of the Friuli—even if, as we shall see, he had encountered them at least once in the course of his readings.

This is even more significant since interest in these questions in Italy was not limited to the upper classes of society.

> The porter, the maidservant, and the bondsman
> dissect free will
> and make hash of predestination,

the satirical poet Pietro Nelli, alias Messer Andrea da Bergamo, wrote in mid-sixteenth century. A few years earlier, Neapolitan tanners had passionately argued over the epistles of St. Paul and the doctrine of justification after listening to the sermons of Bernardino Ochino. An echo of the debates concerning the importance of faith and works for salvation turns up in the most unexpected quarters, for example, in a prostitute's appeal to Milanese authorities. These are random examples to which we could easily add. Nevertheless, there is a common element among them: almost all have an urban setting. It is one indication, among many, of the growing separation in Italy between the city and the country. The religious conquest of Italian rural areas, which the Anabaptists might have attempted if they had not been crushed almost at once by political and religious repression, was achieved a few decades later under a quite different banner by the religious orders of the Counter-Reformation, principally the Jesuits.

This doesn't mean that the Italian countryside failed to experience religious unrest during the sixteenth century. But behind this thin fabric of themes and issues of contemporary events one glimpses the massive presence of different and much more ancient traditions. What did a cosmogony such as the one described by Menocchio—the primordial cheese from which the worm-angels are produced—have to do with the Reformation? How can one trace back to the Reformation statements such as those attributed to Menocchio by his fellow villagers: "everything that we see is God, and we are gods," "the sky, earth, sea, air, abyss, and hell, all is God"? Provisionally, it's best to attribute them to a substratum of peasant beliefs, perhaps centuries old, that were never wholly wiped out. By breaking the crust of religious unity, the Reformation indirectly caused these old beliefs to emerge; the Counter-Reformation, attempting to restore unity, brought them into the light of day in order to sweep them away.

On the basis of this hypothesis, then, Menocchio's radical statements will not be explained by tracing them to Anabaptism or, worse yet, to a generic "Lutheranism." Rather, we should ask if they don't belong within an autonomous current of peasant radicalism, which the upheaval of the Reformation had helped to bring forth, but which was much older.

10

It seemed impossible to the inquisitors that Menocchio, uninfluenced, should have formulated ideas so different from current ones. Witnesses were asked if Menocchio "had spoken sincerely or in mockery, or whether he was repeating what he heard other people saying." Menocchio was asked to give the names of his "companions." But the replies in both cases were negative. Menocchio, in particular, declared decisively, "Sir, I have never met anyone who holds these opinions; my opinions came out of my own head." But, in part at least, he was not telling the truth. In 1598 don Ottavio Montereale (who, as we remember, had been indirectly responsible for the intervention of the Holy Office) said that he had understood "this Menocchio learned his heresies from a M. Nicola, a painter of Porcía" who had gone to Montereale to paint in the home of a signor de Lazzari, don Ottavio's brother-in-law. Actually, Nicola's name had emerged even during the first trial, provoking a visibly embarrassed reaction from Menocchio. First he related having met him during Lent, when he had heard Nicola declare that indeed he was fasting, but "out of fear." (Menocchio instead had been consuming "a little bit of milk, cheese, and an occasional egg," excusing himself by the weakness of his constitution.) But immediately afterward, changing the subject, he began to speak in what seemed to be a distracted way of a book that Nicola owned. Nicola had been called in turn before the Holy Office but was released immediately following favorable testimony as to his character given by two ecclesiastics of Porcía. In the second trial, however, evidence emerged concerning the influence on Menocchio's heterodox opinions by an unknown person. During the interrogation of the 19th of July 1599, the inquisitors asked him how long he had believed—on the basis of a novella from the *Decameron,* as we shall see—that every man could be saved through his own religion, and accordingly, that a Turk was right to remain a Turk and not be converted to Christianity. Menocchio replied, "It may be fifteen or sixteen years that I have held these opinions, since we began to discuss such things, and the devil put them in my head." "With whom did you discuss this?" the inquisitor immediately asked. Only after a long pause *("post longam moram")* did Menocchio reply, "I don't know."

It seems, then, that Menocchio must have spoken with someone about religion fifteen or sixteen years before–in 1583, probably, because at the beginning of the following year he had been imprisoned and tried. In all probability it was the same person who had lent Menocchio the incriminated book, the *Decameron.* Menocchio named him a couple of weeks later: Nicola de Melchiori. In addition to the name, the dates (coincidences that escaped the inquisitors) lead us to identify this person with Nicola da Porcia, whom in 1584, Menocchio had not seen for precisely a year.

Don Ottavio Montereale was well informed: Menocchio must actually have discussed religious questions with Nicola da Porcia. We don't know if Nicola had been part of the group of artisans who gathered to read the Gospel more than twenty-five years before. In any case, despite the statements obtained in his favor in 1584, he had been known for some time as "a great heretic." At least this is the way he had been described in 1571 by a nobleman of Pordenone, Fulvio Rorario, in reference to an event of eight or ten years before. Nicola "said that he had personally broken some tablets that had been placed as a decoration in a church not far from Porcia, declaring it was wrong, and that they did not belong there and were . . . merchandise . . . and that figures should not be placed in church." Menocchio's sharp condemnation of sacred images immediately comes to mind. But this wasn't all he learned from Nicola da Porcia.

"I know," said Menocchio to the vicar general "that [Nicola] had a book called *Zampollo,* a buffoon, according to him, who died and went to hell and joked with the demons there; and if I remember he said that he was with a companion, and that a demon had taken a liking to the buffoon, and when his companion learned that the demon was fond of the buffoon he said to him that he should pretend to be unhappy; and as he was doing this, the demon said to him: 'Why do you look unhappy? Speak honestly, regardless, because one should be honorable even in hell.' " To the vicar general this speech must have sounded like a lot of foolishness. He immediately brought the interrogation back to more serious questions—for example, had Menocchio ever asserted that all men go to hell?—

thereby allowing an important lead to slip by. In fact, Menocchio had absorbed the book that Nicola da Porcia had given him to read to the point where he had permanently assimilated its themes and expressions, even if mistakenly he had substituted a perversion of the name of the protagonist, Zanpolo, for the title, *Il sogno dil Caravia.*

In the *Sogno* the Venetian jeweler, Alessandro Caravia, portrays himself and the celebrated buffoon Zanpolo Liompardi, his close friend, who had died a short time before at a great age.

> You appear to me to be *melancholia*
> Depicted by a good master painter,

Zanpolo says at the beginning to Caravia (who, in fact, in an engraving on the title page is represented in the pose of Dürer's *Melancholia)*. Caravia is sad. He sees about him a world filled with injustice and is grieved by it. Zanpolo comforts him, and reminds him that the true life is not on this earth.

> Oh how dearly I should love to have news
> Of someone who is in the other world,

exclaims Caravia. Zanpolo promises that after his death he will try to return and appear before him. He dies shortly after; most of the verses of the poem describe the jeweler's dream in which Zanpolo, the buffoon, relates his journey to paradise where he converses with St. Peter, and to hell where, through his clowning, he first forms a friendship with the devil, Farfarello, and later meets another famous buffoon, Domenego Taiacalze. The latter suggests a plan that will enable Zanpolo to appear before Caravia, as he had promised:

> I know that Farfarel loves you very much
> And soon I think will come to visit you;
> He will ask you if you feel great misery:
> You, when you see him, must pretend to be
> More unhappy than you really are,
> And he will try to please you.
> Then you will tell him what you are thinking
> And perhaps he will do everything your heart desires.

"Then I pretended . . . " Zanpolo relates,

> To be in great torment
> And sat myself down in a corner
> Before Farfarel should come upon me.

But the ruse didn't work, and Farfarello scolds him:

> I've seen through your pretense:
> My mind is now confused about you

Because you tried such a trick on me.
I had your promise to obey every commandment
And to keep the faith even in hell.

Nevertheless, he forgives him. Zanpolo appears to Caravia, who upon awakening, offers a prayer on his knees before the crucifix.

Farfarello's exhortations to tell the truth even in hell, which Menocchio seized upon, certainly represent one of the fundamental themes in the *Sogno,* namely, the polemic against hypocrisy, especially that of monks. Its printing was concluded in May 1541, while the colloquies that seemed destined to restore religious peace between Catholics and Protestants were taking place in Regensburg. The *Sogno* is, in fact, a typical voice of Italian evangelism. The "*sgnieffi, berleffi, ceffi,* and twisted faces" of the two buffoons Zanpolo and Taiacalze, who began to dance even in front of Beelzebub's tribunal, "showing him their naked buttocks," in fact accompany—and the mixture is carnivalesque—a broad and persistent religious discourse. Taiacalze openly praises Luther:

A certain Martin Luther has been turned up
Who esteems priests little and monks less
And is by the Germans much beloved;
He never tires of calling for a council [. . .]
This Martin, from what we hear,
Excells in all branches of learning:
He abandons not the pure Gospel.
Luther has confused the minds of many;
One says that only Christ can pardon us,
Another that Paul III and Clement may.
There are those who pull and those who yield,
Who speak the truth, who lie through their teeth.
All desire that the council take place
Only to clarify these heresies now:
The hot sun melts the snow,
So may God any evil thought . . .

Altogether, Luther's position is judged favorably since he calls for a council to restore doctrinal clarity and he reasserts the "pure Gospel":

Unwillingly did I see death come
For me, friend, since I was not clear
On the different opinions arisen in great number
Each unsteadily holding sway in the world.
Men would like to remain steadfast in their faith
And not be confused by empty words
But to read well in the Gospels' text
And not care about Martin for the rest.

What is meant by "the pure Gospel" is explained later, in turn by Zanpolo, St. Peter, and Taiacalze. There is, in the first place, justification by faith in Christ's sacrifice:

> The first cause that saves the Christian
> Is to love God and have faith only in him.
> The second, to hope that the human Christ
> By his blood saves whoever believes in him.
> The third, to keep the heart sound by charity.
> And to act in the light of the Holy Spirit, if he wishes
> To obtain reward from the only God in three Persons.
> Together these three save you from hell.

No theological subtleties here, such as those preached by monks, that had become fashionable even among the unlearned.

> Many fools who think themselves scholars
> Speak constantly of Holy Scripture,
> Barbers, smiths, and tailors,
> Theologizing beyond measure,
> Causing people to fall into many errors,
> About predestination they are really frightening
> Concerning the judgment, and free will too.
> Let them be burned by the powder of saltpeter.
> It would be enough for these small artisans
> To believe in the Creed, and say Our Father
> And not commit a thousand errors against the faith
> Searching for things that were never written
> With ink, nor with sharpened pen.
> The Evangelists have shown the way
> Right and simple, for him who wishes to go to Heaven.
> One need not, Zanpol, be so subtle
> As to see the membrane of an egg inside the hen [. . .]
> Oh how many friars, who know next to nothing
> Use their minds to confuse
> This poor wretch and that one.
> Know that they would do better to preach
> The pure Gospel and leave the rest alone.

The clear-cut contrast between a religion reduced to an essential core on the one hand and theological subtleties on the other recalls statements by Menocchio—who, even though he had read in this passage a word like "predestination," actually said he didn't know its meaning. Still more definite is the similarity between the condemnation of the "laws and commandments of the Church" as "merchandise" (*mercantie,* a term used, as we saw, also by Nicola da Porcía) and the invective against priests and monks that the *Sogno* puts in the mouth of St. Peter:

They make a business of burying the dead
As though they were a sack of wool, or peppercorns:
In these matters they are very shrewd
In not wanting to receive the deceased
If first the money is not delivered into their hands;
Then they go to eat and drink it up
Laughing about those who made such payments
And enjoying good beds and heavy-laden boards.
Business of even greater importance
They make of the Church that was mine,
Among themselves drawing in every abundance
Not bothering about those who go without.
In my opinion this is an evil practice
To turn my Church into a marketplace
And to think blessed he who has more benefices
And yet says few masses, and fewer offices still.

There's an implicit denial of purgatory and thus of the utility of Masses for the dead; condemnation of the use of Latin by priests and monks ("Purposefully they perform all their ceremonies/If only they would speak to you in the vernacular, and not in Latin"); rejection of "sumptuous churches"; limitations on the cult of saints:

Saints should be honored, my son,
Because they have taken their precepts from Christ [. . .]
Whoever does as they do, it is God's desire
That they dwell with him in the heaven of the elect:
But he does not dispense their grace,
And who believes that makes a mistake.

And about confession:

Every faithful Christian should confess
With his mind and heart every hour before God
And not only once at the New Year
Just to show that he is not a Jew.

These are all recurring motifs, as we've seen, in Menocchio's statements. And yet he had read the *Sogno* more than forty years after its publication, in a completely different situation. The council that should have healed the conflict between "the papists" and Luther—a conflict that Caravia compared to that between the two Friulian factions of the *Strumieri* and the *Zamberlani*—had indeed taken place, but it had been a council of condemnations and not of concord. For men like Caravia, the Church outlined by the Tridentine decrees was certainly not the Church "made straight" and based on the "pure Gospel" about which they had dreamed. And even Menocchio must have read the *Sogno* as a book that on many counts was tied to an age long since passed. Of course, the anticlerical or antitheological polemics still had a contemporary ring, for reasons that we have already seen: but the more radical elements of Menocchio's religion went well beyond the *Sogno*. In the latter there was no trace of a denial of Christ's divinity, of the rejection of the integrity of Scripture, of the condemnation of baptism (although it was defined as "merchandise"), nor of the indiscriminate exaltation of tolerance. Had it been Nicola da Porcía who had spoken to Menocchio about all this? In regard to tolerance, apparently, yes—if the identification of Nicola de Melchiori with Nicola da Porcía is correct. But all the evidence furnished by the inhabitants of Montereale indicates that the complex of Menocchio's ideas had formed long before the date of the first trial. It's true that we don't know how far back his relations with Nicola went: but Menocchio's obstinacy demonstrates that we aren't dealing with a passive reception of someone else's ideas.

11

"Would you like me to teach you the true way? Try to do good and walk in the path of my ancestors, and follow what Holy Mother Church commands": These were the words, as we recall, that Menocchio maintained (although he was probably lying) he had spoken to his fellow villagers. In fact, Menocchio had taught exactly the opposite: disassociation from the faith of one's forefathers, rejection of the doctrines preached by the priest from the pulpit. Maintaining this deviant position for such a long time (perhaps for almost thirty years), first in such a small community as Montereale and later before the tribunal of the Holy Office, called for moral and intellectual strength that can be described as nothing less than extraordinary. The diffidence of his relatives and friends, the reproaches of the priest, the threats of the inquisitors, none had succeeded in shaking Menocchio's self-confidence. But what made him so sure of himself? With what authority was he speaking?

In the early exchanges of the trial he ascribed his opinions to diabolical inspiration: "I uttered those words because I was tempted . . . it was the evil spirit that made me believe those things." But he had already become less submissive by the end of the first interrogation: "What I said came either through the inspiration of God or of the devil. . . . " Fifteen days later he added yet another possibility: "The devil or something tempted me." Shortly after, he clarified what this "something" was that nagged at him: "My opinions came out of my head." Thereafter he never deviated from this idea during the entire course of the first trial. Even when he decided to ask his judges to forgive him, he attributed his errors to his own "artful mind."

So, Menocchio was not claiming special revelations or illumination. It was to his own intelligence that he gave the chief credit. This alone was enough to distinguish him from the prophets, visionaries, and itinerant preachers who had proclaimed obscure revelations in the public squares of Italian cities between the end of the fifteenth and beginning of the sixteenth centuries. Even as late as 1550, a former Benedictine, Giorgio Siculo, had tried to communicate to the fathers assembled at the Council of Trent truths that Christ himself, appearing "in his own person," had revealed to him. But by the time of Menocchio's trial, twenty years had passed since the Council had ended. The hierarchy had spoken and the long period of uncertainty about what the faithful could and should believe was over. And yet this miller lost in the hills of the Friuli continued to mull over "exalted things," opposing his own religious views to the decrees of the Church: "I believe . . . according to what I think and believe. . . . "

In addition to his own reason, there were books. The *Sogno dil Caravia* was not an isolated case. "On confessing several times to a priest of Barcis," Menocchio declared during his first interrogation, "I said to him, 'Can it be that Jesus Christ was conceived by the Holy Spirit and born of the Virgin Mary?' I added, however, that I believed this, but sometimes the devil tempted me." The attribution of his own doubts to demoniacal temptation reflected Menocchio's relatively cautious attitude at the beginning of the trial; in fact, he promptly expounded the two premises supporting his position: "I based my belief on the fact that many men have been born into the world, but none of a virgin woman; and when I read that the glorious Virgin was married to St. Joseph, I believed that our Lord Jesus Christ was the son of St. Joseph, because I have read some histories where St. Joseph called our Lord Jesus Christ his son, and I read this in a book called *Il Fioreto della Bibia.*" This is an example chosen at random; Menocchio frequently indicated that this or that book was the source (not the only one in this particular case) of his "opinions." But what had Menocchio actually read?

12

Unfortunately, we don't have a complete list of his books. At the moment of his arrest the vicar general had his house searched. A few volumes were found, but since they were neither suspected nor prohibited, they weren't inventoried. We can reconstruct a partial picture of Menocchio's readings only on the basis of the brief references that he made during the interrogations. The following books were mentioned during the first trial:

1. The Bible in the vernacular, "a large part of it in red letters" (an unidentified edition);
2. *Il Fioretto della Bibbia* (the translation of a medieval Catalan chronicle compiled from various sources among which were, besides the Vulgate of course, the *Chronicon* of Isidore, the *Elucidarium* of Honorius of Autun, and several apocryphal gospels; of this work, which circulated widely in manuscript between the fourteenth and fifteenth centuries, we know of twenty-odd editions variously entitled *Fioretto della Bibbia, Fiore di tutta la Bibbia, Fiore novello,* reprinted until mid-sixteenth century);
3. *Il Lucidario* (or *Rosario?) della Madonna* (probably to be identified with the *Rosario della Gloriosa Vergine Maria,* by the Dominican Albert da Castello, which also was frequently reprinted in the sixteenth century);
4. *Il Lucendario (sic,* for *Legendario) de santi* (the translation of the widely diffused *Legenda aurea* by Jacopo da Voragine, edited by Niccolò Malermi, which appeared under the title *Legendario delle vite de tutti li santi);*
5. *Historia del giudicio* (an anonymous fifteenth-century poem in *ottava rima* that circulated in numerous versions of varying length);
6. *Il cavallier Zuanne de Mandavilla* (the Italian translation of the famous book of travels written in the mid-fourteenth century and attributed to a Sir John Mandeville, reprinted many times throughout the sixteenth century);
7. "A book called *Zampollo"* (actually *Il sogno dil Caravia,* printed in Venice in 1541).

To these titles should be added others mentioned in the second trial:

8. *Il supplimento delle cronache* (the vernacular translation of the chronicle compiled by the Augustinian of Bergamo, Jacopo Filippo Foresti, at the end of the fifteenth century. It was reprinted and enlarged many times until the late sixteenth century with the title *Supplementum supplementi delle croniche . . .);*
9. *Lunario al modo di Italia calculato composto nella città di Pesaro dal ecc. mo dottore Marino Camilo de Leonardis* (many reprintings are known of this also);
10. the *Decameron* of Boccaccio in an unexpurgated edition;

11. an unidentified book that a witness supposed was the Koran (an Italian translation had appeared in Venice in 1547).

13

First of all, let's see how Menocchio managed to get hold of these books. The only one that we are certain was purchased is the *Fioretto della Bibbia,* "which," Menocchio said, "I bought in Venice for 2 soldi." We have no information about three others—the *Historia del Giudicio,* the *Lunario,* and the presumed Koran. Foresti's *Supplementum* was given to Menocchio as a gift by Tomaso Mero da Malmins. All the rest—six out of eleven, more than half—were loaned to him. These are important facts that permit us to perceive in this tiny community a network of readers who overcame the obstacle of their meager financial resources by passing books to one another. The *Lucidario* (or *Rosario) della Madonna* was loaned to Menocchio by a woman, Anna de Cecho, during his exile at Arba in 1564. Her son, Giorgio Capel, when summoned to testify (his mother had died), said that he had a book entitled *La vita de santi;* other books of his had been confiscated by the priest of Arba, who returned only two or three to him declaring that they (the inquisitors, evidently) "will want to burn the rest." The Bible and the *Legendario de santi* had been loaned to Menocchio by his uncle, Domenico Gerbas, but since the *Legendario* "had become wet, it tore." The Bible, instead, ended up in the hands of Bastian Scandella from whom Menocchio, who was his cousin, borrowed it from time to time. Six or seven months before the trial, however, Bastian's wife, Fior, had taken the Bible and had burned it in the oven: "But it was a sin to have burned that book!" Menocchio exclaimed. The Mandeville had been loaned to him five or six years before by the priest Andrea Bionima, curate of Montereale, who had discovered it by chance at Maniago while going through "some notarial documents." (At any rate, Bionima prudently stated that he had not been the one to give Menocchio the book, but rather that it was Vincenzo Lombardo, who knew "how to read a little" and must have taken it home.) The *Sogno dil Caravia* had been loaned to Menocchio by Nicola da Porcia, who may be identified perhaps, as we have seen, with that Nicola de Melchiori from whom he had received the *Decameron* through Lunardo della Minussa of Montereale. Menocchio, in turn, had loaned the *Fioretto* to a young man of Barcis, Tita Coradina, who claimed that he had read only one page of it. Then the priest told him that it was a forbidden book and he burned it.

It was a lively network involving not only priests (which was foreseeable) but women as well. We know that in Udine, at the beginning of the sixteenth century, a school was opened under the direction of Girolamo Amaseo, "for reading and teaching, without exception, children of citizens as well as those of artisans and the lower classes, old as well as young, without any set payment." Elementary schools, where even a little Latin was taught, also existed in such places as Aviano and Pordenone not far from Montereale. Just the same, it's astonishing that so much reading went on in this small town in the hills. Unfortunately, only rarely are we provided with information that permits us to identify the social position of these readers. We have already mentioned the painter Nicola da Porcía. Menocchio's cousin, Bastian Scandella, appears in the 1596 assessment mentioned above as a person who held (but we don't know in what capacity) many sections of land; he was also the mayor of Montereale in the same year. But almost all the others are just names. It seems to be clear, at any rate, that books were part of daily life for these people. They were objects to be used, treated without excessive regard, sometimes exposed to the dangers of water and tearing. Significant, however, is Menocchio's scandalized reaction over the Bible that finished in the fire (undoubtedly so that it would not be found in a possible search by the Holy Office). In spite of his ironic comparison of Scripture with "the books of battle that grew and grew," to him the former was a book different from all others because it contained an essential element provided by God.

14

The fact that more than half the books mentioned by Menocchio had been borrowed should be kept in mind in analyzing the contents of this list. Only for the *Fioretto della Bibbia,* in fact, can we claim with certainty that it was a real and actual choice on Menocchio's part that had led him to buy precisely *that* book out of the many gathered in the shop or stall of the unknown Venetian bookseller. It is of significance, as we shall see, that for him the *Fioretto* had been a sort of bedside book, a *livre de chevet.* On the other hand, chance alone had led the priest Andrea Bionima to stumble upon the Mandeville volume among the "notarial papers" in Maniago; and an indiscriminate appetite for reading matter, rather than a particular interest, must have brought it into Menocchio's hands. This is probably also the case with all the books borrowed from the other villagers. The list that we have reconstructed reflects chiefly the books Menocchio might have had at his disposal, but certainly not a picture of intentional preferences and choices.

Furthermore, it's an incomplete list. This explains, for example, the prevalence of religious texts: six out of the eleven. It's natural that during his two trials Menocchio should refer above all to readings of this type to justify his own ideas. A complete list of the books he had either possessed or read probably would have presented a more varied picture and would have included, for example, some of those "books of battle" that he had provocatively compared to the Bible—perhaps the *Libro che tratta di bataglia, chiamato Fioravante* (Venice, 1506) or one similar to it. But even this handful of titles, fragmentary and one-sided as it may be, permits a certain amount of discussion. Besides Scripture there are works of piety, versions of Scripture in verse and prose, saints' lives, an almanac, a semi-comical poem, a book of travels, a chronicle, a collection of stories (the *Decameron):* all vernacular texts (we've said that Menocchio knew little more Latin than what he had learned serving Mass) composed two or three centuries before that were widely diffused and read by people of various social levels. The Foresti and the Mandeville, for example, had also been in the library of another, very different "unlettered man" ("omo sanza lettere"), in other words, one almost totally ignorant of Latin, namely, Leonardo da Vinci. And the *Historia del Giudicio* appears among the books owned by the famous naturalist Ulisse Aldrovandi (who, incidentally, had had dealings with the Inquisition for his association with heretical groups in his youth). Certainly, the Koran (if Menocchio really did read it) stands out on this list: but it's an exception that we'll consider separately. The rest are fairly obvious titles that appear incapable of shedding light on how Menocchio had happened to formulate what one of his fellow villagers called "fantastic opinions."

15

Once again we have the impression of being in a blind alley. Earlier, faced by Menocchio's extravagant cosmogony, we stopped to ask ourselves just as the vicar general had, whether this was not the talk of a madman. After discarding this hypothesis, the examination of his ecclesiology suggested another, that Menocchio might have been an

Anabaptist. Rejecting this as well we confronted the problem of his ties to the Reformation, on the basis of the information that Menocchio considered himself a "Lutheran" martyr. However, the attempt to fit Menocchio's ideas and beliefs within a deeply-rooted current of peasant radicalism brought to the surface by the Reformation (but independent of it) now seems to be emphatically contradicted by the list of readings we've reconstructed from the trial records. To what extent can we consider as typical such an unusual figure as that of a sixteenth-century miller who knew how to read and write? And typical of what? Certainly not of a current in peasant culture, seeing that Menocchio himself pointed to a group of printed books as sources for his ideas. By dint of running up against the walls of this labyrinth, we've returned to the point of departure.

Almost, that is. We have seen what books Menocchio read. But how did he read them?

When we compare, one by one, passages from the books mentioned by Menocchio with the conclusions that he drew from them (if not with the manner in which he reported them to the judges), we invariably find gaps and discrepancies of serious proportions. Any attempt to consider these books as "sources" in the mechanical sense of the term collapses before the aggressive originality of Menocchio's reading. More than the text, then, what is important is the key to his reading, a screen that he unconsciously placed between himself and the printed page: a filter that emphasized certain words while obscuring others, that stretched the meaning of a word, taking it out of its context, that acted on Menocchio's memory and distorted the very words of the text. And this screen, this key to his reading, continually leads us back to a culture that is very different from the one expressed on the printed page—one based on an oral tradition.

This doesn't mean that for Menocchio the book was incidental, or a pretext. He himself declared, as we shall see, that at least one book had moved him deeply, encouraging him to think new thoughts by its startling assertions. It was the encounter between the printed page and the oral culture, of which he was one embodiment, that led Menocchio to formulate—first for himself, later for his fellow villagers, and finally for the judges—the "opinions . . . [that] came out of *his* head."

16

We might illustrate Menocchio's manner of reading by a series of examples of progressively increasing complexity. In the first interrogation he repeated that Christ had been a man like all other men, born of St. Joseph and the Virgin Mary. And he explained that Mary "was called a Virgin, having been in the temple of the virgins, because there was a temple where twelve virgins were kept, and as they grew up they were married off, and I read this in a book called the *Lucidario della Madonna.*" This book, which he called the *Rosario* elsewhere, was probably the *Rosario della gloriosa Vergine Maria* by the Dominican Alberto da Castello. Menocchio would have been able to read in it: "Contemplate here zealous soul, how after making an offering to God and to the priest, St. Joachim and St. Anne left their most precious daughter in the temple of God, where she was to be cared for with the other virgins who had been dedicated to God. In that place she dwelt in sublime devotion contemplating divine things, and she was visited by the Holy Angels, as though she were their queen and empress, and she was always engaged in prayer."

What may have led Menocchio to pause over this page in the *Rosario* was the fact that he had frequently seen the scenes of Mary at the temple and of Joseph with the pretenders in frescoes executed in 1566 by a follower of Pordenone, Calderari, on the walls of the church of St. Rocco in Montereale. In any case, he changed the significance without actually distorting the literal meaning. In the text, the appearance of the angels set Mary apart from her companions, conferring a supernatural aura upon her. But in Menocchio's mind, the significant element was the presence of "the other virgins," which explained in the simplest manner the title given to Mary by linking her with her companions. Thus, what was originally a detail ended by becoming the central issue, thereby altering the general sense.

17

At the end of the interrogation held on 28 April, after having, without restraint, poured out his accusations against the Church, priests, the sacraments, and ecclesiastical ceremonies, Menocchio declared, in reply to a question by the inquisitor: "I believe that in this world the empress was greater than the Madonna, but in the hereafter the

Madonna is greater, because there we are invisible." The inquisitor's question originated in an episode reported by a witness that Menocchio promptly confirmed: "Yes sir, it is true that when the empress passed by I said that she was greater than the Madonna, but I meant in this world; and in that book about the Madonna many honors were neither given nor paid to her and, in fact, when she was brought to be buried she was treated with dishonor, because someone wanted to pull her off the shoulders of the apostles, and he remained attached to her by his hands, and this was in the life of the Madonna."

To what text was Menocchio referring? The expression "book of the Madonna" again might suggest the *Rosario della gloriosa Vergine Maria:* but the reference doesn't fit. Instead, the passage occurs in another book read by Menocchio, the *Legendario delle vite de tutti li santi* by Jacopo da Voragine, in the chapter entitled "On the Assumption of the blessed Virgin Mary," which is a revision of "a certain apocryphal booklet ascribed to blessed John the Evangelist." This is Voragine's description of Mary's last rites:

> And the angels and the apostles were singing and filling the earth with the news of her wonderful life. All those who were awakened by such a sweet melody went out of the city, and having diligently inquired what was happening, someone said: "The disciples are carrying that Mary who died, and they are singing the melody that you hear about her." Then they all ran to take up arms, inciting one another by saying: "Come, let us kill all the disciples, and let us consume with fire the body that once bore that seducer." And beholding this the prince of the priests, also astonished and filled with anger, exclaimed scornfully: "Here is the tabernacle of the one who troubled us and our generation, [see] now what glory she has received." And after he had said this, he laid his hand on the bier and tried to cast it to the ground together with the body, but when he placed his hands on the bier they withered instantly and remained attached to it: tortured by great suffering he cried out with loud laments, and the rest of the people were struck blind by the angels who were in the clouds. Then the prince of the priests cried out, "I beg you, oh St. Peter, do not abandon me in this tribulation, I beg you to intercede for me with the Lord; don't you remember how I forgave you the times you were accused by the maidservant." To this Peter said: "We are being disturbed in the obsequies to our Lady, and at the moment we cannot attend to curing you. But if you will believe in the Lord Jesus and in the one who bore him, I trust that you will promptly receive the gift of health." And the priest replied: "I believe the Lord Jesus to be the true son of God, and that this is his most holy mother." Instantly his hands were released from the bier, but the dryness remained in his arms and the severe pain had not left him. Then Peter said: "Kiss the bier and say I believe in God Jesus Christ, whom she carried in her womb, remaining a virgin after his birth." And when he did this he was restored. . . .

For the author of the *Legendario,* the chief priest's insult to the corpse of Mary was resolved in the description of a miraculous cure and, finally, in the exaltation of the Virgin Mary, Christ's mother. But evidently, for Menocchio, the account of the miracle was unimportant, and the reaffirmation of Mary's virginity, which he repeatedly rejected, even less so. He singles out only an action by the priest, the "dishonor" to Mary during her burial, evidence of her miserable condition. Through the filter of Menocchio's memory Voragine's story is transformed into its very opposite.

18

The mention of the passage from the *Legendario* was almost incidental. The one that we have already cited from the *Fioretto della Bibbia,* however, was much more important. In the first interrogation, we recall, Menocchio had insisted that he didn't believe in the immaculate conception of Mary by virtue of the Holy Spirit "because many men have been born into the world, but none of a virgin woman," and also because in a book called *Fioretto della Bibbia* he had read "that St. Joseph called our Lord Jesus Christ his son." He argued from this that Christ was the son of St. Joseph. Now in chapter 166 of the *Fioretto,* "How Jesus was sent to school," one reads that Jesus cursed the teacher who slapped him, and caused him to be stricken dead on the spot. Viewing the anger of the bystanders, "Joseph said, 'Control yourself my son, can you not see how many people hate us?' " "My son" Menocchio noted. But on the same page, in the chapter immediately preceding, which is entitled "How Jesus, while playing with other children, revived a child who had died," Menocchio could have read the following reply from Mary to a woman who had asked her if Jesus was her son: "Yes, he is my son, his father is the one God."

Menocchio's manner of reading was obviously one-sided and arbitrary—almost as if he was searching for confirmation of ideas and convictions that were already firmly entrenched. In the present instance, the conviction was that "Christ was born a man like us." It was irrational to believe that Christ was born of a virgin, and that he died on the cross: "If he was God eternal he should not have let himself be taken and crucified."

19

We shouldn't be surprised by Menocchio's use of passages in the *Legendario* and the *Fioretto,* taken from the apocryphal gospels. In view of the contrast he drew between the laconic simplicity of God's Word—"four words"— and the immoderate growth of Scripture, the very notion of apocryphal had to be abandoned. Apocryphal and canonical gospels alike were placed on the same level and were regarded as purely human texts. On the other hand, contrary to what we might have expected in view of the testimony given by the people of Montereale ("he is always arguing with one person or another, and he has the vernacular Bible and imagines that he bases his reasoning on it"), Menocchio made very few specific references to Scripture during his trial. In fact, such parascriptural adaptations as the *Fioretto della Bibbia* would seem to be better known to him than the vernacular Bible. Thus, on 8 March, replying to an unspecified question put to him by the vicar general, Menocchio proclaimed, "I say that it is a greater rule to love one's neighbor than to love God." Even this statement was based on a text. Menocchio added immediately afterward: "because I read in a *Historia del Giudicio* that when judgment day comes, [God] will say to that angel: 'You are wicked, you have never done a good deed for me'; and that angel replies: 'My lord, I have never seen you so that I could do you a good deed.' [And God said] 'I was hungry and you did not feed me, I was thirsty and you did not give me drink, I was naked and you did not clothe me, when I was in prison you did not come to visit me.' And because of this I believed that God was that poor neighbor, because he said 'I was that beggar.' "
And this is the corresponding passage from the *Historia del Giudicio:*

> Oh, you who have already been blessed by my father
> Come to possess my glory:
> Hungry and thirsty was I,
> And you gave me to eat and drink;
> In prison I suffered bitter torment,
> And always you came to see me;
> I was infirm, and was visited
> And I died, and I was buried by you.
>
> And after each one has been gladdened
> They will come to Jesus Christ to ask
> "When, Lord, were you hungry
> That we gave you to drink and eat?
> When, infirm, were you visited
> And, dead, did we come to bury you?
> When, in prison, did we visit you,
> And when did we give you clothing?"

Christ will reply in joyful countenance:
"That beggar who came to the door
Famished, afflicted, and overcome
Was asking for charity in my name,
He was not driven off or cut down by you,
But he ate and drank of what was yours,
To him you gave for love of God:
Know that I was that beggar."

From the left they will then seek to speak
But God will drive them off with great anger,
Saying: "Sinners of evil life
Go dwell amidst the eternal flames of hell.
From you I received nothing to drink or eat
Nor did you do anything good for love of me.
Go, damned ones, to the everlasting fire
Where you will abide in eternal grief."

Those sorrowful peoples will respond:
"When, Lord, did we ever see you
Famished, afflicted, and in distress,
When did you suffer such travails in prison?"
And then Christ glorious will reply:
"When you drove off the miserable beggar.
You did not have pity for the downtrodden
Or ever show charity toward them."

One can see that these crude octaves prosaically copy a passage from the Gospel of Matthew 25:41–46. But it's to these verses, rather than to the biblical text, that Menocchio is referring. Here, too, the borrowing from the printed page—which is basically accurate except for a curious slip that attributes the protestations of the damned to the "angel"—actually becomes a revision of it. But if distortion of the meaning in the preceding cases had occurred essentially by way of omissions, the procedure here is more complex. Menocchio takes one more step in respect to the text that, though small in appearance, is actually enormous: if God is our neighbor, "because he said, 'I was that beggar,' " it's more important to love our neighbor than to love God. It was a conclusion that heightened in a radical direction the insistence on a practical, active religiosity common to almost all Italian heretical groups at this time. Even the Anabaptist Bishop Benedetto d'Asolo taught the belief in "only one God, only one Jesus Christ our Lord the mediator" and charity toward one's neighbor, because "on the day of judgment . . . we shall be asked only if we gave food to the hungry, drink to the thirsty, clothed the naked, visited the sick, sheltered travelers . . . these are the foundations of charity." But Menocchio's attitude toward preaching of this type—if it actually reached his ears, as seems possible—was not simply a passive one. A decided tendency to reduce religion to morality appears frequently in his utterances. In a remarkable line of reasoning, packed as usual with vivid images, Menocchio explained to the inquisitor that to blaspheme is not sinful "because it only hurts oneself and not one's neighbor, just as if I have a cloak and tear it, I injure only myself and no one else, and I believe that he who does no harm to his neighbor does not commit sin; and because we are all children of God, if we do not hurt one another, as for example, if a father has several children, and one of them says 'damn my father,' the father may forgive him, but if this child breaks the head of someone else's child he cannot pardon him so easily if he does not pay: therefore have I said that it is not sinful to blaspheme because it does not hurt anyone." Thus, the person who doesn't injure his neighbor is not committing a sin: man's relationship to God becomes unimportant compared to his relationship with his neighbor. And if God is that neighbor, why then do we need God?

Certainly, Menocchio didn't take this final step that would have led him to affirm an ideal of a just human society wholly devoid of religious values. For him, love toward a neighbor remained a religious precept, or, better yet, the very essence of religion. And, generally, his attitude wasn't without vacillation (for this reason, in his case one should speak only of a tendency to reduce religion to morality). He was accustomed to say to his compatriots (according to the witness Bartolomeo d'Andrea): "I teach you not to do evil, not to take the property of others, and this is the good that we can do." But during the interrogation that took place on the afternoon of 1 May, the inquisitor asked him to specify what were "the works of God" by means of which one went to heaven, to which Menocchio—who, in fact, had spoken simply of "good works"—replied: "love [God], adore him, sanctify him, revere and thank him; and also one should be charitable, merciful, peaceful, loving, honorable, obedient to one's superiors, pardon injuries, and keep promises: and for doing this one goes to heaven, and this is all we need to go there." In this instance, duties toward one's neighbor were placed alongside duties to God, without stating the superiority of the first over the second. But the list of the "bad works" immediately following—"to rob, assassinate, commit usury, commit cruelties, dishonor, vituperate, and murder: these are seven works that displease God, do harm to the world, and are pleasing to the devil"—dealt exclusively with human relationships, with man's capacity to be unjust toward his fellow man. And Menocchio's simplified religion ("and for doing this one goes to heaven, and this is all we need to go there") couldn't be accepted by the inquisitor: "What are God's commandments"? "I believe," Menocchio replied, "they are the ones I mentioned before." "To call out God's name, to sanctify holy days, are these not precepts of God"? "This I do not know."

In reality, it was just this exclusive insistence on the Gospel message in its most meager and simple form that permitted extreme conclusions such as Menocchio's. This danger had been foreseen with exceptional insight almost fifty years earlier in one of the most important writings produced by Italian evangelism—an anonymous booklet published in Venice with the title *Alcune ragioni del perdonare.* The author, Tullio Crispoldi, was a faithful companion of the celebrated bishop of Verona, Gian Matteo Giberti. Building upon a series of the bishop's sermons, Crispoldi endeavored to demonstrate with a variety of arguments that the essence of Christianity was "the law of forgiving," the forgiving of one's neighbor so as to be forgiven by God. At a certain point, however, he came to see clearly that this "law of forgiving" could be interpreted exclusively in a human sense, thus "endangering" the worship owed to God: "The prescription to forgive is so powerful and so prevalent that by making this law, God has endangered the devotion that is his due. In fact, it has the semblance of a law made only by men for the salvation of all men, by means of which it is openly declared that God does not want to consider the offenses that we have committed against him, however numerous, so long as we forgive and love one another. And indeed, if he did not grant grace to those who forgive and allow them to leave behind their sins and become good men, everyone would have cause to judge this not as being a law of God intended for governing men, but rather as a law devised by men who, for the sake of being and living in peace, do not concern themselves with offenses or sins committed secretly or in company so as not to disturb the peace and well-being of the world. But seeing that he who forgives for the honor of God, obtains what he desires from God and is favored by God and becomes disposed to do good works and to turn away from evil ones, people become strengthened in their awareness of the goodness of God toward us."

Only the supernatural intervention of divine grace, then, prevents taking the core of Christ's message (the "law of forgiving") as a purely human political bond. The possibility of such a worldly interpretation of religion is clearly very much on the mind of the author of the booklet. He is familiar with (and partly influenced by) its most coherent expression, Machiavelli's—and not the Machiavelli diminished by over-simplification into the theoretician of the *religio instrumentum regni,* but rather the Machiavelli of the *Discorsi,* who sees religion primarily as a powerful factor contributing to political unity. But the target being attacked in the passage that we have quoted seems to be different: not so much the tendency to consider religion objectively *from without,* but rather that which corrodes its foundations *from within.* Crispoldi's anxiety that the "law of forgiving" could be understood as "a law made only by men for the salvation of all men, by means of which it is openly declared that God does not want to consider the offenses that we have committed against him, however numerous, so long as we forgive and love one another," recalls almost to the letter Menocchio's words to the inquisitor: "I believe that he who does no harm to his neighbor does not commit sin; and because we are all children of God, if we do not hurt one another, as for example, if a father has several children, and one of them says 'damn my father,' the father may forgive him, but if this child breaks the head of someone else's child he cannot pardon him so easily if he does not pay . . . ."

Naturally, there's no reason to suppose that Menocchio was familiar with the *Ragioni del perdonare.* In sixteenth-century Italy, however, in the most heterogeneous circles a tendency existed (recognized with remarkable perception by Crispoldi) to reduce religion to nothing more than worldly reality—to a moral or political bond. This tendency found different modes of expression, based on very different premises. However, even in this instance, it may be possible to discern a partial convergence between the most progressive circles among the educated classes and popular groups with radical leanings.

At this point, if we should return to the rough verses of the *Historia del Giudicio* cited by Menocchio in order to justify his own belief ("I say that it is a greater rule to love one's neighbor than to love God") it seems clear that once again his interpretative filter was far more important than the "source" itself. Even if Menocchio's interpretation was triggered by contact with this text, its roots had distant origins.

20

And yet, there were some texts that really had meant a lot to Menocchio: and first among them, by his own admission, was "the knight Zuanne de Mandavilla," namely, the *Travels* of Sir John Mandeville. When the trial reopened in Portogruaro the inquisitors, threateningly this time, reiterated the usual exhortation to name "all his accomplices, or else more rigorous measures would be taken against him; because it seems impossible to this Holy Office that he should have learned so many things alone, and that he does not have companions." "Sir, I am not aware that I ever taught anyone," was Menocchio's reply, "nor has anyone shared my opinions; and what I have said came from that book of Mandeville that I read." More precisely, Menocchio, in a letter to his judges from prison, listed second among the causes of his errors "having read that book of Mandeville about many kinds of races and different laws that sorely troubled me." What was the reason for this "troubling," for this agitation? To answer this we shall have to consider, first of all, what this book actually contained.

The *Travels,* probably originally written in French at Liège, in mid-fourteenth century, and attributed to a Sir John Mandeville, is basically a compilation based on geographical texts and on such medieval encyclopedias as the *Speculum* by Vincent of Beauvais. After circulating widely in manuscript, the work passed through many printed editions, both in Latin and in the principal European languages.

The *Travels* is divided into two parts very different in content. The first is a journey to the Holy Land, a sort of pilgrim's tourist guide. The second is the description of a voyage to the Orient. It touches ever more distant islands—as far away as India, as far away even as Cathay, that is, China. The book ends with a description of the earthly paradise and of the islands that border the kingdom of the mythical Prester John. Both parts are presented as eyewitness reports: but whereas the first abounds in precise and documented observations, the second is mostly imaginary.

Doubtless, the contents of the first part were largely responsible for the book's extraordinary success. It's well known that throughout the sixteenth century the circulation of descriptions of the Holy Land continued to outnumber those of the New World. And Mandeville's reader could acquire a series of facts both about the holy places and the locations of the principal relics preserved there, as well as about the practices and customs of the inhabitants. Menocchio, as we know, was completely indifferent to relics: but the minute description of the theological or ritual peculiarities of the Greek church and of "the different manners of Christians" (Samaritans, Jacobites, Syrians, Georgians) living in the Holy Land, and of their schisms with the Church of Rome, must have aroused his interest. His denial of the sacramental efficacy of confession would have found confirmation, or perhaps stimulus, in Mandeville's description of the doctrines of the "Jacobites," who bore this name because they had been converted by St. James: "They say that a man shall make his confession only to God and promise to make amends only to him; and therefore when they want to confess they light a fire next to themselves and cast incense and other aromatic spices into it and in the smoke they confess to God and ask for mercy." Mandeville termed this kind of confession "natural" and "primitive" (two adjectives filled with significance for a sixteenth-century reader), hastening to recognize that "the holy Fathers and popes who came later ordered man to make confession to another man, and with good reason, because they perceived that as no sickness can be cured nor good medicine administered if first one does not know the nature of the illness, similarly, a good penance cannot be imposed if one does not first know the nature of the sin, because sins are not the same, neither are places nor times. Therefore it is necessary to know the nature of the sin and the places and the times, and then impose the proper penance." Now, Menocchio—although he contemptuously placed confession to a priest and confession to a tree on the same level—admitted that the priest could impart "the knowledge of penance" to one who lacked it: "if that tree could give the knowledge of penance, it would be good enough; and if some men seek out priests because they do not know what penance has to be made for their sins, in order that the priests may teach it to them, if they had understood this matter, there would be no need to go to them, and for those who already know, it is useless." Was this a recollection from Mandeville?

Mandeville's long exposition of the religion of Mohammed would have fascinated Menocchio even more. It appears from the second trial that he attempted (but, as we said, the evidence is unconfirmed) to satisfy his curiosity on the subject by directly reading the Koran, which had been translated into Italian in mid-sixteenth century. But Menocchio would have been able to learn even from Mandeville's travels certain beliefs of the Mohammedans that coincide in part with his own. Mandeville reported that, according to the Koran, "among all the prophets Jesus was the most excellent and the one closest to God." And Menocchio, practically echoing him: "I doubted that . . . he was God, instead he must have been some prophet, some great man sent by God to preach in this world." In Mandeville, again, he had been able to find a clear rejection of Christ's crucifixion, considered to be impossible because it contradicted the justice of God: "but he was never crucified as they say; on the contrary, God caused him to ascend to him without death and without blemish, but his body was transformed into one called Judas Iscariot whom the Jews crucified thinking he was Jesus, who had ascended alive to heaven to judge the world: and therefore they say . . . that in this article we err, because the great righteousness of God would not suffer such a thing. . . ." It seems that Menocchio believed something similar, according to the testimony of one of his fellow villagers: "it is not true that Christ was crucified, but rather it was Simon of Cyrene." Indeed, even for Menocchio, the crucifixion, the paradox of the cross, was unacceptable: "it seemed a strange thing to me that a lord would allow himself to be taken in this way, and so I suspected that since he was crucified he was not God, but some prophet. . . . "

These are obvious, if partial, similarities. But it doesn't seem possible that reading these pages could have troubled Menocchio. He would have been even less fazed by the severe judgment of Christianity that Mandeville attributed to the sultan: "they [the Christians] should set an example of good behavior for common people; they should go to the temples to serve God, and instead they pass the whole day in taverns, gambling, drinking, gourging themselves like animals. . . . And they should be simple and humble and gentle and worthy and charitable as was Jesus Christ in whom they believe. But instead they do the contrary and the opposite, and they all incline to do evil, and are so greedy and avaricious that for small gain they sell their children, their sisters, and their own wives to be prostitutes, and they take each other's wives, and do not keep the faith, in fact do not abide by the law that Jesus Christ provided for their salvation. . . ."

This picture of the corruption of Christianity, written two hundred years earlier, must certainly have been read by Menocchio as an absolutely contemporary and relevant text. The greediness of priests and monks, the privileges and deceptions of those who styled themselves followers of Christ were his to behold every day. At most Menocchio could have found in the words of the sultan a confirmation and a justification for his own implacable criticism of the Church, but not a reason for feeling deeply troubled. This must be sought elsewhere.

21

"The peoples of these lands have different laws, because some worship the sun, some fire, some the trees, some serpents, and others the first thing they encounter in the morning. Still others worship images and idols. . . ." Mandeville related these facts at the beginning of the second part of his travels in speaking of Chana, a small island off the Indian coast. Here he mentions, and later repeats many times, the "different laws," the variety of beliefs and religious customs that had so badly "troubled" Menocchio. By means of Mandeville's accounts, his largely imaginary descriptions of distant lands, Menocchio's mental universe expanded enormously. It no longer consisted only of Montereale, or Pordenone, or even Venice—the places of his world as a miller—but rather, India and Cathay and islands inhabited by cannibals, Pigmies, and men with the heads of dogs. It was on the subject of Pigmies that Mandeville wrote a page destined to enjoy an extraordinary success:

"they are people short in stature, who are about three spans long: and they are beautiful and graceful, both men and women, because of their smallness. They marry when they are six months of age and beget children when they are two or three years old and generally they do not live beyond six or seven years: and those who live eight years are considered ancient. These Pigmies are extremely skillful and great masters in working with silk and cotton and in everything that there is in the world. And they frequently battle against the birds in their country and are often taken and eaten by them. These small people work neither land nor vineyards, but have large people of our stature dwelling among them who cultivate the land. They [the Pigmies] . . . despise them just as we would despise the Pigmies if they lived among us. . . . "

The scorn of the Pigmies for the "large people of our stature" is the key to the confusion that this book caused Menocchio to experience. The diversity of beliefs and practices described by Mandeville led Menocchio to ask himself about the foundations of his own beliefs and acts. These largely imaginary islands furnished him with an Archimedean point from which to look at the world where he was born and had lived. "So many kinds of races and . . . different laws," "many islands where some lived in one way and some in another," "out of many different kinds of nations, some believe in one way, some in another"; Menocchio stressed this point repeatedly in the course of the trial.

In these same years a nobleman of Périgord, Michel de Montaigne, had experienced a similar relativistic shock while reading accounts of the natives in the New World. But Menocchio was not Montaigne, he was only a self-taught miller. His life had been passed almost completely within the walls of the village of Montereale. He knew neither Greek nor Latin (at the most some snatches of prayers); he had read only a few books and these largely by chance. He had chewed upon and squeezed meaning out of every word in these books. He pondered them for years; for years words and phrases had fermented in his memory. One example will illustrate the process of his long and laborious development. In chapter 148 of Mandeville's *Travels* entitled "Of the island of Dondun where they eat one another when they cannot escape, and of the power of its king, who rules over 54 other islands, and of many types of men who inhabit these islands," Menocchio had come upon this page:

> In this island there are peoples of different natures, since the father eats his son and the son his father, and the husband his wife, and the wife her husband. When the father or the mother or one of their friends becomes ill, the son or someone else among them goes at once to the priest of their law and begs him to question their idol, which by virtue of the devil behind him replies, saying he will not die on this occasion, and teaches them how

> he must be cured: and then the son returns and serves the father and carries out what the idol has commanded until he has cured him. Husbands do the same for their wives and friends for one another. But if the idol declares that he (the sick person) must die, then the priest goes with the son and with the wife or with the sick friend, and they lay a cloth over his mouth to stop his breath, and by suffocating him they kill him, and then they slice up the body into pieces and invite all their friends to come and eat from his dead body, and they summon as many pipers as they can, and thus eat with great rejoicing and with great solemnity. And when they have consumed him they take the bones and bury them singing and making great celebration and melody: and all their relatives and friends who did not attend this celebration are reproved and they suffer great shame and sorrow, because they are no longer considered friends. The friends say that they eat his flesh to free him from suffering: and they say that if the flesh is too lean, they committed a great sin to have allowed him to languish and suffer so much pain without reason; and when the flesh is fat, they say that it is well and that they have sent him to paradise quickly, and he has not suffered at all. . . .

This description of ritual cannibalism affected Menocchio powerfully (as it had Leonardo, whom it drove to inveigh against the evil in men). This emerges clearly from the interrogation of 22 February. The vicar general asked for the umpteenth time, "Tell me who were the companions with whom you shared these opinions." To which Menocchio replied: "Sir, I have never met anyone who holds these opinions; my opinions came out of my head. It's true that I once read a book lent to me by our chaplain, Father Andrea da Maren, who now lives in Monte Real. That book was entitled *Il cavalier Zuanne de Mandavilla;* I believe it was French, printed in the vernacular Italian language. It may be five or six years ago that he lent it to me, but I returned it to him at least two years ago. And this book dealt with a journey to Jerusalem, and certain differences between the Greeks and the pope; and it also dealt with the great Khan, with the city of Babylon, with Prester John, and Jerusalem, and also with many islands where some lived in one way and some in another. And it told how this knight went to the sultan, who asked him about priests, cardinals, the pope, and the clergy; and he related how Jerusalem once belonged to the Christians and God took it from them because of bad government by Christians and the pope. He also discussed in one place how when one died . . . " At this point the inquisitor impatiently interrupted Menocchio to ask him "if this book did not have something to say about chaos." And Menocchio replied: "No sir, but I read about that in the *Fioretto della Bibia;* the other things I have said about this chaos I made up in my own head." Immediately after, he resumed the thread of the interrupted discussion: "This same book by the knight Mandeville also related how when men were sick and near death they would go to their priest, and that priest beseeched an idol, and that idol told them whether he had to die or not, and if he had to die the priest suffocated him, and they ate him in company: and if he tasted good he was sinless, and if he tasted bad he had many sins, and they had done wrong to let him live so long. And from there I got my opinion that when the body dies, the soul dies too, since out of many different kinds of nations, some believe in one way and some in another."

Once again, Menocchio's vivid memory had assimilated, transposed, and remolded words and phrases. The lean corpse had become bad (to eat), the fat one good (to eat). The moral as well as gastronomic interchange of these terms (good, bad) transferred the attribution of sin from the killers to the killed. Thus, one who was good (to eat) was sinless, one who was bad (to eat) was sinful. At this point Menocchio burst forth with his conclusion: the hereafter doesn't exist, future punishments and rewards don't exist, heaven and hell are on earth, the soul is mortal. As usual, he aggressively distorted the text (but obviously in a wholly involuntary manner). The flood of questions that he brought to his books went far beyond the written page. But in this particular case the function of the text was not at all secondary: "*And from there I got* my opinion that when the body dies, the soul dies too, *since out of many different kinds of nations, some believe in one way some in another.*"

22

Nevertheless, the insistence on the variety of laws and customs was only one aspect of Mandeville's narrative. At the opposite extreme was the recognition of an element that remained virtually constant in the midst of such great diversity: namely, a rationality that was always joined to faith in a God who was creator of the world, a "God of nature." So, after having spoken of the worshippers of idols and images on the island of Chana, Mandeville stated: "And you should know that everyone who adores images does so out of respect for some valiant man who once lived, such as Hercules, and many others who performed great marvels in their time. However, these people say they know well that these valiant ones of old are not gods, that, in fact, there is only one God of nature who made all things and [is] in the sky; and the people know well that these heroes could not have performed their marvels, except for the special grace of God, and because these men were loved by God, they are adored by the people. And they say the same about the sun, because it changes the time and gives heat and nourishment to everything on earth, and because the sun has so much power they know full well that this comes of God's loving it more than other things, and thus has bestowed on it greater worth than on anything else that is in the world. So, it is reasonable, as they say, that it should be honored and revered. . . . "

"Reasonable." With a restrained, detached, almost ethnographic tone Mandeville described exotic facts and beliefs, showing how a rational core lay hidden behind their monstrosity or absurdity. Indeed, the inhabitants of the island of Chana worshipped a deity who was half ox, half man. But they considered the ox "the holiest beast on earth, and most useful among all others," while man "is the most noble of the creatures and has dominion over all beasts." Couldn't there also be some Christians who superstitiously attributed beneficial or malicious powers to certain animals? "Now there is no reason to marvel if pagans, who possess no other doctrine than what is of nature, should, in their simplicity, believe in them more widely." The inhabitants of the island Nacumera (Mandeville related) all had, men and women alike, "the heads of dogs and they are called Cynocephales"—but he added immediately afterward: "they are reasonable people with good understanding." Thus, in the final chapter of the book, at the conclusion of the account of his extraordinary travels, Mandeville could solemnly declare to his readers: "you should know that in all that country (Cathay) and in all those islands made up of diverse peoples and diverse laws and faiths, which I have described, there are none among them who, if they have reason and understanding, do not also have some article of our faith and some good point of our belief, and who do not believe in God who created the world, whom they call *Iretarge,* that is to say, God of nature, in agreement with what the prophet declared: *'et metuent eum omnes fines terrae,'* and elsewhere: *'omnes gentes servient ei, etc.'*; but they do not know how to speak perfectly of God the Father or of the Son or of the Holy Spirit; nor do they know how to speak of the Bible and especially of Genesis and of the other books of Moses, of Exodus, of the prophets, because they have no one to teach them and they know nothing except through their natural intelligence. . . . " Mandeville urged a boundless tolerance toward these people: "although they [the inhabitants of the islands Mesidarata and Genosaffa] do not possess the articles of the faith totally as we do, nevertheless because of their good intentions I believe, in fact, I am certain, that God loves them and welcomes their services, as he did Job's. And for this reason the Lord used to say through the mouth of Hosea the prophet: *'ponam eis multiplices leges meas'*; and elsewhere it is stated in Scripture: *'qui totum subdit orbem legibus.'* Similarly, our Lord said in the Gospel: *'alias oves habeo quae non sunt ex hoc ovili,'* that is to say that he had other servants than those who are Christians by nature under the law . . . we must not hate or feel scorn for any Christian people due to the difference of their law, nor judge any of them. On the contrary, we must pray to God for them because we neither know whom God loves nor whom he hates, since God does not hate any creature that he has made. . . . "

Thus, through Mandeville's *Travels,* this innocent tale interwoven with mythical elements, translated and reprinted countless times, an echo of medieval religious tolerance, reached even the age of the wars of religion, of excommunications, and of the burning of heretics. It was probably only one of several channels feeding into a popular current—of which so far very little is known—favoring toleration, a few traces of which can be discerned in the course of the sixteenth century. Another consisted in the enduring success of the medieval legend of the three rings.

23

This legend had so greatly affected Menocchio that he related it at length during the second trial (12 July 1599) to the inquisitor sitting in judgment, who on this occasion was the Franciscan Gerolamo Asteo. After admitting having said in the past ("but I do not know to whom") that he had been "born a Christian, and so desired to live as a Christian, but if he had been born a Turk, he would have wanted to remain a Turk," Menocchio added: "I beg you, sir, listen to me. There was once a great lord who declared his heir would be the person found to have a certain precious ring of his; and drawing near to his death, he had two other rings similar to the first one made, since he had three sons, and he gave a ring to each son; each one of them thought himself to be the heir and to have the true ring, but because of their similarity it could not be known with certainty. Likewise, God the Father has various children whom he loves, such as Christians, Turks, and Jews and to each of them he has given the will to live by his own law, and we do not know which is the right one. That is why I said that since I was born a Christian I want to remain a Christian, and if I had been born a Turk I would want to live like a Turk." "Do you believe then," the inquisitor retorted, "that we do not know which is the right law?" To which Menocchio replied: "Yes sir, I do believe that every person considers his faith to be right, and we do not know which is the right one: but because my grandfather, my father, and my people have been Christians, I want to remain a Christian, and believe that this is the right one."

This is an extraordinary moment, even in a trial like this, extraordinary from beginning to end. The roles have been temporarily reversed, Menocchio had seized the initiative and attempted to persuade the judge: "I beg you, sir, listen to me." Who here is taking the side of a higher culture, who the side of popular culture? It's not easy to say. The way Menocchio had heard of the story of the three rings made the situation even more paradoxical. He declared that he had read it "in some book or other." The inquisitor discovered what sort of book it was only in the following interrogation: "It is in a prohibited book." Menocchio revealed the title almost a month later: "I read it in the book of the *Cento novelle* by Boccaccio" borrowed from "the late Nicola de Melchiori,"—probably to be identified with the painter Nicola da Porcía from whom Menocchio had, according to a witness, "learned his heresies."

But everything that we have seen thus far shows that Menocchio didn't parrot the opinions or ideas of others. His way of dealing with books, his contorted and awkward statements, are the sure signs of an original approach. Of course, all this didn't occur in a vacuum. More and more clearly we see intellectual and popular currents converging in ways and forms that remain to be explained. It may have been Nicola da Porcía who placed a copy of the *Decameron,* as well as the *Sogno dil Caravia,* into Menocchio's hands. The *Decameron,* or at least part of it— the third story of the first day in which the legend of the three rings is told—made a profound impression on Menocchio. Unfortunately, we don't know how he reacted to Boccaccio's other *novelle.* Certainly, Menocchio's religious attitude, so intolerant of confessional restrictions, must have found support in the story of Melchisedec the Jew. But that very page of Boccaccio's that dealt with the legend of the three rings had fallen under the scissors of the Counter-Reformation censor, notoriously much more concerned with passages offensive to religion than with presumed obscenities. Menocchio must have used an older edition, at any rate one untouched by censorship. The clash between Gerolamo Asteo, inquisitor and canonist, and the miller Domenico Scandella, nicknamed Menocchio, over the story of the three rings and its glorification of tolerance, is in some way symbolic. The Catholic Church at this time was engaged in a two-front war: against high culture, both old and new, which wouldn't conform to Counter-Reformation patterns, and against popular culture. As we saw, subterranean convergences could develop between these two very different opponents.

To the inquisitor's question—"Do you believe then that we do not know which is the right law?"—Menocchio gave a shrewd reply: "Yes sir, *I believe that each person holds his faith to be right, but we do not know which is the right one. . . .* " This was the theory of the advocates of tolerance, a tolerance that Menocchio extended, as had Sebastian Castellio, no longer only to the three great historic religions, but to heretics as well. And just as it did for those contemporary thinkers, Menocchio's position on tolerance had a positive content: "the majesty of God has given the Holy Spirit to all, to Christians, to heretics, to Turks, and to Jews; and he considers them all dear, and they are all saved in the same manner." More than toleration in a strict sense, this was an explicit recognition of the equivalence of all faiths, in the name of a simplified religion, free of dogmatic or confessional considerations. It was something akin to that faith in the "God of nature" that Mandeville had encountered in all peoples, even among the most remote, dissimilar, and monstrous—although, as we shall see, Menocchio, in fact, rejected the idea of a God who was creator of the world.

But in Mandeville that recognition was accompanied by a firm declaration of the superiority of Christianity over the partial truths of the other religions. Thus, once again, Menocchio was going beyond his texts. His religious radicalism, even if it occasionally drew from motifs of medieval tolerance, had more in common with the sophisticated religious theories of contemporary, humanistically trained heretics.

24

We have seen how Menocchio read his books: isolating words and phrases, sometimes distorting them, juxtaposing different passages, firing off rapid analogies. Each time, a comparison between the texts and Menocchio's responses to them has led us to suggest a hidden key to his reading that possible relations with one heretical group or another aren't sufficient to explain. Menocchio mulled over and elaborated on his readings outside any preexistent framework. And his most extraordinary declarations originated from contact with such innocuous texts as Mandeville's *Travels* or the *Historia del Giudicio.* It was not the book as such, but the encounter between the printed page and oral culture that formed an explosive mixture in Menocchio's head.

25

Let's return then to Menocchio's universe, which had appeared incomprehensible to us at the beginning. Now we can reconstruct its complex stratification. It began by departing at once from the Genesis account and its orthodox interpretation by affirming the existence of a primordial chaos: "I have said that, in my opinion, all was chaos, that is, earth, air, water, and fire were mixed together. . . . " (7 February). In a subsequent interrogation, as we saw, the vicar general interrupted Menocchio, who was talking about Mandeville's *Travels*, to ask him "if this book did not have something to say about chaos." Menocchio replied negatively, reiterating (consciously, this time) the previously mentioned interweaving of written and oral culture: "No sir, but I read about that in the *Fioretto della Bibia;* the other things I have said about this chaos I made up in my own head."

Actually, Menocchio hadn't remembered correctly. The *Fioretto della Bibbia* doesn't exactly speak of chaos. Nevertheless, the biblical account of creation is preceded there, without any concern for coherence, by a series of chapters taken largely from the *Elucidarium* of Honorius of Autun, where metaphysics is mixed with astrology and theology with the doctrine of the four temperaments. Chapter 4 of the *Fioretto,* "How God created man out of four elements," begins: "As it is said, in the beginning God made a great substance, which had neither form nor style: and he made so much that he could take and do what he wanted with it, and he divided it and apportioned it so that he made man out of it composed of four elements. . . . " Here, as we see, a primordial confusion of elements is postulated, which, in fact, excludes creation *ex nihilo:* but chaos is not mentioned. It is probable that Menocchio took this learned term from a book that he mentioned incidentally during the second trial (but which, as we shall have occasion to say, was already known to him in 1584): the *Supplementum supplementi delle croniche* by the Augustinian hermit Jacopo Filippo Foresti. This chronicle, written at the end of the fifteenth century but deriving from foundations that were still clearly medieval, begins with the creation of the world. After citing Augustine, the patron of his order, Foresti wrote: "and it is said in the beginning God made heaven and earth: not that this already existed, but there was the potential, because afterward it is written that the heavens were made; it is as if considering the seed of a tree we were to say here is the root, the trunk, the branches, the fruits, and the leaves: it is not that they are already present, but they must grow from this. And so it is said, in the beginning God made heaven and earth, really the seed of heaven and earth, since the substance of heaven and earth was still in a state of confusion; but as it was certain that this was to become heaven and earth, therefore that substance was already called heaven and earth. Our Ovid, at the beginning of his major work, along with other philosophers, called this extensive form, which then lacked a specific shape, Chaos, which Ovid mentions in that aforesaid volume when he says: 'Before earth, sea, and the sky, which covers everything, existed, nature had an appearance throughout its expanse that the philosophers called Chaos, a great and inchoate matter: and it was nothing but an uncertain and sluggish weight, and discordant seeds of things not well combined gathered in that same expanse.' "

Beginning with the idea of harmonizing the Bible with Ovid, Foresti had ended by proposing a universe that was more Ovidian than biblical. The concept of a primordial chaos, of a "great and inchoate matter" made a strong impression on Menocchio. He drew from it, by dint of long cogitation, "the other things . . . about this chaos . . . made up in *his own* head."

These "things" Menocchio attempted to communicate to his fellow villagers. "I heard him say," Giovanni Povoledo related, "that in the beginning this world was nothing, and that it was thrashed by the water of the sea like foam, and it curdled like a cheese, from which later great multitudes of worms were born, and these worms became men, of whom the most powerful and wisest was God, to whom the others rendered obedience. . . . "

This was very indirect testimony, no less than third hand. Povoledo was reporting what a friend had told him eight days before while "walking along the road on the way to the market at Pordenone"; and the friend, in turn, was relating what he had heard from another friend, who had spoken with Menocchio. In fact, Menocchio himself gave a somewhat different version at his first interrogation: "I have said that, in my opinion, all was chaos . . . and out of that bulk a mass formed—just as cheese is made out of milk—and worms appeared in it, and these were the angels. The most holy majesty decreed that these should be God and the angels, and among that number of angels, there was also God, *he too having been created out of that mass at the same time. . . .* " Apparently, as a result of passing from mouth to mouth, Menocchio's account had been simplified and distorted. A difficult word such as "chaos" had disappeared, replaced by a more orthodox alternative ("in the beginning this world was nothing"). The sequence cheese-worms-angels-holy majesty-God, the most powerful of the men-angels, had been abbreviated along the way into that of cheese-worms-men-God, the most powerful among men.

On the other hand, in Menocchio's version the reference to foam lashed by the water of the sea didn't appear at all. It was impossible that Povoledo could have invented it. During the course of the trial it became increasingly evident that Menocchio was prepared to vary this or that element of his cosmogony while leaving its essential character intact. Thus, to the vicar general's question—"What was this most holy majesty?"—he replied, "I conceive that most holy majesty to have been *the spirit of God who was from eternity.*" In a subsequent interrogation he explained further: on the last day men would be judged by "that most holy majesty that I mentioned before, *which existed even before there was chaos.*" And in another version he substituted God for the "most holy majesty," the Holy Spirit for God: "I believe that the eternal God, out of that chaos that I mentioned before, removed the most perfect light in the way that is done with cheese, where the most perfect is taken, and from that light he made those spirits that we call angels, then he chose the noblest among them and bestowed on him all his knowledge, all his will, and all his power, and this one is he whom we call the Holy Spirit, and God placed him over the creation of the whole word. . . ." He also changed his opinion about the precedence of God in respect to chaos: "This God was in the chaos like one who is in water and wants to expand, and like one who is in a forest and wants to expand: thus, this intellect having received knowledge wanted to expand to create this world." But then, asked the inquisitor, "Was God eternal and always with the chaos?" "I believe," Menocchio replied, "that they were always together, that they were never separated, that is, neither chaos without God, nor God without chaos." In the face of this muddle the inquisitor tried (it was 12 May) to achieve a little clarity, before concluding the trial definitively.

26

INQUISITOR: It appears that you contradicted yourself in the previous examinations speaking about God, because in one instance you said God was eternal with the chaos, and in another you said that he was made from the chaos: therefore clarify this circumstance and your belief.

MENOCCHIO: My opinion is that God was eternal with chaos, but he did not know himself nor was he alive, but later he became aware of himself, and this is what I mean that he was made from chaos.

INQUISITOR: You said previously that God had intelligence; how can it be then that originally he did not know himself, and what was the cause that

afterwards he knew himself? Relate also what occurred in God that made it possible for God who was not alive to become alive.
MENOCCHIO: I believe that it was with God as with the things of this world that proceed from imperfect to perfect, as an infant who while he is in his mother's womb neither understands nor lives, but outside the womb begins to live, and in growing begins to understand. Thus, God was imperfect while he was with the chaos, he neither comprehended nor lived, but later expanding in this chaos he began to live and understand.
INQUISITOR: Did this divine intellect know everything distinctly and in particular in the beginning?
MENOCCHIO: He knew all the things that there were to be made, he knew about men, and also that from them others were to be born; but he did not know all those who were to be born, for example, those who tend herds, who know that from these, others will be born, but they do not know specifically all those that will be born. Thus, God saw everything, but he did not see all the particular things that were to come.
INQUISITOR: This divine intellect in the beginning had knowledge of all things: where did he acquire this information, was it from his own essence or by another way?
MENOCCHIO: The intellect received knowledge from the chaos, in which all things were confused together: and then it [chaos] gave order and comprehension to the intellect, just as we know earth, water, air, and fire and then distinguish among them.
INQUISITOR: Did this God not have will and power before he made all things?
MENOCCHIO: Yes, just as knowledge increased in him, so will and power also increased.
INQUISITOR: Are will and power the same thing in God?
MENOCCHIO: They are distinct just as they are in us: where there is will there must also be the power to do a thing. For example, the carpenter wants to make a bench and needs tools to do it, and if he does not have the wood, his will is useless. Thus we say about God, that in addition to will, power also is needed.
INQUISITOR: What is this power of God?
MENOCCHIO: To operate through skilled workers.
INQUISITOR: These angels that you think are God's ministers in the creation of the world, were they made directly by God, or by whom?
MENOCCHIO: They were produced by nature from the most perfect substance of the world, just as worms are produced from a cheese, and when they emerged received will, intellect, and memory from God as he blessed them.

INQUISITOR: Could God have done everything by himself without the assistance of the angels?
MENOCCHIO: Yes, just as someone who is building a house uses workers and helpers, but we say that he built it. Similarly, in making the world God used the angels, but we say that God made it. And just as that master carpenter in building the house could also do it by himself, but it would take longer, so God in making the world could have done it by himself, but over a longer period of time.
INQUISITOR: If there had not been that substance from which all those angels were produced, if that chaos had not been there, could God have created the entire apparatus of the world by himself?
MENOCCHIO: I believe that it is impossible to make anything without matter, and even God could not have made anything without matter.
INQUISITOR: That spirit or supreme angel that you call Holy Spirit, is he of the same nature and essence as God?
MENOCCHIO: God and the angels are of the same essence as chaos, but there is a difference in perfection, because the substance of God is more perfect than that of the Holy Spirit, since God is the more perfect light: and I say the same about Christ, who is of a lesser substance than that of God and that of the Holy Spirit.
INQUISITOR: This Holy Spirit is he as powerful as God? And Christ also is he as powerful as God and the Holy Spirit?
MENOCCHIO: The Holy Spirit is not as powerful as God, and Christ is not as powerful as God and the Holy Spirit.
INQUISITOR: Is what you call God made and produced by someone else?
MENOCCHIO: He is not produced by others but receives his movement within the shifting of the chaos, and proceeds from imperfect to perfect.
INQUISITOR: Who moves the chaos?
MENOCCHIO: It moves by itself.

27

Thus, in his thick speech, redolent with metaphors from everyday life, and with quiet assurance, Menocchio explained his cosmogony to the inquisitors whom he had amazed and whose curiosity he had aroused. Why else would they have conducted the interrogations in such detail? Amidst such a great variety of theological terms one point remained constant: the refusal to attribute the creation of the world to the divinity—and also, the stubborn recurrence of the apparently most bizarre element: the cheese and the worms born in the cheese.

There may be an echo here of the *Divine Comedy (Purgatory,* X, 124–25):

> . . . worms
> born to produce the angelic butterfly,

especially when we remember that Vellutello's commentary on these verses ("Angelic, that is to say divine, created by God *to fill the seats lost by the black angels who were driven from heaven. . . .* ") is reproduced literally in another passage of Menocchio's cosmogony: "And this God then made Adam and Eve, and people in great number *to fill those seats of the expelled angels.*" It would be strange indeed if the occurrence of two coincidences in a single page came about by chance. But if Menocchio had read Dante—perhaps as a key to knowledge and as a master of religious and moral truths—why did precisely those verses ("worms/ born to produce the angelic butterfly") stick in his mind?

Actually, Menocchio hadn't taken his cosmogony from books: "From the most perfect substance of the world [the angels] were produced by nature, *just as worms are produced from a cheese,* and when they emerged received will, intellect, and memory from God as he blessed them": it seems clear from Menocchio's reply that the repeated mention of the cheese and the worms was intended to serve simply as an explanatory analogy. He used the familiar experience of maggots appearing in decomposed cheese to elucidate the birth of living things of which the first and most perfect were the angels—from chaos, that "great and crude" matter, *without resorting to divine intervention.* Chaos preceded the "most holy majesty," which is not further defined; from chaos came the first living beings—the angels, and God himself who was the greatest among them—by spontaneous generation, "produced by nature." Menocchio's cosmogony was basically materialistic—and tendentiously scientific. The doctrine of the spontaneous generation of life from inanimate matter, fully accepted by all the intellectuals of the day (and which would hold the field until Francesco Redi's experiments disproved it more than a century later), was in fact more scientific than the doctrine of the Church concerning creation, which was based on Genesis. A Walter Raleigh in the name of "experience without art" could relate the woman who made cheese (cheese!) and the natural philosopher: they both knew that the rennet made cheese coagulate in the churn, even if they couldn't explain why.

And yet harking back to Menocchio's daily experience doesn't explain everything: in fact, it may not explain anything. A quick analogy between the coagulation of cheese and the thickening of the nebula destined to form the terrestrial globe may seem obvious to us, but it certainly wasn't for Menocchio. And there's still more. In suggesting this analogy he unknowingly echoed ancient and distant myths. The origin of the universe is explained in an Indian myth in the Vedas by the coagulation—similar to that of milk—of the waters of the primordial sea, beaten by the creator gods. According to the Kalmucks, at the beginning of time, the waters of the sea were covered by a solid layer, similar to that which forms on milk, from which plants, animals, men, and gods issued. "In the beginning this world was nothing, and . . . it was thrashed by the water of the sea like foam, and it curdled like a cheese, from which later great multitudes of worms were born, and these worms became men, of whom the most powerful and wisest was God": more or less, these had been Menocchio's words except for the possible simplifications that have been mentioned.

It's an astonishing coincidence—even disquieting, unless one is willing to go along with quite unacceptable theories, such as the collective unconscious, or simplistic ones, such as chance. Certainly, Menocchio was speaking of a very real, not at all mythical, cheese—cheese that he had often seen being made (or perhaps that he himself had made). The shepherds of Altai, instead, had translated the same experience into a cosmogonic myth. But despite this difference, which shouldn't be underestimated, the coincidence remains. It can't be excluded that it may constitute one of the proofs, even though fragmentary and partly obliterated, of the existence of a millenarian cosmological tradition that, beyond the difference of languages, combined myth with science. It's curious that the metaphor of the revolving cheese recurs, a century after Menocchio's trial, in a book that would provoke considerable controversy—the attempt by the English theologian Thomas Burnet to harmonize Scripture with the science of his day. It may have been an echo, perhaps an unconscious one, of that ancient Indian cosmology to which Burnet dedicated a few pages in his work. But in Menocchio's case it's impossible not to think of a direct transmission—an oral transmission from generation to generation. This hypothesis appears less improbable if we think of the diffusion, during these very years in the Friuli itself, of a cult with shamanistic undercurrents such as that of the *benandanti*. Menocchio's cosmogony fits into this little-explored area of cultural relations and transmissions.

28

In Menocchio's talk we see emerging, as if out of a crevice in the earth, a deep-rooted cultural stratum so unusual as to appear almost incomprehensible. This case, unlike others examined thus far, involves not only a reaction filtered through the written page, but also an irreducible residue of oral culture. The Reformation and the diffusion of printing had been necessary to permit this *different* culture to come to light. Because of the first, a simple miller had dared to think of *speaking out*, of voicing his own opinions about the Church and the world. Thanks to the second, *words* were at his disposal to express the obscure, inarticulate vision of the world that fermented within him. In the sentences or snatches of sentences wrung out of books he found the instruments to formulate and defend his ideas over the years, first with the other villagers, later even against judges armed with learning and authority.

In this manner he had experienced in his own person the historic leap of incalculable significance that separates the gesticulated, mumbled, shouted speech of oral culture from that of written culture, toneless and crystallized on the page. The first is almost an extension of the body, the second "a thing of the mind." The victory of written over oral culture has been, principally, a victory of the abstract over the empirical. In the possibility of finding release from particular situations one has the root of the connection that has always indissolubly bound writing and power. This is clear in cases such as those of Egypt and China, where for millennia priestly and bureaucratic classes monopolized hieroglyphic and ideographic writing. The invention of the alphabet, which broke this monopoly for the first time about fifteen centuries before Christ, wasn't enough, however, to make the written word accessible to everyone. Only printing made this a more concrete possibility.

Menocchio was proudly aware of the originality of his ideas: because of this he wanted to expound them to the highest religious and secular authorities. But at the same time he felt the need to master the culture of his adversaries. He understood that the written word, and the ability to master and to transmit written culture, were sources of power, so he didn't confine himself to denouncing a "betrayal of the poor" in the use of a bureaucratic (and sacerdotal) language such as Latin. The scope of his polemic was broader. "Can't you understand, the inquisitors don't want us to know what they know!" he exclaimed to a fellow villager, Daniel Iacomel, many years after the events we are recounting here. The distinction between "we" and "they" was a sharp one. "They" were the "superiors," the powerful ones—not just those at the pinnacle of the ecclesiastical hierarchy. "We" were the peasants. Almost certainly Daniel was illiterate (when he reported Menocchio's words during the second trial he didn't sign his deposition). Menocchio, instead, knew how to read and write: but he didn't think because of this that his long struggle against authority concerned him alone. The desire "to seek exalted things," which Menocchio had vaguely disavowed twelve years earlier, before the inquisitor at Portogruaro, continued to seem to him not only legitimate but also within everybody's reach. Instead, the pretension of priests to maintain their monopoly over a knowledge that could be bought for "2 soldi" on Venetian book sellers' stalls must have appeared to him unjustified, in fact, absurd. The idea of culture as privilege had been seriously impaired (but certainly not killed off) by the invention of printing.

29

Menocchio had found in that *Fioretto della Bibbia* bought in Venice for "2 soldi" the learned terms that he used in his confessions alongside words from everyday life. Thus, in the interrogation of 12 May, we find "infant in the mother's womb," "herds," "carpenter," "bench," "workmen, "cheese," "worms"; but also "imperfect," "perfect," "substance," "matter," "will, intellect and memory." A medley of words expressing the humble and the sublime, which at first glance seems to resemble this, characterizes especially the first part of the *Fioretto.* Take as an example chapter 3, "How God cannot want evil, or receive it": "God cannot want evil or receive it because he has regulated these elements so that one does not interfere with the other, and they will remain like this as long as there shall be a world. Some say that the world will exist eternally, reasoning that when a body dies, flesh and bones will turn into that matter from which they were created. . . . We can readily see the function of nature, how it reconciles discordant things in such a fashion that it reduces all the differences to unity and combines them into one body and one substance: and also it combines them in plants and in seeds, and by the joining of male and female engenders beings according to the natural course. Jove produces other creatures, who through him engender according to their order. And therefore you see that nature is subject to God. . . . "

"Matter," "nature," "unity," "elements," "substance"; the origin of evil; the influence of the stars; the relationship between creator and creature. Examples such as these could be multiplied. Some of the key concepts and some of the most debated themes in the cultural history of antiquity and the Middle Ages reached Menocchio by way of such a poor and disorganized compilation as the *Fioretto della Bibbia.* The importance of this cannot be overemphasized. First of all, it provided Menocchio with the linguistic and conceptual tools to develop and express his view of the world. Moreover, with an expository method based in the manner of the scholastics on the enunciation and successive refutation of erroneous opinions, it certainly contributed to the unleashing of his voracious intellectual curiosity. The doctrinal inheritance that the priest of Montereale presented as a compact and unassailable structure showed itself to be subject to various interpretations in the *Fioretto.* In chapter 26, for example, "How God inspires souls in bodies," Menocchio could read: "Now many philosophers have been deceived and have fallen into great error about the creation of souls. Some have said that souls have all been made eternally. Others say that all souls are one and that the elements are five, the four mentioned above and one other that is called *orbis:* and they say that out of this *orbis* God made the soul of Adam and all the others. And for this reason they say that the world will never end, because when man dies he returns to his elements. Others say that souls are those evil, fallen spirits, and they say that they enter human bodies and when one body dies they enter into another, and in doing this are saved: and they say that at the end of the world they will be saved. Others say that the world will never end and a new life will begin in thirty-four thousand years and every soul will return to its body. And these are all errors and those who have uttered them have been pagans, heretics, schismatics, and enemies of the truth and of the faith who did not know divine things." But Menocchio wasn't one to allow himself to be intimidated by the invectives in the *Fioretto.* He didn't hesitate to speak his mind even on this question. Instead of causing him to submit to the interpretation of authority, the example of the "many Philosophers" induced him "to seek exalted things," to follow the trend of his own thoughts.

Thus a mass of composite elements, ancient and not so ancient, came together in a new construction. An almost unrecognizable fragment of a capital, or the half-obliterated outline of a pointed arch, might jut out from a wall: but the design of the edifice was his, Menocchio's. With an unselfconscious and open mind he made use of remnants of the thinking of others as he might stones and bricks. But the linguistic and conceptual tools that he tried to acquire were neither neutral nor innocent. This is the explanation for most of the contradictions, uncertainties, and incongruities of his speeches. Using terms infused with Christianity, neo-Platonism, and scholastic philosophy, Menocchio tried to express the elemental, instinctive materialism of generation after generation of peasants.

30

We have to break through the surface of this terminology in order to release the living stream of Menocchio's deepest thoughts. What did Menocchio really mean when he spoke of God, of the most holy majesty of God, of the spirit of God, of the Holy Spirit, of the soul?

Let's begin with the most obvious element in Menocchio's language: the abundance of metaphors. These are metaphors that introduce the words of everyday experience we have already noted—"infant in the mother's womb," "herds," "carpenter," "cheese," and so forth. Now, the images that adorn the *Fioretto della Bibbia* have an obvious and exclusive didactic purpose: namely, they illustrate with directly comprehensible examples the arguments that are to be transmitted to the reader. The function of metaphors in Menocchio's speech is different—in a sense, opposed. In his mental and linguistic world, marked as it was by the most absolute literalism, even metaphors must be taken in a rigorously literal sense. Their content, which is never accidental, allows the thread of the real and inexpressed speech of Menocchio to show through.

31

We might begin with God. For Menocchio, he is above all a father. The play of metaphors gives a new meaning to such a worn-out and traditional epithet. God is a father to men: "We are all children of God and of the same nature as he who was crucified." All: Christians, heretics, Turks, Jews—"they are all dear to him and they are all saved in the same way." Whether they desire it or not, they always remain children of the father: "He claims all, Turks, Jews, Christians, heretics, and all equally in the same way as a father who has several children and claims them all equally; even if there are some who do not want to be, they belong to the father." In his love the father doesn't even mind being cursed by his children: to blaspheme "only hurts oneself and not one's neighbor, just as if I have a cloak and tear it, I injure only myself and no one else, and I believe that he who does no harm to his neighbor does not commit sin; and because we are all children of God, if we do not hurt one another, as for example, if a father has several children, and one of them says 'damn my father,' the father may forgive him, but if this child breaks the head of someone else's child he cannot pardon him so easily if he does not pay:

therefore have I said that it is not sinful to blaspheme because it does not hurt anyone."

All this is tied, as we saw, to the assertion that it is less important to love God than to love one's neighbor—a neighbor who should also be understood as concretely and literally as possible. God is a loving father but removed from the life of his children.

But besides being a father, God also seems to be the very image of authority for Menocchio. At various times he speaks of a "most high majesty," sometimes distinguished from God, sometimes identified with the "spirit of God" or with God himself. Moreover, God is compared to a "great captain" who "sent his son as an ambassador to men in this world." Or, he is compared to a gentleman: in paradise "he who will sit on those seats will want to be able to see everything, and resembles that gentleman who lays out all things to be seen." The "Lord God" is first of all, and literally, a lord: "I said that if Jesus Christ was God eternal he should not have allowed himself to be taken and crucified, and I was not certain about this article but had doubts as I have said, because it seemed a strange thing to me that a lord would allow himself to be taken in this way, and so I suspected that since he was crucified he was not God. . . . "

A lord. But the principal quality of lords is that of not having to work, because they have people to work for them. This is the case with God: "as for indulgences, I believe that they are good because if God has put a man in his place as pope to grant a pardon, that is good, because it is as if we are receiving it from God since these indulgences are given by one who is acting as his steward." But the pope isn't God's only steward. The Holy Spirit also "is like a steward of God; this Holy Spirit selected four captains, or should we say stewards, from among those angels who were created. . . . " Men were made by "the Holy Spirit through the will of God and by his ministers; it is the same as when a steward joins in the work of his agents, just so the Spirit lent a hand."

Thus God is not only a father, but a master—a landowner who doesn't soil his hands working, but assigns the wearisome tasks to his stewards. Even the latter, for that matter, "lend a hand" only rarely. The Holy Spirit, for example, made the earth, trees, animals, man, fish, and all other creatures "by means of the angels, his workers." True, Menocchio doesn't rule out (replying to a question on this subject by the inquisitors) that God could have made the world even without the assistance of the angels: "Just as someone who is building a house uses workers and helpers, but we say that he built it. Similarly, in making the world God used the angels, but we say that God made it. And just as that master carpenter in building the house could also do it by himself, but it would take longer, so God in making the world could have done it by himself, but over a longer period of time." God has the "power": "where there is will there must also be the power to do a thing. For example, the carpenter wants to make a bench and needs tools to do it, and if he does not have the wood, his will is useless. Thus we say about God, that in addition to will, power also is needed." But this "power" consists of operating "through skilled workers."

These recurring metaphors certainly are a response to the need of making the principal figures of religion more familiar and comprehensible by talking about them in terms of daily experience. Menocchio, who had told the inquisitor that his trades, besides that of miller, were "carpenter, sawyer, mason," compared God to a carpenter, to a mason. But a deeper content emerges from the abundance of metaphors. The "making of the world" is, once again, literally, a material act—"I believe that it is impossible to make anything without matter, and even God could not have made anything without matter"—this was manual labor. But God is a lord, and lords don't work with their hands. "Has this God himself created or produced any beings?" the inquisitors asked. "He has arranged to provide the will through which all things have been made," Menocchio replied. Even if compared to a carpenter or mason, God always had "assistants" or "laborers" in his service. Only once, carried away by his enthusiasm while inveighing against the adoration of images, did Menocchio speak of "God alone who has made the heavens and the earth." Actually, for him, God hadn't made anything, just as his "steward," the Holy Spirit also had not. It was the "workmen," the "laborers"—the angels—who had set their hands to "making the world." As for the angels, who had made them? Nature: "they were produced by nature from the most perfect substance of the world, just as worms are produced from a cheese. . . . "

Menocchio had been able to read in the *Fioretto della Bibbia* that "the angels were the first creatures to have been created in the world, and because they were created from the most noble matter that existed, they sinned in their pride and were deprived of their places." But he had also been able to read: "And so you see that nature is subject to God just as the hammer and anvil are to the smith who newly makes whatever he desires, sometimes a sword, sometimes a knife, sometimes other things: and although he makes them with the hammer and anvil, it is not the hammer that makes them, but the smith." But Menocchio couldn't accept this. His stubbornly materialistic view didn't admit the existence of God the creator. Of a God, yes—but he was a distant God, like a master who has left his fields in the hands of stewards and "laborers."

Distant—or (and it was really the same) a God who was very close, dissolved among the elements, identical with the world. "I believe that the entire world, that is, air, earth and all the beautiful things of this world are God. . . : this is because we say that man is made in God's image and likeness, and in man there is air, fire, earth, and water, and it follows from this that air, earth, fire, and water are God."

And it follows from this: once again Menocchio's imperturbable reason dealt with its texts (Scripture, the *Fioretto*) with the most extraordinary license.

32

But Menocchio spoke much more hastily in discussions with the other villagers: "What is this Almighty God? It's a betrayal on the part of Scripture to deceive us and if he really was God Almighty he would let himself be seen"; "what do you imagine God to be? God is nothing else than a little breath, and whatever man imagines him to be"; "what is this Holy Spirit? . . . This Holy Spirit can't be found." When he was reminded of these words in the course of the trial, Menocchio cried out indignantly: "You will never find I said there is no Holy Spirit. In fact, the strongest faith I have in the world is my belief in the Holy Spirit, which is the Word of the highest God to enlighten the entire world."

There is a striking contrast between the testimony of the inhabitants of Montereale and the trial records. One may be tempted to resolve it by attributing Menocchio's confessions to fear, to the desire to escape Holy Office condemnation. The "real" Menocchio would have been the one who roamed the streets of Montereale denying the existence of God—and the other, the Menocchio of the trial, a simple hypocrite. But this hypothesis runs up against a serious difficulty. If Menocchio really wanted to conceal the more radical aspects of his thinking from the judges, why did he doggedly insist on the mortality of the soul? Why did he steadfastly persist in denying the divinity of Christ? Actually, with the exception of occasional reticence during the first interrogation, Menocchio's behavior during the trial seems guided by anything but caution or dissimulation.

Let's try to formulate a different hypothesis following a lead suggested by Menocchio's own statements. He presented a simplified, exoteric view of his ideas to the ignorant villagers: "If I could speak I would, but I do not want to speak." The more complex, esoteric view, instead, was reserved for the religious and secular authorities whom he so eagerly wished to approach: "I said," he informed his judges at Portogruaro, "that if I had permission to go before the pope, or a king, or a prince who would listen to me, I would have a lot of things to say; and if he had me killed afterwards, I would not care." Thus the most complete presentation of Menocchio's ideas must be sought in the statements he made during the trial. But we must also try to explain how Menocchio managed to say things that were apparently contradictory to the people of Montereale.

Unfortunately, the only solution we're able to suggest is purely conjectural, namely, that Menocchio might have had indirect knowledge of Servetus's *De Trinitatis erroribus,* or had read the now lost Italian translation introduced into Italy about 1550 by Giorgio Filaletto, called *Turca* or *Turchetto.* This is certainly a risky conjecture, since we are dealing with a very complicated text, bristling with philosophical and theological terms—a book infinitely more difficult than the ones Menocchio had read. But it may just be possible to discover an almost inaudible echo of it, however feeble and disfigured, in Menocchio's utterances.

At the heart of Servetus's first work there is a vindication of Christ's full humanity—a humanity deified through the Holy Spirit. Now, in the first interrogation, Menocchio stated: "I doubted that he . . . was God, instead he must have been some prophet, some great man sent by God to preach in this world. . . . " He clarified this subsequently: "I think that he is a man like us, born of man and woman like us, and that all he had he received from man and woman: but it is quite true that God sent the Holy Spirit to elect him as his son."

But what was the Holy Spirit for Servetus? He began by listing the various meanings ascribed to this expression in Scripture: "For by Holy Spirit it means now God himself, now an angel, now the spirit of a man, a sort of instinct or divine inspiration of the mind, a mental impulse, or a breath; although sometimes a difference is marked between breath and Spirit. And some would have the Holy Spirit mean nothing other than the right understanding and reason of man." This diversity of meanings corresponds closely to what one encounters in Menocchio: "I believe . . . he is God. . . . It is that angel to whom God has given his will. . . . I believe that our Lord God gave us free will and the Holy Spirit in our body. . . . [I believe that] the spirit comes from God, and is the one, when we have to do something, who inspires us to do this or that thing or not to do it."

This discussion about terms was intended by Servetus to demonstrate the inexistence of the Holy Spirit as a person distinct from that of the Father: "As though Holy Spirit denoted not a separate thing, but an activity of God, a certain energy or inspiration of the power of God." The assumption behind this pantheism was the thesis of the living presence of the Spirit in man and in the whole of reality. "In speaking of the Spirit of God," Servetus wrote recalling a time when he still espoused the errors of the philosophers, "it was enough for me if I understood that the third being was in a sort of corner. But now I know, what he himself said: 'I am a God at hand, and not a God afar off'; now I know that God's universal spirit fills the earth, encompasses all things, and produces virtues in every man. With the prophet I would cry out, 'O Lord, whither shall I go from thy spirit?' since neither above nor below is there any place without the spirit of God." As for Menocchio he had been going around telling his fellow villagers, "What do you think God is? Everything that can be seen is God. . . . " "The sky, earth, sea, air, abyss, and hell, all is God."

Servetus had used every tool at his disposal to dismantle a philosophical and theological system that had endured for more than a millennium: Greek, Hebrew, Valla's philology and the Cabala, Tertullian's materialism and Ockham's nominalism, theology and medicine. He ended up restoring the original meaning by dint of scraping away the incrustations that had formed about the word "Spirit." The difference betwen "spiritus," "flatus," and "ventus," seemed to him to be merely conventional, tied to linguistic usage. There was a profound analogy between "spirit" and breath: "Again, all that is made by the power of God is said to be made by his breath and inspiration; for there can be no uttering of a word without a breathing of the spirit, just as we can not utter speech without exhaling; and therefore we say the breath of the mouth and the breath of the lips. . . . I say, therefore, that our spirit dwelling in us is God his very self; and that this is the Holy Spirit in us. . . . Outside man there is no Holy Spirit." This should be compared with Menocchio's "What do you imagine God to be? God is nothing else than a little breath. . . . Air is God. . . . We are gods. . . . I believe that the [Holy Spirit] is in everybody. . . . What is this Holy Spirit?. . . This Holy Spirit can't be found."

To be sure, the leap from the words of the Spanish physician to those of the miller of the Friuli is enormous. On the other hand, we know that Servetus's writings circulated widely in sixteenth-century Italy and not only among the learned. Menocchio may provide a clue as to how these writings might have been read, understood and misunderstood. This hypothesis would permit us to resolve the discrepancy between the testimony of the people of Montereale and the records of the trial. It would actually appear to be more a case of intentionally choosing to operate on different levels than of a contradiction. In the rough explanations that Menocchio cast at the villagers we would be obliged to see a conscious attempt to translate the obscure Servetian ideas, as he had understood them, into something that would be comprehensible to ignorant listeners. He reserved expounding the doctrine in all its complexity for a different audience: the pope, a king, a prince, or, for lack of anyone better, the inquisitor of Aquileia and the mayor of Portogruaro.

33

We had identified, behind the books mulled over by Menocchio, a method he used in his reading; and behind this a solid stratum of oral culture, which, at least in the case of the cosmogony, we had seen rise directly to the surface. But to suggest that some of Menocchio's ideas were a distant echo of such a sophisticated text as the *De Trinitatis erroribus* doesn't mean that we have to retrace our steps. That echo, if it's real, should be considered as a translation of a learned conception, containing a powerful materialistic component, into terms of popular materialism (further simplified for his fellow villagers). God, the Holy Spirit, the soul—none exist as separate substances. Only matter imbued with divinity, the mixture of the four elements, exists. Once again we're scraping against the foundations of Menocchio's oral culture.

His was a religious materialism. A remark such as that about God—"it's a betrayal on the part of Scripture to deceive us, and if he really was God Almighty he would let himself be seen"—was simply the rejection of that God about whom priests and their books spoke to him. He saw his own God everywhere: "What is this Almighty God?— besides earth, water, and air," he added quickly (always according to the same witness, the priest Andrea Bionima). God and man, man and the world seemed to him interwoven in a web of revelatory relationships: "I believe that [men] are made of earth, but, however, of the most beautiful metal that can be found and this is why one sees man desiring these metals and above all gold. We are composed of the four elements, participate in the seven planets. So one partakes more of one planet than another and is more mercurial and more jovial, depending under which sign he is born." In this view of a reality pervaded by the divine, even priestly benedictions were acceptable because "the devil is accustomed to enter things and poison them," and "the holy water of the priest drives away the devil"—even if, he added, "I believe that all water has been blessed by God," and "if a layman knew the words they would be worth as much as [those] of the priest, because God has given his power (virtú) equally to all and not to one more than another." This, in short, was a peasant religion that had very little in common with that preached by the priest from his pulpit. Certainly, Menocchio went to confession (outside the village, however), received communion, and, undoubtedly, had his children baptized. And yet, he rejected divine creation, the incarnation, and redemption. He denied the efficacy of the sacraments for salvation and affirmed that to love one's neighbor was more important than to love God. He believed that the entire world was God. But there was one flaw in this so thoroughly coherent complex of ideas: the soul.

34

Let's return to the identification of God with the world. "We say," Menocchio had exclaimed, "that man is made in the image and likeness of God, and in man there is air, fire, earth, and water, and it follows from this that air, earth, fire, and water are God." The *Fioretto della Bibbia* was the source for this assertion. He had borrowed from it—making one decisive change in the process—the ancient concept of the correspondence between man and world, microcosm and macrocosm: "and therefore man and woman who were the last to be made were made of earth and of base matter, so that they should ascend to heaven not in arrogance but in humility; inasmuch as the earth is a base element that is stomped upon all day long, and is in the midst of other elements, which are joined and bound together and surrounded in the same way as an egg where you see the yolk in the middle of the egg, and which has albumen about it and the shell outside it; and the elements are similarly together in the world. The yolk corresponds to the earth, the albumen to the air, the thin tissue that is between the albumen and the shell to the water, the shell to the fire: and they are joined together in this way, so that cold and heat, dry and moist may work on each other. And our bodies are made out of and composed of these elements: by our flesh and bone we mean earth, by blood we mean water, by breathing air, and by heat fire. Our bodies are composed of these four elements. Our body is subject to the things of this world, but the soul is subject only to God, *because it is made in his image* and composed of more noble matter than the body. . . . " It was a refusal, then, to admit the existence of an immaterial principle in man—the soul—distinct from the body and from its operations that had led Menocchio to identify not only man with the world, but the world with God. "When man dies he is like an animal, like a fly," he used to repeat to the villagers, perhaps echoing, more or less knowingly, the verses in Ecclesiastes, "and . . . when man dies his soul and everything else about him also dies."

However, at the beginning of the trial Menocchio denied ever having said anything of the kind. He was trying, without much success, to be cautious and follow the advice of his old friend, the vicar of Polcenigo.

And to the question "What is your belief concerning the souls of faithful Christians?" he had answered: "I said that our souls return to the majesty of God who deals with them as he pleases, depending on how they have acted, assigning paradise to the good and hell to the bad and purgatory to some." He thought he had found cover in the orthodox doctrine of the Church (a doctrine that he didn't share in the least). Actually, he had plunged himself into a terrible labyrinth.

35

In the subsequent interrogation (16 February) the vicar general began with a request for clarification concerning "the majesty of God." This led up to a direct attack: "You say that our souls return to the majesty of God, and you have already stated that God is nothing other than air, earth, fire, and water: how then can these souls return to the majesty of God?" The contradiction was indeed real; Menocchio didn't know how to reply: "It's true I said that air, earth, fire, and water are God, and I cannot deny what I said; and as for souls, these came from the spirit of God, and therefore they must return to the spirit of God." Pressing on, the vicar general inquired, "Are the spirit of God and God the same thing? And is this spirit of God incorporated in these four elements?"

"I don't know," Menocchio said. He remained silent for a moment. He may have been tired. Or perhaps he didn't know what "incorporated" meant. Finally, he replied: "I believe that we men all have a spirit from God, which if we do good is cheerful, and if we do evil, that spirit is angry."

"Do you mean that this spirit of God is the one born from that chaos?"

"I don't know."

"Confess the truth," the vicar general began again, unrelenting, "and resolve this question; namely, if you believe that souls return to the majesty of God, and that God is air, water, earth, and fire, how then do they return to the majesty of God?"

"I believe that our spirit, which is the soul, returns to God since he gave it."

How stubborn this peasant was! Fortified by all his patience and all his logic, the vicar general, Giambattista Maro, doctor of canon and civil law, again urged him to reflect and state the truth.

"I said," Menocchio then replied, "that all things in the world are God, and as for myself I believe that our souls revert into all the things of the world and receive benefits, as it pleases God." He was silent momentarily. "These souls are like those angels depicted with God whom he keeps by him, according to their merits, and some who were evil he disperses about the world."

36

And so the interrogation closed on yet another of Menocchio's many contradictions. After making an assertion that, for lack of a better term, we can describe as pantheistic ("all things in the world are God")—a statement that obviously denied the possibility of individual survival ("I believe . . . that our souls revert into all the things of the world . . . ")—Menocchio probably was seized by a doubt. Fear or uncertainty silenced him briefly. Then, from the depths of his memory there had flashed before him a picture that he must have seen in a church, perhaps in some country chapel: God surrounded by a chorus of angels. Was this what the vicar general wanted?

But the vicar general was asking for something very different from a fleeting allusion to the traditional image of paradise—accompanied, moreover, by an echo of the popular belief, pre-Christian in origin, that the souls of the dead are "dispersed about the world." In the subsequent interrogation he immediately put Menocchio on the spot, listing for him his previous denials of the soul's immortality: "so, tell the truth and speak more openly than you did in the preceding examination." At this point Menocchio made an unexpected statement that contradicted what he had said in the first two interrogations. He admitted having spoken of the immortality of the soul with certain friends (Giuliano Stefanut, Melchiorre Gerbas, Francesco Fasseta), but he clarified: "I said these very words, that when the body dies the soul dies but the spirit remains."

Up to that point Menocchio had ignored this distinction: in fact, he had spoken explicitly of "our spirit, which is the soul." Now, in the face of the vicar's astonished query, "whether he believed that there are a body, soul, and spirit in man, and that these things are distinguished from one another, and that the soul is one thing and the spirit another," Menocchio replied: "Yes sir, I do believe that the soul is one thing and the spirit another. The spirit comes from God, and is the one, when we have to do something, who inspires us to do this or that thing or not to do it." The soul, or better still (as he explained in the course of the trial) souls, are nothing else than the various operations of the mind, and perish with the body: "I will tell you there are in man intellect, memory, will, thought, belief, faith, and hope. These seven things God gave to man, and they are like souls through which works are to be done, and this is what I meant saying when the body dies the soul dies." The spirit instead "is separated from man, has the same will as man, and sustains and governs this man": after death it returns to God. This is the good spirit: "I believe," Menocchio explained, "that all men in this world can be tempted, because our heart has two parts, one bright, and the other dark; in the dark one there is the evil spirit, and in the bright one the good spirit."

Two spirits, seven souls, and a body composed of four elements: how had such an abstruse and complicated anthropology cropped up in Menocchio's head?

37

As in the case of the relationship between the body and the four elements, the enumeration of the various "souls" could also be found in the *Fioretto della Bibbia:* "And it is true that the soul has as many names in the body as it has functions there. So, when the soul animates the body, it is called substance; when it desires, it is called the heart; when the body breathes, it is called spirit; when it comprehends and feels, it can be called judgment; when it imagines and thinks, it can be called imagination or memory; therefore, intelligence is located in the highest reaches of the soul, where we receive reason and knowledge, since we are in the image of God. . . . " This is a sequence that corresponds to Menocchio's only in part: but the similarities are unquestionable. The chief difference is the presence of the spirit among the names of the soul—traced back etymologically, moreover, to the bodily act of breathing. Where then did Menocchio's distinction between a mortal soul and an immortal spirit originate?

The distinction had reached him through a long and complicated process. We must go back to the discussions on the problem of the immortality of the soul that began in Averroist circles during the first decades of the sixteenth century, especially among the faculty of the University of Padua, who had been influenced by the thought of Pietro Pomponazzi. Philosophers and physicians openly asserted that at the death of the body, the individual soul—distinguished from the active intellect postulated by Averroes—also perished. Elaborating upon these themes in a religious context, the Franciscan Girolamo Galateo (who had studied at Padua and was later condemned to life imprisonment for heresy) maintained that after death the souls of the saved slept until Judgment Day. Probably following in his footsteps the ex-Franciscan Paolo Ricci, later better known as Camillo Renato, restated the doctrine of the sleep of the soul, distinguishing between the *anima,* condemned to perish with the body, and the *animus,* destined to be revived at the end of time. Through the direct influence of Renato, an exile in the Valtellina, this doctrine was adopted, although not without some opposition, by Venetian Anabaptists, who "believed that the soul *(anima)* was life and that although man died this *spirit* that sustained life in man went into God, and life went into the earth and no longer knew either good or evil, but slept until the day of Judgment when our Lord would revive all men"—except for the wicked, for whom there is no future life of any kind, since there is "no other hell besides the grave."

From professors at the University of Padua to a miller in the Friuli: this chain of influences and contacts is indeed peculiar, although historically plausible because we know, very probably, who constituted its final link—the priest of Polcenigo, Giovanni Daniele Melchiori, Menocchio's childhood friend. In 1579–80, a few years before Menocchio's trial, he too had been prosecuted for heresy by the tribunal of the Inquisition in Concordia and had been found to be "lightly suspect." The accusations made against him by his parishioners were many and varied: from that of being a "whoremonger and ruffian" to that of treating sacred things (for example, the consecrated hosts) without respect. But it's another point that interests us: a statement allegedly made by Melchiori in the village square that "we go to paradise only on Judgment Day." At his trial Melchiori denied having said this but he admitted having spoken of the difference between physical and spiritual death on the basis of what he had read in a book entitled *Discorsi predicabili* by "a priest of Fano" whose name he didn't remember. And to his inquisitors, with great self-confidence, he unburdened himself of a true and proper sermon: "I remember having said, speaking of bodily and spiritual death, that there are two kinds of death, each very different from the other. Although bodily death is common to all, spiritual death is only for the wicked; bodily death deprives us of life, spiritual death deprives us of life and grace; bodily death deprives us of friends, spiritual death of saints and angels; bodily death deprives us of earthly goods, spiritual death of celestial goods; bodily death deprives us of earthly gain, spiritual death deprives us of every merit of Jesus Christ our savior; bodily death deprives us of the terrestrial kingdom, spiritual death of the celestial kingdom; bodily death deprives us of sensibility, spiritual death deprives us of sensibility and intellect; bodily death deprives us of this physical motion, and spiritual death immobilizes us like stone; bodily death causes the body to stink, spiritual death causes the soul to stink; bodily death gives the body to the earth, spiritual death the soul to hell; the death of the wicked is called terrible, as we read in David's Psalm *'mors peccatorum pessima,'* the death of the good is called precious as we read in the same [source] *'pretiosa in conspettu Domini mors sanctorum eius'*; the death of the wicked is called death, the death of the good is called sleep, as we read in St. John the Evangelist, *'Lazzarus amicus noster dormit,'* and in another place *'non est mortua puella sed dormit'*; the wicked fear death and would rather not die, the good do not fear death but say with St. Paul *'cupio dissolvi et esse cum Christo.'* And this is the difference between the bodily death and the spiritual death about which I reasoned and preached: and if I have fallen into error, I am ready to recant and be corrected."

Even if he didn't have the book at hand, Melchiori remembered its contents perfectly—to the letter, in fact. He had read these things in the 34th discourse of the *Discorsi predicabili per documento del viver christiano,* a widely circulated manual for preachers compiled by the Augustinian hermit (not priest) Sebastiano Ammiani of Fano. But in that calculated play of innocent rhetorical contrasts Melchiori had isolated the very phrase that lent itself to a heretical interpretation: "the death of the wicked is called death, the death of the good is called sleep." Undoubtedly, he was aware of the implications of these words, since he had gone so far as to say that "we go to Paradise only on Judgment Day." The inquisitors instead revealed themselves to be much less aware and informed. With what heresy should Melchiori's ideas be connected? Their accusation that he had adhered *"ad perfidam, impiam, eroneam, falsam et pravam hereticorum sectam . . . nempe Armenorum, nec non Valdensium et Ioannis Vicleff"* reflected this bewilderment. It would seem that the Anabaptist implications of the doctrine of the sleep of the soul were not apparent to the inquisitors of Concordia. Faced with theses that were suspect but of obscure origin they dug century-old definitions out of their manuals of controversy. The same thing occurred in Menocchio's case, as we shall see.

There is no mention of the distinction between mortal "soul" and immortal "spirit" in Melchiori's trial. Nevertheless, this was the basic assumption in his argument that souls slept until Judgment Day. This distinction must have reached Menocchio through the vicar of Polcenigo.

"I believe that our spirit, which is the soul, returns to God who gave it to us," Menocchio had said on 16 February (second interrogation). "When the body dies the soul also dies but the spirit remains," he corrected himself on 22 February (third interrogation). The morning of 1 May (sixth interrogation) he seemed to return to the original position: "soul and spirit are one thing."

He had been interrogated about Christ: "What was the Son: man, angel or God?" "A man," Menocchio had replied, "but the spirit was in him." Later, he added: "The soul of Christ either was one of those angels made in times past, or it was newly made by the Holy Spirit from the four elements, or from nature herself. Things cannot be done well except in threes, and therefore since God had given knowledge, will, and power to the Holy Spirit, he gave them also to Christ, so that later they could be a comfort to one another. . . . When there are two who cannot agree in an opinion, if there is a third, when two of the three agree, the third goes along: and therefore the Father has given will and knowledge and power to Christ because he has to judge. . . . "

The morning was almost over; the interrogation would be interrupted shortly for dinner and adjourned until the afternoon of the same day. Menocchio was talking on and on, mixing proverbs with recollections from the *Fioretto della Bibbia,* intoxicated by his own words. He was probably also tired. He had spent part of the winter and spring in prison and must have been looking forward impatiently to the conclusion of a trial that had already dragged on almost three months. And yet, to be questioned and listened to so attentively by such learned monks (there was even a notary to take down his replies) must have been a heady experience for someone who previously had only enjoyed a public made up almost exclusively of semiliterate peasants and artisans. His audience wasn't the popes, kings, and princes before whom he had dreamed of speaking—but, it was something. Menocchio was repeating things he had already said, adding new ones, omitting others, and contradicting himself. Christ was "a man like us, born of man and woman like us . . . but it is quite true that God had sent the Holy Spirit to elect him as his son. . . . After God had appointed him to be a prophet and had given him great wisdom and sent the Holy Spirit to him, I believe he performed miracles. . . . I believe he has a spirit like ours, because soul and spirit are the same thing." But what did it mean to say that soul and spirit are the same thing? "Earlier you said," interrupted the inquisitor, "that when the body dies the soul dies: therefore we should like to know if the soul of Christ also perished when he died." Menocchio hesitated, listed the seven souls given to man by God: intellect, memory.... During the afternoon's interrogation the judges persisted: did the intellect, memory, and will of Christ perish with the death of his body? "Yes my lords because up above, there is no need for their operations." Well then, had Menocchio dropped his idea of the survival of the spirit, identifying it with the soul destined to perish with the body? No, because a little later, while speaking of Judgment Day, he stated that "the seats were filled with celestial spirits but they will be refilled with the most select and intelligent terrestrial spirits," among which will be Christ's, "because the spirit of his son Christ is terrestrial." Now what?

It seems impossible—perhaps pointless—to try to make sense out of this muddle of words. And yet there was a real contradiction behind the verbal contradictions into which Menocchio had locked himself.

39

He couldn't help but imagine an otherworldly life. He was certain that at death man reverted to the elements of which he was composed. But an irrepressible yearning drove him to picture some sort of survival after death. For this reason the abstruse contrast between mortal "soul" and immortal "spirit" had become fixed in his head. Thus the vicar general's clever question—"earlier you affirmed that God is nothing other than air, earth, fire, and water: how then do these souls return to the majesty of God?"—had silenced Menocchio who was always so ready to reply, argue, and ramble on. Certainly, the resurrection of the flesh seemed absurd and untenable to him: "No sir, I do not believe that we can be resurrected with the body on Judgment Day. It seems impossible to me, because if we should be resurrected, bodies would fill up heaven and earth: and the majesty of God will see our bodies with the intellect, no differently than when we, shutting our eyes and wanting to make something, put it in our mind and intellect, and thus see it with that intellect." As for hell, it seemed a priestly invention to him: "Preaching that men should live in peace pleases me but in preaching about hell, Paul says one thing, Peter another, so that I think it is a business, an invention of men who know more than others. I have read in the Bible," he added, trying to get the point across that the real hell was here on this earth, "that David made the Psalms while he was being pursued by Saul." But afterwards, contradicting himself, Menocchio admitted the validity of indulgences ("I think they are good") and of prayers for the dead ("because God gives such a one a small advantage and enlightens him a little more"). Above all, he daydreamed about paradise: "I believe it is a place that surrounds the entire world, and from it one sees all the things in the world, even the fish in the sea: and for those who are in that place it is like being at a feast. . . ." Paradise is a feast—the end of work, the negation of daily toil. "Intellect, memory, will, thought, belief, faith, and hope," in other words, "the seven things . . . given by God to man, in the manner of a carpenter who wants to work—a carpenter with an ax and saw, wood and other tools—so God has given something to man to do his work," but in paradise all these are useless: "up above, there is no need for operations." In paradise matter becomes pliable, transparent: "with our bodily eyes we cannot see everything, but with the eyes of the mind all things will be transfixed, mountains, walls, and everything . . . "

"It is like being at a feast." Menocchio's peasant paradise probably took more from the Mohammedan (rather than the Christian) hereafter about which he had read in Mandeville's lively description: "paradise is a gentle place where one finds every kind of fruit in every season and rivers forever flowing with milk, honey, wine, and sweet water; and . . . there are beautiful and lordly houses befitting the merit of each, decorated with precious stones, gold, and silver. Each person will have maidens and make use of them and will find them always more beautiful. . . ." In any case, to the inquisitors who asked Menocchio "do you believe in an earthly paradise?" he replied with obvious sarcasm: "I believe that the earthly paradise is where there are gentlemen who have many possessions and live without working."

40

Besides fantasizing about paradise Menocchio also desired a "new world": "my mind was lofty" he said to the inquisitor, "and wished for a new world and way of life, because the Church did not act properly, and because there should not be so much pomp." What did Menocchio mean by these words?

In societies founded on oral tradition, the memory of the community involuntarily tends to mask and reabsorb changes. To the relative flexibility of material life there corresponds an accentuated immobility of the image of the past. Things have always been like this; the world is what it is. Only in periods of acute social change does an image emerge, generally a mythical one, of a different and better past—a model of perfection in the light of which the present appears to be a deterioration, a degeneration. "When Adam delved and Eve span, who was then the gentleman?" The struggle to transform the social order then becomes a conscious attempt to return to this mythical past.

Even Menocchio contrasted the rich and corrupt Church he saw with the poverty and purity of a mythical primitive Church: "I wish that [the Church] were governed lovingly as it was when it was founded by our Lord Jesus Christ . . . now there are pompous Masses, and the Lord Jesus Christ does not want pomp." But unlike the majority of the other villagers, he had the ability to read, and it had given him the chance to acquire a view of the past that went beyond this summary antithesis. The *Fioretto della Bibbia* to some extent, but especially Foresti's *Supplementum supplementi delle croniche,* in fact offered an analytical account of human events that went from the creation of the world to the present, mixing sacred and profane history, mythology and theology, descriptions of battles and of countries, lists of princes and philosophers, of heretics and artists. We lack specific information about Menocchio's reactions to these texts. Certainly, they didn't leave him "troubled" as had Mandeville's *Travels.* The crisis of ethnocentricity in the sixteenth century (and for a long time afterward) came about through geography, however fantastic, not through history. Nevertheless, an almost imperceptible trail perhaps may allow us to understand something of the mood in which Menocchio read Foresti's chronicle.

The *Supplementum* was translated into the vernacular and reprinted both before and after the death of its author (1520). Menocchio must have had a posthumous translation that had been brought up to date by an unknown hand to include events close to his own time. Thus, he read the pages dedicated to the schism of "Martin known as Luther monk of the order of hermits of St. Augustine" by the anonymous editor—most likely one of Foresti's brother-members in the Augustinian order. The tone of these pages was singularly benevolent, although it turned into a clear-cut condemnation at the end: "The reason why he [Luther] broke out in such iniquity," wrote the unknown editor, "would appear to have been the supreme pontiff (although *in rei veritate* that is not so) but was rather certain malignant and evil men who, under guise of sanctity, performed enormous and excessive things." These men were the Franciscans, to whom first Julius II and later Leo X entrusted the preaching of indulgences. "And because ignorance is the mother of all error, and the habit of wealth had perhaps unduly inflamed the hearts of these friars toward the acquisition of money, these Observant monks erupted into great madness and became the cause of grave scandal to the people because of the follies they uttered while preaching these indulgences. And among other parts of Christianity, they spread widely in Germany. When they said some folly and certain men (of upright conscience and doctrine) sought to reprove them, the monks instantly declared these men excommunicated. Among them was this Martin Luther, who was a truly learned and literate man. . . . " The causes of the schism, then, for the anonymous writer, were the "follies" of the rival order, which, when confronted by Luther's righteous reaction, had him excommunicated. "After which the aforesaid Martin Luther, who was of quite noble blood and was held in great esteem among all people, publicly began to preach against these indulgences, saying they were false and unjust. As a result he had everything turned upside down in very short order. And because the larger part of almost all wealth was in the hands of the clergy and there was ill will between the spiritual and temporal estates, he easily found a following among the latter and started a schism within the Catholic Church. And seeing that he was getting great support, he separated himself completely from the Roman Church and created a new sect and a new way of life through his various and diverse opinions and imaginings. And this is how it came about that a large number of those countries rebelled against the Catholic Church and do not render it obedience in anything. . . . "

"He created a new sect and a new way of life"; "I wished for a new world and way of life, because the Church did not act properly, and because there should not be so much pomp." The instant Menocchio uttered his aspirations for a reformation in religion (later we'll speak of his allusion to a "new world") dictated to him by his "lofty mind," he was echoing, knowingly or not, the portrayal of Luther that he had read in Foresti's chronicle. Certainly he wasn't repeating the religious ideas—on which, for that matter, the chronicle didn't dwell since it limited itself to condemning the "new kind of doctrine" that Luther had proposed. But, more than anything else, he couldn't be satisfied with the anonymous writer's cautious and perhaps ambiguous conclusion: "And in this way he has befuddled the ignorant populace; and those of knowledge and learning, hearing about the evil doings of the ecclesiastical state, join him, without considering that this proposition is not valid: clerics and ecclesiastics lead a low life, therefore the Church of Rome is not good. Because even if they do lead a low life, the Church of Rome is, nevertheless, good and perfect; and even if Christians are of low life, the Christian faith is, nevertheless, good and perfect." To Menocchio, as to Caravia, the "law and commandments of the Church" seemed to be "all a business" designed to enrich priests: for him the moral renewal of the clergy and a profound reformation in doctrine went hand-in-hand. By the unforseen vehicle of Foresti's chronicle, Luther was being presented to him as the prototype of the religious rebel—as the person who had known how to rally "the ignorant populace, and those of knowledge and learning" against the ecclesiastical hierarchy, exploiting the "ill will" that "the temporal state" had nurtured against the latter "because the larger part of almost all wealth was in the hands of the clergy." "Everything belongs to the Church and to priests" Menocchio has exclaimed to the inquisitor. Who knows if he had also reflected on the similiarities between conditions in the Friuli and those in lands beyond the Alps, where the Reformation had triumphed.

41

Menocchio's possible contacts with "those of knowledge and learning" aren't known to us—except for one case that we'll examine later. We are familiar, instead, with his stubborn attempts to spread his own ideas among "the unlearned populace." But apparently no one paid any attention to him. In the sentence that terminated the first trial, this lack of success was interpreted as a sign of divine intervention that had prevented the corruption of the simple minds of the inhabitants of Montereale.

Actually, there had been an illiterate carpenter, Melchiorre Gerbas, "considered to be a person of little wit," who had listened to Menocchio. The talk about him "in the inns was that he does not believe in God and blasphemes vehemently." More than one witness had linked Melchiorre's name to Menocchio's because he had "slandered and spoken ill about the things of the Church." Then the vicar general had wanted to know about his dealings with Menocchio, who had just been imprisoned. At first Melchiorre insisted that they were simply matters connected with their occupations ("he provides me with wood to work on and I pay him"): but afterwards he admitted having blasphemed in the inns of Montereale, repeating a sentence he had learned from Menocchio: "Menocchio told me that God is nothing but air and this I too believe. . . . "

This attitude of blind dependence isn't difficult to understand. Because of Menocchio's ability to read, write, and orate it seemed to Melchiorre as if there was an almost magical quality about him. After he had loaned him a Bible that he had at home, Melchiorre had gone about saying with a mysterious air that Menocchio had a book with which he was capable of "working marvelous things." But the people had no trouble understanding the difference between them: "This one . . . is suspected of heresy, but he is not the same as Domenego," someone had said, speaking about Melchiorre. And another had remarked, "he says things one would expect from a madman, and also he gets drunk." Even the vicar general readily understood that he had before him a man of a very different stamp than the miller. "When you were saying that God does not exist did you really believe in your heart that there was no God?" he asked kindly. And Melchiorre promptly replied: "No father, because I believe that there is God in heaven and on earth, and that he can have me die any time he wishes; and I uttered those words because they had been taught to me by Menocchio." A few light penances were imposed on Melchiorre and they let him go. This was Menocchio's only follower in Montereale—at least, the only confessed follower.

Apparently, Menocchio hadn't wanted to confide even in his wife and children: "God forbid that they should have had such opinions." Despite all his ties to the village, he must have felt very much alone: "That night," he admitted, "when the father inquisitor told me 'Come away tomorrow to Maniago' I was almost beside myself, and I wanted to go out and cause some harm . . . I wanted to kill priests and set fire to churches and do something crazy: but because of my two little children, I restrained myself. . . . " This outburst of powerless desperation speaks eloquently about his isolation. In the face of the injustice afflicting him, his only reaction was one that he had suppressed instantly, that of individual violence: to revenge himself on his persecutors, lash out against the symbols of the oppression, and become an outlaw. A generation before, the peasants had set fire to the castles of the Friulian nobility. But times had changed.

42

Only the dream of a "new world" now remained to him. These are words that the passing of time have dulled, like coins that have passed through too many hands. Let's try to recapture their original meaning.

Menocchio didn't believe that the world had been created by God. In addition, he explicitly rejected original sin, declaring that man "begins to sin when he first takes his mother's milk, after he leaves the womb." And to him Christ was simply a man. Consistently, then, any notion of religious millenarism was alien to him. He never alluded to the Second

Coming in the course of his confessions. The "new world" for which he longed was thus an exclusively human reality, attainable by human means.

However, we tend to take for granted the banal metaphorical use of an expression that, when Menocchio used it, still retained all its original force. It was really a powerful metaphor on a metaphor. At the beginning of the century a letter had been printed under the name of Amerigo Vespucci directed to Lorenzo di Pietro de' Medici and entitled precisely *Mundus novus*. Giuliano di Bartolomeo del Giocondo, who translated the letter from Italian into Latin, explained the significance of the title in the preface: "A few days ago I wrote to you in detail about my return from those new regions . . . *which it is appropriate to call a new world* since there was no knowledge of them among our ancestors, and is a completely new thing to all listeners." These weren't the Indies, then, as Columbus had thought, and not even some new lands, but actually a new world unknown up to that time *"Licet appellare* [which it is appropriate to call] . . .": the metaphor was very new and he was almost offering an excuse to the reader. Taken in this sense the term began to circulate widely until it entered into everyday use. But Menocchio, as we saw, employed it differently, applying it not to a new continent but to a new society yet to be established.

We don't know who was first responsible for this shift. At any rate, the image of a radical and rapid transformation of society was behind it. In a letter that Erasmus wrote to Martin Bucer in 1527, he spoke bitterly of the violent turn taken by the Lutheran Reformation. He observed that, first, the assent of princes and bishops should have been sought, and any kind of seditious activity avoided; moreover, a number of things, among them the Mass, should have been "changed without disorder." There are people today, he concluded, who no longer accept anything that has to do with tradition *("quod receptum est")*, as if a new world could be brought into being virtually instantaneously *("quasi subito novus mundus condi posset")*. A slow and gradual transformation on the one hand, a rapid and violent upheaval (revolutionary, we'd call it) on the other: the contrast was distinct. But nothing having to do with geography was suggested by Erasmus with the expression *"novus mundus"*: the emphasis was rather on the term *"condere"* used to indicate the foundation of cities.

The shift of the metaphor "new world" from a geographical to a social context is, however, explicit in utopian literature at various levels. Let's take the *Capitolo, qual narra tutto l'essere d'un mondo nuovo, trovato nel mar Oceano, cosa bella, et dilettevole (A chapter that narrates everything about a new world, discovered in the Ocean sea, a beautiful and enjoyable account)*, which appeared anonymously in Modena about the middle of the sixteenth century. It is one of many variations on the old theme of the land of Cockaigne (referred to specifically in the *Begola contra la Bizaria,* which precedes it, rather than in the *Capitolo)* located in this account among the lands discovered beyond the Ocean:

> Anew a beautiful place has been discovered
> By sailors in the Ocean Sea
> Which had never before been seen, and never heard about . . .

The description follows the usual motifs of this grandiose peasant utopia:

> A mountain of grated cheese
> Is seen standing alone in the middle of the plain,
> A kettle has been brought to its summit . . .
> A river of milk gushes forth from a cave
> And goes flowing through the town
> Its embankments are made of ricotta . . .
> The king of the place is called Bugalosso,
> They have made him king because he is the laziest,
> Like a haystack he is big and fat . . .
> And from his arse manna comes forth
> And when he spits, out come marzipans,
> Instead of lice, he has fish in his head.

But this "new world" isn't only the land of abundance: it's also a place without the constraint of social institutions. There is no family, because total sexual liberty prevails there:

> Neither skirts nor cloaks are needed there,
> Nor shirts, nor pants at any time:
> They all go naked, modest maids and stable boys.
> There is neither heat nor cold at any time,
> Everybody sees and touches the other as much as he desires:
> Oh, what a happy life, oh what a good time . . .
> There it does not worry us to have many children,
> To mind them, as it does among us here,
> And when it rains, it rains ravioli.
> Nor about their girls and marrying them off
> Is there any worry, since they go as booty,
> Everyone satisfies his own appetites.

There is no property, because there is no need to work, and everything is in common:

> Everyone has what he wants in every way,
> And who should ever dare speak about working
> They would hang him, so that the heavens couldn't save him . . .
> There are no peasants or villeins in that place,
> Everyone is rich, everyone has what his heart desires,
> Because table-tops are laden with goods . . .
> Neither fields nor land are divided,

There is an abundance of things for everyone,
And so the place is totally free.

These elements, which are encountered (although not at such length) in almost all sixteenth-century versions of the *Land of Cockaigne*, are most probably an exaggeration of the already mythologized image furnished by the first explorers of the lands discovered beyond the ocean and their inhabitants: nudity and sexual freedom, absence of private property and of all social distinctions, an extraordinarily fertile and hospitable natural setting. In this way, the medieval myth of the land of milk and honey *(Bengodi)* took on a strong element of primitive utopianism. Not only serious but even prohibited subjects could circulate freely as long as they were in a comical, paradoxical, exaggerated context such as owls excreting cloaks, donkeys tied with sausages—and duly mocked at the end with the ritual formula:

Who wants to travel there, I shall tell him the way:
Go embark at the port of the simpleton,
And then navigate through the sea of lies,
Whoever arrives is king over every dolt.

Totally different language is used by Anton Francesco Doni in the dialogue included in one of the first and most famous sixteenth-century Italian utopias: the *Mondi* (1552) specifically entitled *Un mondo nuovo.* Here the tone is extremely serious and even the subject matter is different. Doni's isn't a peasant utopia as is the *Land of Cockaigne* but a thoroughly urban one, located in a city with a star-shaped layout. Moreover, the inhabitants of the "new world" described by Doni lead a sober existence far removed from the revelry of Cockaigne ("I enjoy this good order of having banished the shame of drunkenness . . . and of gorging oneself for five and six hours at the table"). Nevertheless, Doni, too, combined the ancient myth of an age of gold with the image of primitive innocence and purity depicted by the first reports of the American continent. But there was only an implicit allusion to those lands: the world described by Doni was simply "a new world different from this one." Thanks to this ambiguous expression it became possible for the first time in utopian literature to project the model of a perfect society into time, into the future, instead of into the space of an inaccessible land. But the principal characteristics of this "new world," the community of women and of property, were taken from the explorers' accounts (as well as from More's *Utopia,* which Doni himself published, with an introduction). As we saw, these features were also part of what was imagined about the land of Cockaigne.

Menocchio could have read about the American discoveries in the scant references in Foresti's *Supplementum.* He may have had them in mind when he declared with his habitual open-mindedness: "Because I have read that there are many kinds of races of men, I believe that many different peoples have been created in various parts of the world." However, Menocchio probably wasn't acquainted with Doni's urban, sober "new world"—whereas at least an echo must have reached him of the rural carnival-like one of the *Capitolo,* or of other similar texts. However, there were elements in both that might have pleased him. In the world portrayed by Doni, religion lacked rites and ceremonies, despite the massive presence of the temple in the center of the city. It was a religion such as Menocchio had described with longing during his trial, reduced to the simple commandment of "know God, thank him, and love your neighbor." In the world described in the *Capitolo,* there was an image of happiness linked to abundance, to the enjoyment of material goods, to the absence of work. Granted, when Menocchio was accused of violating Lenten commandments, he defended fasting, even if he did so on dietary rather than religious grounds: "Fasting has been established by the mind so that those humors would not form, and as for me I wish we could eat three or four times a day, but not drink wine so as not to bring on those humors. . . ." But this apology for sobriety was transformed instantly into a polemical attack, intended perhaps (the notary's transcription is incomplete at this point) for the monks facing him: "and not to be like these . . . who eat more in one meal than they should in three." In a world filled with social injustices, gripped by a constant fear of starvation, the picture of a uniformly sober life had a ring of protest:

> I dig holes in the ground
> Searching for varied and strange roots
> So we may stuff our faces with them:
> Still if we had some each new day
> It would go much less badly with us.
> A terrible thing is famine.

These are lines in a contemporary verse, "Lamento de uno poveretto huomo sopra la carestia," to which the next poem, "L'Universale allegrezza dell'abondantia," immediately replies:

> Today we enjoy and celebrate
> All of us in company
> Because the impious famine
> No longer causes us grief . . .
> Three cheers for bread and grain,
> Plenty and abundance,

Come, poor things, let us sing
That hope has at last arrived . . .
After darkness comes the light,
After evil comes the good,
Our guide and leader, Abundance,
Comes to lead us away from misery;
And brings with herself grain aplenty:
This alone is what sustains us,
The beautiful and good white bread.

This poetical contrast provides us a counterpoise in the real world to the exaggerated fantasies about the land of Cockaigne. Opposite the "varied and strange roots" of the times of famine, "the beautiful and good white bread" eaten in company in times of plenty is a "feast." "It is like being at a feast," Menocchio had said about paradise: a feast without end, free from the periodic alternation of "darkness and light," of famine and abundance, of Lent and Carnival. The land of Cockaigne beyond the ocean was also a single enormous feast. Who knows how much Menocchio's longed-for "new world" resembled it?

In any case, his words momentarily bring to the surface the deeply rooted *popular* origins of the utopias, both of the scholarly and popular varieties, which all too often have been considered to be purely literary exercises. Perhaps that image of a "new world" had a core that was ancient and tied to mythical tales of a remote age of prosperity. In other words, it didn't break the cyclical view of human history, typical of an age that had seen the establishment of the myths of *re*naissance, *re*formation, and of the New Jerusalem. None of this can be ruled out. But the fact remains that the image of a more just society was consciously projected into a noneschatological future. It wasn't the Son of Man high up in the clouds, but men like Menocchio—the peasants of Montereale, whom he had vainly tried to convince—who, through their struggles, would have to be the bearers of this "new world.'

43

The interrogations ended on the 12th of May. Menocchio was conducted back to his cell. A few days passed. Finally, on the 17th, he refused the services of a lawyer, which had been offered him, and submitted a long letter to his judges in which he asked to be forgiven for his past errors—the letter that his son had asked him to write three months before, in vain.

44

"In the name of the Father and of the Son and of the Holy Spirit. I, Domenego Scandella, called Menocchio of Montereal, am a baptized Christian and have always lived in a Christian way and have always performed Christian works, and I have always been obedient to my superiors and to my spiritual fathers to the best of my power, and always, morning and night, I crossed myself with the sign of the holy cross, saying, 'in the name of the Father and of the Son and of the Holy Spirit." And I recited the Pater Noster and the Ave Maria and the Credo with a prayer to our Lord and one to the Madonna. It is indeed true that I thought and believed and said, as appears in the trial records, things against the commandments of God and of the holy Church. I said them through the will of the false spirit who blinded my intellect and memory and will, making me think, believe, and say what was false and not true, and so I confess that I thought and believed and said what was false and not true and so I gave my opinion but I did not say that it was the truth. I want to take four words briefly as an example from Joseph, son of Jacob, when he was speaking with his father and with his brothers about certain dreams that revealed that they should adore him. For this his brothers became angry with him and wanted to kill him, but it did not please God that they should kill him, but, rather, that they should sell him. And so they sold him to certain Egyptian merchants who took him to Egypt where he was thrown in prison because of some transgressions. And the king Pharaoh had a dream where he thought he saw seven fat cows and seven lean ones, and no one could interpret this dream for him. He was told that there was a youth in prison who would know how to explain it, and so [Joseph] was taken from prison and led before the king. [Joseph] told him that the fat ones meant seven years of plenty, and the lean ones seven years of famine in which it would not be possible to find grain even to buy. And so the king believed him and made him chief and governor over the entire kingdom of Egypt. Then came the abundance and Joseph set aside enough grain to last for more than twenty years; then came the famine when it was not possible to find grain, even to buy. And Jacob knew that grain was being sold in Egypt and sent ten of his sons with their animals to Egypt. They were recognized by their brother, and with the king's permission he had his father summoned with all his family and goods. And so they lived together in Egypt and the brothers stayed unwillingly, fearful because they had sold him. When Joseph saw that they were staying unwillingly he said to them: 'Do not be unhappy because you sold me, it was not your doing but the will of God so that he could provide for our needs; so be of good cheer because I forgive you with all my heart.' Similarly, I had been speaking with my brothers and spiritual fathers and they accused me, sold me as it were to the most reverend father inquisitor, and he had me brought to this Holy Office and put in prison. But I do not blame them, because it was the will of God. Although I do not know if they are spiritual brothers or fathers, however, I pardon them all who were the cause of it, so that God may forgive me just as I forgive them. There are four reasons why God wanted me to be taken to this Holy Office: first, to confess my errors; second, to do penance for my sins; third, to free me from the false spirit; fourth, to give an example to my children and to all my spiritual brothers,so that they would not fall into these errors. Therefore, if I thought and believed and said and worked against the commandments of God and of the Holy Church, I am sad and sorrowful, repentant and unhappy. So I say *'mea colpa, mea masima colpa,'* and for the remission of all my sins I ask forgiveness and mercy of the most Holy Trinity, Father and Son and Holy Spirit, and next of the glorious Virgin Mary and of all the saints in paradise, and also of your most holy and most reverend and most illustrious justice, so that you will want to pardon me and have mercy on me. And so I beg you in the name of the passion of our Lord Jesus Christ that you should not want to sentence me either in anger or in justice, but rather with love and with charity and with mercy. You know that our Lord Jesus Christ was merciful and forgiving, and is and always will be forgiving to Mary Magdalen who was a sinner, to St. Peter who denied him, to the thief who stole, to the Jews who crucified him, and to St. Thomas who would not believe until he had seen and touched. And so I firmly believe that he will forgive me and will have mercy on me. I have done penance in a dark prison one hundred and four days, in shame and disgrace and with the ruin and desperation of my house and my children. Therefore, I beg you for love of our Lord Jesus Christ and of his glorious mother the Virgin Mary that you repay it in charity and in mercy and not be the cause of separating me from the company of my children whom God gave to me for my happiness and my comfort. And so I promise never again to fall into these errors, but instead to be obedient to all my superiors and to my spiritual fathers in everything they will command me to do, and nothing else. I await your most holy, revered, and illustrious sentence with its lesson to live as a Christian, so that I may teach my children to be true Christians. These have been the causes of my errors: first, I believed in the two commandments love God and love your neighbor, and that this was enough; second, because I read that book of Mandeville about many kinds of races and different laws, which sorely troubled me; third, my mind and thought were making me know things that were improper; fourth, the false spirit was always tormenting me teaching me what was false and was not the truth; fifth, the disagreement that existed between me and the parish priest; sixth, that I worked and exhausted myself and became weak and because of this I could not obey the commandments of God and of the holy Church in all things. And so I make my defense with a plea for pardon and mercy, and not anger or justice, and I ask of our Lord Jesus Christ and of you mercy and forgiveness and not anger or justice. And do not pay attention to my falseness and ignorance."

45

The appearance itself of the pages on which Menocchio had written, with the letters set side by side, almost without ligatures (as is usually done by "ultramontanes, women, and the aged" according to a contemporary writing manual), clearly demonstrates that their writer didn't have great familiarity with the pen. We get a very different first impression from the flowing and nervous writing of don Curzio Cellina, notary of Montereale, who seems to have been among Menocchio's accusers at the time of the second trial.

Menocchio surely had not gone beyond an elementary level of schooling: learning to write must have cost him an enormous effort—a physical effort as well, from the evidence of certain marks that give the impression of having been cut in wood rather than written on paper. He obviously found reading much easier. Although he had been confined "in a dark prison one hundred and four days," certainly without books at his disposal, he had dug out of his memory details, absorbed slowly and over a long period, of the story of Joseph, which he had read in the Bible and in the *Fioretto.* To this familiarity with the written page we owe the singular features of his letter to the inquisitors.

The following passages can be distinguished in it: 1) Menocchio states that he had always lived as a good Christian, although he recognizes that he has violated the commandments of God and of the Church; 2) he declares that the origin of this contradiction is in the "false spirit" that led him to believe and say what was false—portrayed by him, however, as an "opinion," not as the truth; 3) he compares himself to Joseph; 4) he gives four reasons why God had wanted him to be imprisoned; 5) he compares the judges to the merciful Christ; 6) he begs forgiveness of the judges; 7) he lists the six causes of his own errors. To this ordered external structure corresponds, internally, a language packed with symmetry, alliteration, and such rhetorical devices as anaphora or *derivatio.* It suffices to look at the first sentence: "I am a baptized *Christian,* and have always lived in a *Christian* way and have always performed the works of a *Christian* . . . "; "and have *always* lived . . . , and *always* . . . , and *always* . . . "; "et *se*npre matina et *se*ra io *so*n *se*gnato col *se*gno de la *sa*nta *croze* . . . " ("and always, morning and night, I crossed myself with the sign of the holy cross . . . "). Of course, Menocchio was being rhetorical unknowingly, just as he wasn't aware that the first four "causes" that he mentioned were final, and the other six efficient, causes. Nevertheless, the wealth of alliteration and rhetorical figures in his letter wasn't accidental, but rather imposed by the necessity of finding a language capable of impressing itself on the memory easily. Before being set down as marks on the page, those words had certainly been thought over carefully. But from the start they had been conceived as written words. Menocchio's "spoken language," to the extent we can speculate about it from the transcripts of the interrogations recorded by notaries of the Holy Office, differed if only because it abounded in metaphors, which are totally lacking in the letter to the inquisitors.

The (established) association between Menocchio and Joseph and the (hoped for) one between the judges and Christ, is not, in fact, metaphorical. Scripture furnishes a network of *exempla* to which existing reality conforms or should conform. But it's the formula of the *exemplum* itself that causes the hidden content of the letter to emerge, independently of Menocchio's intentions. Menocchio considers himself a sort of Joseph, not only because he is an innocent victim, but also because he is capable of revealing truths unknown to anyone. The people, such as the priest of Montereale who had accused him and had him imprisoned, can be compared to Joseph's brothers, involved in God's inscrutable designs. But the protagonist is he, Menocchio-Joseph. It is he who forgives the evil brothers, who actually are the blind instruments of a superior will. This parallelism belied in advance the pleas for mercy with which the letter closes. Even Menocchio noticed the incongruity: "although I do not know if they are brothers or spiritual fathers," he added, attempting to reestablish a relationship of filial reverence that his various assumptions, in fact, denied. Nevertheless, he refrained from following blindly the advice of his son who had counseled him, through the priest, to promise "complete obedience to Holy Church." While recognizing his own errors, on the one hand Menocchio put them into a providential perspective, and on the other explained them with reasons that, with the exception of the mention of "the false spirit," didn't concede much from the inquisitors' point of view. These reasons in all likelihood were listed according to an order of decreasing importance. First of all, there were two textual citations, one implicit, the other explicit: to a Scriptural passage (Matthew

22: 36–40) interpreted literally, and to the *Travels* of Mandeville, read in the manner we observed above. Then there were two reasons of an internal sort: the goading by "mind and thought" and the temptation by that "false spirit," which, he stated in his trial, dwells in the "dark" recesses of men's hearts. Finally, two external circumstances: the hostility between himself and the priest, the physical weakness that he had appealed to on other occasions to justify his violations of obligations to fast. Then, we have books; reactions to books ("I believed in the two commandments . . . which sorely troubled me"); the deductions made from the books; and conduct. There was an undoubted connection in this apparently disparate list of causes. Despite his pathetic final plea ("and do not pay attention to my falseness and ignorance") Menocchio wasn't renouncing discussion and argument.

46

The same day that Menocchio sent off his letter, the judges gathered to pronounce sentence. Their attitude had changed imperceptibly in the course of the trial. At first, they had pointed out Menocchio's contradictions; later, they had tried to lead him back to the straight and narrow path; finally, in view of his obstinacy, they had given up any attempt to convert him and had limited themselves to exploratory questions, as if they were trying to obtain a complete picture of his errors. Now, unanimously, they declared that Menocchio was "not only a formal heretic . . . but even a heresiarch." On the 17th of May, they came to pass sentence.

One is immediately struck by its length, four or five times longer than ordinary sentences. It's an indication of the importance attributed to Menocchio's case by the judges and especially of the difficulty of fitting his extraordinary statements into the standard *formulae* for documents of this type. The astonishment of the judges shows through the dry judicial language: "we find you have fallen into manifold *and almost unmentionable* heretical pravity." Thus, this exceptional trial closed with an equally exceptional sentence (accompanied by an equally lengthy abjuration).

From the very beginning the judges had underscored the fact that Menocchio had spoken of his heretical opinions and argued against the Catholic faith "not only with men of religion, but also with simple and ignorant people," jeopardizing their faith. This undoubtedly was an aggravating circumstance: the peasants and artisans of Montereale had to be kept out of reach of such dangerous doctrines at any price. This was followed by a detailed refutation of Menocchio's ideas. With a completely rhetorical crescendo, altogether unusual in an inquisitorial trial, the judges stressed the audacity and obstinacy of the offender: "thus pertinacious in these heresies," "you persevered with an obdurate heart," "audaciously you denied," "you mutilated . . . with profane and impious words," "with diabolical mind you affirmed," "you did not keep holy fasting unbroken," "did we not find that you raged even against holy sermons?" "you damned . . . with your profane judgement," "the evil spirit led you to that which you have dared to affirm," "you strove with your polluted mouth," "you contrived this most wicked thing," "and you denied that there remained nothing unpolluted and not contaminated by you . . ." "you were accustomed to say . . . twisting with your malicious tongue," "finally you raged," "you served up poison," "and things not testified but heard by all were execrable," "and your malicious and perverse spirit was not content with all this . . . but raised horns, and like one of the giants *(gigantes)* you commenced to battle against the most holy ineffable Trinity," "the heavens were greatly troubled, all were distressed and listeners trembled at the inhuman and horrible things that were uttered by that profane mouth of yours about Jesus Christ the Son of God." There's no doubt that the judges were trying to express a very real sentiment with this exaggerated literary verbiage: their astonishment and horror in the face of an unheard of mass of heresies, which in their eyes must have appeared as nothing less than hell spilling over.

But "unheard of" isn't quite exact. Unquestionably, these inquisitors had held innumerable trials in the Friuli involving Lutherans, witches, *benandanti,* blasphemers, even Anabaptists, without ever encountering anything like this. Only with regard to Menocchio's remark that for confession it sufficed to tell one's sins to God, did they recall the similar teaching of the "heretics," namely, the followers of the Reformation. For the rest, they sought occasional analogies and precedents from a more distant past, falling back on their own theological and philosophical education. Thus, Menocchio's reference to chaos was connected with the doctrines of an unnamed ancient thinker: "You brought again to light and firmly asserted as true that elsewhere censured opinion of an ancient philosopher that there was an eternal chaos from which everything of this world originated." The statement that "God is author of good but does not do evil, but the devil is author of evil and does not do good," was traced to the Manichean heresy: "finally, you resurrected the opinion of the Manichees about the twofold generation of good and evil. . . . " Similarly, the notion of the equivalence of all religions was identified with Origen's doctrine of apocatastasis: "You brought again to light Origen's heresy that all peoples would be saved, Jews, Turks, pagans, Christians, and all infidels, since the Holy Spirit has been given equally to them all. . . . " Several of Menocchio's assertions not only appeared heretical to the judges, but even opposed to natural reason. This was the case, for example, with the idea that "when we are in the mother's womb we are just like nothing, dead flesh," or the other about the non-existence of God: "Regarding the creation of the soul, you went against not only the holy Church, but also all philosophers. . . . That on which all agree, and which no one has ever dared to deny, you dared when you foolishly said 'God does not exist.' "

In Foresti's *Supplementum supplementi delle croniche,* Menocchio could have encountered fleeting references to the teachings of Origen and the Manichees. But to look upon them as precedents for Menocchio's own ideas was obviously a mistake. The sentence confirmed the gulf, evident throughout the trial, separating Menocchio's cultural world from the inquisitors'.

The duty of the latter was to compel the offender to reenter the Church. Menocchio was condemned to publicly abjure all his heresies, to fulfill various salutary penances, to wear forever a penitential garment, the *habitello,* decorated with a cross, and to spend the rest of his life in prison at the expense of his children ("we solemnly condemn you to be confined between two walls, where you will remain for the entire duration of your life").

47

Menocchio languished in the prison at Concordia for almost two years. On the 18th of January 1586 his son Ziannuto, in the name of his brothers and his mother, presented a petition to Bishop Matteo Sanudo and Fra Evangelista Paleo, inquisitor of Aquileia and Concordia at that time. Menocchio himself had written it:

"Although I, poor Domenego Scandella prisoner, have on other occasions beseeched the Holy Office of the Inquisition to ask if I might be worthy of pardon, to permit me to do more penance for my error, now compelled by my extreme need I return to implore you to consider that more than two years have passed since I was taken from my home and condemned to such a cruel prison. I do not know why I did not die because of the foulness of the air, deprived of being able to see my dear wife due to the distance from here, burdened with family, with children who because of their poverty will be forced to abandon me, so that I will necessarily have to die. Therefore, I, repentant and grieving over my great sin, beg forgiveness, first from our Lord God, and then from this holy Tribunal, and ask them for the gift of my release. I offer proper guarantee that I will live in the teachings of the Holy Roman Church, and also that I will do whatever penance shall be imposed on me by this Holy Office, and I pray to Our Lord for their every happiness."

The assistance of a lawyer can be seen behind the stereotyped expressions of humility, purged of the customary provincialisms (for example, "*Chiesa*" is used instead of "*Gesia*"). Menocchio had expressed himself very differently two years before when he had taken pen in hand to write his defense. But this time the bishop and the inquisitor decided to exercise the mercy that they had refused in the past. First of all they summoned the jailer, Giovan Battista de' Parvi. He informed them that the prison in which Menocchio was confined was "strong and secure," barricaded by three "strong and safe" doors, so that no "other prison stronger or more severe than it can be found in the city of Concordia."

Menocchio had never left it, except to recite his abjuration, candle in hand, at the entrance of the cathedral of the city on the day sentence was passed and on the day of the fair of St. Stephen, and also to attend Mass and receive communion (but usually he had received it in prison). He had fasted many Fridays "except when he was so violently ill that it was thought he would die." Menocchio interrupted his fasting after his illness, "but many times on the eve of other holy days, many times he told me, 'Tomorrow bring me only some bread, because I want to fast, and don't bring me meat or anything else fat.' " "Many times," the jailer added, "I quietly went up to the door of his cell to hear what he was doing or saying, and I heard him praying." Other times Menocchio had been seen reading a book that had been brought to him by a priest, or "an *Office of the Madonna* containing the seven psalms and other prayers"; also he had asked for "an image before which he could say his prayers, and so his son bought him one." Only a few days before [Menocchio] had said "that he always resigned himself to God, and recognized that he was suffering for his sins and errors, and that God had helped him, because he didn't believe he could survive fifteen days suffering as he did in prison, and yet he had come this far." He had talked to the jailer frequently "about those follies of his that he had believed in previously, saying that he knew well that they really had been follies, but he had never adhered to them so that he really firmly believed them, but that it was through temptation of the devil that such extravagant thoughts had come into his head." In conclusion , he seemed to be sincerely repentant, even though (the jailer cautiously observed) "the hearts of men are not so easily known except by God." Then the bishop and the inquisitor had Menocchio summoned. He wept and pleaded. Prostrate on the ground he humbly asked forgiveness: "I am deeply repentant that I have offended my Lord God, and I wish now that I had not said the follies that I said, into which I stupidly fell blinded by the devil and not understanding myself what he told me. . . . Not only have I not regretted doing the penance that was imposed upon me and to be in that prison, but I felt such a great happiness, and God comforted me always while I was praying to his Divine Majesty, that I felt I was in paradise." If it hadn't been for his wife and children, he exclaimed clasping his hands and raising his eyes to heaven, he would have wanted to remain in prison the rest of his life to expiate his offenses against Christ. But he was "very poor": he had to support his wife, seven children, and a number of grandchildren with two mills and two rented fields. His prison, "harsh, earthen, dark, and humid," had ruined his health completely: "I lay four months without getting out of bed, and this year I had swollen legs, and I also became puffy in the face, as you can see, and I almost lost my hearing, and became weak and almost beside myself." "And truly," the notary of the Holy Office recorded, "while he was saying this, he was very pale in appearance, and an invalid in his body, and in a poor way."

The bishop of Concordia and the inquisitor of the Friuli recognized the signs of an authentic conversion in all this. They immediately summoned the mayor of Portogruaro and a few local nobles (among whom was the future historian of the Friuli, Giovan Francesco Palladio degli Olivi) and commuted his sentence. They assigned the village of Montereale to Menocchio as his perpetual prison with instructions not to leave it. He was expressly forbidden to speak of or to mention his dangerous ideas. He had to confess regularly, and wear over his clothing the *habitello* with the painted cross, the sign of his infamy. A friend of his, Daniele de Biasio, made himself a bondsman guaranteeing to pay 200 ducats in case the sentence was violated. Menocchio returned to Montereale, broken in body and spirit.

48

He resumed his place in the community. Despite his troubles with the Holy Office, the defamatory condemnation, and prison, in 1590 he was reappointed administrator *(cameraro)* for the church of Santa Maria in Montereale. The new priest, Giovanni Daniele Melchiori, Menocchio's childhood friend, must have had a hand in the appointment. (We shall see later what had become of the previous priest, Odorico

Vorai, who had denounced Menocchio to the Holy Office.) Apparently no one found it scandalous that a heretic, a heresiarch in fact, should administer the funds of the parish: and, for that matter, as we recall, even the priest had had dealings with the Inquisition.

The position of *cameraro* was frequently entrusted to millers, perhaps because they were in a position to advance the money needed to administer the parish. In any case, the *camerari* tended to make good their expenditures by delaying to turn over the tithes collected from the faithful. In 1593, when Matteo Sanudo, Bishop of Concordia, came to Montereale in the course of a visitation of the entire diocese, he examined the account books that had been kept by *camerari* for the seven previous years. It emerged that among the debtors there was Domenico Scandella, our Menocchio, owing 200 lire—the largest single debt after one of Bernardo Corneto. This was a common phenomenon, one regularly deplored in pastoral visitations in the Friuli during this period. The bishop (who probably didn't connect the name Scandella with the man whom he had condemned nine years before) now attempted to introduce a more rigorous and accurate administration. He disapproved of "the lack of order observed in the keeping of accounts, although good instructions had been given about this on the last visit. If they had been followed, there is no doubt that the affairs of the church would have fared much better"; he ordered that a "large book" should be purchased in which the priest, under threat of suspension from divine services *(a divinis)*, was to register from year to year the income collected "lot by lot, and respectively for those who paid, for the distribution of the grain day by day, for the expenses of the church, and, finally, for the settlement with the *camerari*"; the latter were to note their income in a "register *(vacchetta)* from which afterwards it was to be transferred into the book." The debtors among the *camerari* were ordered to settle their accounts "under penalty of being deprived entry into the church and of ecclesiastical burial in case of death"; within six months the priest was to bring the accounts for the year 1592 to Portogruaro, or face a fine and—once again—suspension *a divinis*. We don't know if Menocchio actually ended up paying his debt. He may have, since in the next pastoral visitation, carried out by Bishop Sanudo himself in 1599–1600, Montereale *camerari* who were in debt turned up only for the years 1592 onwards.

There is evidence from this same period (1595) that confirms Menocchio's unimpaired prestige among his fellow citizens. "A small difficulty" had arisen between Count Giovan Francesco di Montereale and one of his tenants, Bastian de Martin, over two pieces of land and a farmhouse. At the count's request, two assessors were appointed to appraise the improvements made to the dwelling by the previous tenants. Piero della Zuanna was chosen to represent the count, Menocchio, the tenant. The case was a difficult one since one of the parties was none other than the local lord. But obviously there was confidence in Menocchio, in his ability to reason and argue.

The same year, Menocchio and his son Stefano rented a new mill in a locality called "beneath the hedges above" *("de sotto le siege de sora")*. The rental was for a period of nine years: the lessees bound themselves to a yearly payment of 4 bushels of wheat, 10 of rye, 2 of oats, 2 of millet, 2 of buckwheat, and, in addition, a pig weighing 150 pounds. A clause specified that the equivalent should be paid in cash (at the rate of 6 soldi per pound) if the animal's weight should be below or above the one stipulated. Furthermore, there was a provision for "gifts": a brace of capons and half a length of linen. The latter was a token tribute since the mill was used for the fulling of cloth. The two lessees received the mill in consignment equipped with two "good and serviceable" asses, a wheel *(leviera)*, and six fulling machines; and they obligated themselves to return the establishment "improved rather than deteriorated" to the owners, who were guardians of the heirs of Pietro de Macris. The previous tenant, Florito di Benedetto, who had become insolvent, promised to pay the back rent to them within five years; and, at his request, Menocchio and Stefano offered themselves as guarantors of this arrangement.

All this suggests that the financial situation of the two Scandellas must have been fairly solid at this time. Menocchio was participating fully in the life of his community. In 1595, he was the bearer of a message from the provincial governor of the *Patria* of the Friuli to the mayor, as well as being chosen one of fourteen representatives, including the mayor, from the "neighborhood" of Montereale entrusted with the selection of assessors.

Some time later, however, Menocchio must have found himself in difficulty following the death of the son (probably Ziannuto) who had been supporting him. He tried to provide for himself by working at other occupations: school teacher and guitar player at festivals. It became more urgent than ever to rid himself of the stigma of the *habitello* and the prohibition against leaving Montereale that had been imposed upon him by the sentence. So he went to Udine to the new inquisitor, fra Giovan Battista da Perugia, asking to be released from both obligations. He received a negative response regarding the *habitello,* "because," the inquisitor explained in a letter to the bishop of Concordia dated 26 January 1597, "a dispensation on this matter should not be granted lightly"; however, he was granted permission to "freely . . . do business anywhere, except in suspected places, so that in some way he may alleviate his own poverty and that of his family."

Little by little the consequences of the old trial were being erased. But, meanwhile, unknown to Menocchio, the Holy Office had begun to renew its interest in him.

49

During the carnival of the previous year Menocchio had left Montereale to go to Udine, with the inquisitor's permission. In the public square at the hour of Vespers he met a certain Lunardo Simon and began to chat with him. The two knew one another because Lunardo made the rounds of festivals playing his violin while Menocchio, as was mentioned, did the same with the guitar. Some time later, after learning of a bull against heretics, Lunardo wrote to the inquisitor's vicar, fra Gerolamo Asteo, to report this conversation; afterwards, orally, with only a few variations, he confirmed the substance of the letter. The exchange in the square had gone more or less like this:

MENOCCHIO: "I hear that you want to become a monk: is it true?"
LUNARDO: "Isn't that a good story?"
MENOCCHIO: "No, because it is a beggarly thing."
LUNARDO (twisting the pun): "Do I need to become a monk to be a beggar?"
MENOCCHIO: "Of the many saints, hermits, and others who have led holy lives, we don't know where they've ended up."
LUNARDO: "The Lord God doesn't want us to know these secrets now."
MENOCCHIO: "If I were a Turk, I wouldn't want to become a Christian, but I am a Christian, and I don't want to become a Turk at all."
LUNARDO: *"Beati qui non viderunt, et crediderunt."*
MENOCCHIO: "I don't believe if I don't see. But I do believe that God is the father of the whole world, and can do and undo."
LUNARDO: "Turks and Jews also believe this, but they don't believe that he was born of the Virgin Mary."
MENOCCHIO: "What does it mean, when Christ was on the cross, and the Jews said to him, 'If you are the Christ descend from the cross,' that he did not descend?"
LUNARDO: "That was so as not to show obedience to the Jews."
MENOCCHIO: "It was because Christ wasn't able to."

LUNARDO: "So then, you don't believe in the Gospels?"
MENOCCHIO: "No, I don't. Who do you think makes these Gospels if not the priests and monks, who have nothing better to do? They think up these things and write them down one after another."

Then Lunardo had objected that "neither priests nor monks made the Gospels; instead they were made long ago." And he had gone on his way, judging his companion to be a "heretical person."

God, father, and master who can "do and undo"; a human Christ; the Gospels produced by idle priests and monks; the equality of religions. So, despite the trial, the defamatory abjuration, imprisonment, the sensational show of repentance, Menocchio had resumed his old ideas, which, clearly, he had never renounced in his heart. But about him Lunardo Simon knew only his name ("a certain Menocchio, miller of Montereale"): and despite the rumor that he was relapsed and had formerly been condemned by the Holy Office "as a Lutheran," the denunciation wasn't acted on. Only two years later, on 28 October 1598, either accidentally or as a result of a systematic review of the existing records, did the inquisitors suspect that Menocchio and Domenico Scandella were, in fact, one and the same person. Then the machinery of the Holy Office was set again in motion. Fra Gerolamo Asteo, who in the meantime had become inquisitor general of the Friuli, began to collect new information concerning Menocchio. It emerged that don Odorico Vorai, whose accusation of Menocchio many years before had resulted in the latter's incarceration, had paid dearly for this act: "he has been persecuted by Menocchio's relatives and driven from Montereale." As for Menocchio "it has been and is still believed that he holds the same false opinions as before." At this point the inquisitor went to Montereale and questioned the new priest, don Giovan Daniele Melchiori. The latter reported that Menocchio had stopped wearing the *habitello* and was traveling outside the confines of the town, violating the decrees of the Holy Office (which, as we saw, was only partly true). However, he did go to confession and receive communion several times a year: "as for me, I consider him to be a Christian and an honorable man," he concluded. He didn't know what the inhabitants of the village thought of Menocchio. But after having made and signed these statements, Melchiori backtracked: obviously, he feared he might have gone too far. After the words "I consider him to be a Christian and an honorable man" he asked that "as far as one can judge externally" be added.

Don Curzio Cellina, chaplain of Saint Rocco and the village notary, was more explicit. "I consider him to be a Christian because I have seen that he goes to confession and takes communion," he affirmed. But don Cellina saw the former restlessness showing through Menocchio's seeming act of submission: "This Menocchio has certain humors so that when he sees the moon or stars or other planets and hears thunder or something, he immediately wants to give his opinion on what has just happened. In the end he submits to the opinion of the majority saying that the whole world knows more than he alone. And I believe that this humor of his is wicked, but that he submits to the opinions of others out of fear." So, condemnation and imprisonment by the Holy Office had left a deep mark on him. Menocchio, it seemed, no longer dared—at least in the village—to speak with the insolent license of former days. But not even fear had succeeded in stifling his intellectural freedom: "he immediately wants to give his opinion." What was new, instead, was the bitter and ironic sense of his isolation: "he submits to the opinion of the majority saying that the whole world knows more than he alone."

It was mostly an inner isolation. Don Cellina himself observed: "I see him associating with many and I believe he is everybody's friend." As for himself, he declared that he felt "for this Menocchio neither a close friendship nor enmity: but I love him as a Christian and I deal with him as I do with others, when I have some task for him." Externally, as we saw, Menocchio had been fully reintegrated into the life of the village: for a second time he had been named *cameraro* of the parish; with his son he had rented a third mill. But, despite all this, he felt he was an outsider—perhaps also as a consequence of the financial difficulties of the later years. The *habitello* was the tangible symbol of this exclusion. Menocchio was obsessed by it. "I know," Cellina said, "that for a long time he had a garment with a cross on it that the Holy Office had given him, and he wore it secretly under his clothing." Menocchio had told him that "he wanted to go and visit the Holy Office to obtain permission not to wear it, because he used to say that as a result of his having that garment with the cross men did not want to associate and speak with him." Of course, he was deceiving himself about this—he associated with everyone, he was friendly with everybody in the village. But the impossibility of expressing his own opinions, as in the past, weighed upon him. "When he was heard talking about the moon and the stars," Cellina observed, "he was told to be silent." Cellina couldn't remember precisely what he had been saying on this subject, not even when the inquisitor suggested that perhaps Menocchio was attributing to planets the power of coercing men's free will. At any rate, he emphatically denied that Menocchio was talking "in jest": "I think that he was speaking seriously and that he has some bad tendencies."

The investigations of the Holy Office broke off once again. It's not difficult to understand why: after all, the heresiarch miller had been reduced to silence and external conformity; he no longer represented a threat to the faith of his fellow villagers. In January 1599, at one of its congregations, the Holy Office of the Friuli decided to summon the "offender," namely Menocchio. But even this resolve was dropped.

50

And yet, the conversation reported by Lunardo suggests that Menocchio's outward obedience to the rites and sacraments of the Church disguised a stubborn loyalty to his old ideas. At about the same time, a certain Simon, a converted Jew who wandered about subsisting on charity, turned up in Montereale and was given shelter by Menocchio. The two talked about religious questions all through the night. Menocchio said "enormous things concerning the faith": that the Gospels had been written by priests and monks "because they have nothing better to do," and that the Madonna before marrying St. Joseph "had borne two other creatures, and because of this St. Joseph did not want to accept her as his bride." Basically, these were the same subjects that he had brought up with Lunardo on the square at Udine: an attack against the parasitism of the clergy, the rejection of the Gospel, the denial of Christ's divinity. In addition to this, however, that night he had also talked of a "most beautiful book," which unfortunately he had lost, and which Simon "judged was the Koran."

It may have been Menocchio's rejection of the central dogmas of Christianity—and principally that of the Trinity—that had led him, like other heretics of this period, to turn with curiosity to the Koran. Unfortunately, Simon's identification isn't definite, and in any case we don't know what Menocchio took from that mysterious "most beautiful book." Certainly, he was convinced that eventually his heresy would be discovered: "he knew that he would die because of it," he had confided to Simon. But he didn't want to flee since a man who had stood as godfather with him, Daniele de Biasio, had offered surety for him with the Holy Office fifteen years before: "otherwise he would have fled to Geneva." So he had decided to stay in Montereale. He was already looking ahead to the end: "at his death, some Lutherans will learn of it, and will come to collect the ashes."

Who knows what "Lutherans" Menocchio had in mind? Perhaps a group with which he had maintained clandestine ties—or some individual he might have met many years before and who had then dropped out of sight. The aura of martyrdom in which Menocchio envisioned his own death makes one think that all this talk was nothing more than the pathetic fancies of an old man. After all, he had nothing left. He was alone now: his wife and his closest son were dead. He must not have been on good terms with his other children: "And if *my* children want to go their own way, good luck to them," he declared disdainfully to Simon. But that mythical Geneva, the home (or so he thought) of religious freedom, was too far away; this, and his tenacious loyalty to a friend who had stood by him in a moment of difficulty, had kept him from flight. Evidently, on the other hand, he couldn't repress his passionate curiosity about things pertaining to the faith. So he lingered there awaiting his persecutors.

51

In fact, a few months later a new denunciation against Menocchio reached the inquisitor. It appears that he had uttered a blasphemy that traveled from mouth to mouth, from Aviano to Pordenone, provoking scandalized reactions. An innkeeper of Aviano, Michele del Turco, called Pignol, was questioned: seven or eight years before (he had been told) Menocchio had exclaimed: "if Christ had been God he would have been a . . . to have allowed himself to be put on the cross. . . ." "He did not express what Christ would have been," the innkeeper added, "but I gathered that he meant to say that Christ would have been an ass *(coglione)*, to use that ugly word. . . . When I heard such words, my hair stood on end, and I changed the subject immediately so as not to hear such things, because I consider him to be worse than a Turk." He concluded that Menocchio "still persisted in those old opinions of his."

By now it was no longer just the inhabitants of Montereale who told one another the things Menocchio had said: the fame of this miller, whom not even the prisons of the Holy Office had succeeded in leading back to the straight and narrow, had gone beyond the small circle of the village. His provocative questions, his blasphemous jests were repeated sometimes after the lapse of years: "Oh, how can you believe that Christ or God Almighty was the son of the Virgin Mary if the Virgin Mary was a whore?" "How can it be that Christ was conceived by the Holy Spirit if he was borne by a whore?" "Saint Christopher is greater than God since he carried the whole world on his back." (Curiously, the same sally occurs in a book that Menocchio certainly never saw, the collection of emblems, riddled with heretical overtones, by the Bolognese humanist Achille Bocchi.) "I believe that he was wrong-headed, and that he did not dare to speak out because he was afraid," said Zannuto Fasseta of Montereale who had heard Menocchio "make music." But the usual impulse again drove Menocchio to talk about religious questions with the other villagers. One day, while returning from Menins to Montereale, he had asked Daniel Iacomel: "What do you think God is?" Embarrassed or taken aback, the other replied, "I don't know." "He is nothing but air," Menocchio instantly interjected. He was turning his old ideas over and over in his mind; he hadn't given up. "Can't you understand, the inquisitors don't want us to know what they know." He, however, felt capable of standing up to them: "I'd like to say four words of the Pater Noster before the father inquisitor, and see what he would say and answer."

This time the inquisitor must have thought that Menocchio had gone too far. Toward the end of June 1599, he was arrested and confined in the prison at Aviano. A little later he was transferred to Portogruaro. On 12 July he appeared before the inquisitor, fra Gerolamo Asteo, the vicar of the Bishop of Concordia, Valerio Trapola, and the mayor of the place, Pietro Zane.

52

"After having led a certain old man from prison . . . " the notary began. Fifteen years had passed since Menocchio had been questioned by the Holy Office the first time. In the interval there had also been the three years spent in prison. He was an old man by now: thin, his hair had turned white, his beard was gray and turning white, and, as always, he was dressed as a miller with a garment and cap pale gray in color. He was sixty-seven years old. He had had many jobs after his condemnation: "I have been a sawyer, miller, innkeeper, I have kept a school for children to learn the abacus and reading and writing, and I also play the guitar at festivals." In other words, he had tried to get along by making use of his skills—including knowing how to read and write, which had helped to get him into trouble. In fact, to the inquisitor who asked him if he had ever been tried by the Holy Office, he replied: "I was summoned . . . and was interrogated on the Creed and about other fantasies that had come into my head because I had read the Bible and because I have a keen mind. But I have always been a Christian, and remain so."

His tone was submissive—"fantasies"—accompanied, however, by the usual prideful awareness of his own intellectual capacities. He explained in detail how he had fulfilled the penances imposed upon him, how he had gone to confession and had taken communion, how he had occasionally left Montereale but always with the inquisitor's permission. He apologized only in regard to the *habitello:* "I swear upon my faith that on feast days sometimes I wore it and sometimes not; and on work days in winter when it was cold I always wore it, but underneath," since by showing it, "I lost a lot of money not being called to do assessments and other jobs . . . because men considered me excommunicated when they saw that garment, and so I did not wear it." In vain he had begged the father inquisitor but "he would not give me permission to remove the habit."

When they asked him if he had continued to have doubts about those questions for which he had been condemned, Menocchio couldn't lie. Rather than uttering an outright denial, he admitted, "many fantasies came into my head, but I never wanted to pay attention to them, nor have I ever taught anyone bad things." And to the inquisitor who pressed him, asking if he had ever "discussed articles of the faith with anyone, and who were they, and on what occasion and where," he replied that he had spoken "jokingly with some about the articles of the faith, but truthfully I do not know with whom, or where, or when." It was an imprudent reply. The inquisitor rebuked him severely: "How is it that you were joking about matters of the faith? Is it proper to joke about the faith? What do you mean by this word 'jokingly'?" "Saying some lie," Menocchio replied lamely. "What lie were you saying? Come, speak up clearly!" "I truthfully cannot say."

But the inquisitor pressed on with his questions. "I don't know," Menocchio said, "someone may have misinterpreted it, but I have never believed anything that is against the faith." He tried to return blow for blow. He hadn't said that Christ had been incapable of descending from the cross: "I believe that Christ had the power to descend." He hadn't said that he didn't believe in the Gospel: "I believe that the Gospel is the truth." And here he took another false step: "I did indeed say that priests and monks who have studied made the Gospels pretending that it came from the Holy Spirit." The inquisitor pounced on this: Had he really said this? When, where, to whom? And who were those monks? Exasperated, Menocchio replied: "How do you expect me to know? Truthfully, no, I don't know this." "Why did you say it if you do not know it?" "Sometimes the devil tempts us to say certain words. . . . "

Once again, Menocchio was trying to attribute his doubts, his anger, to diabolical temptation—only, however, to promptly reveal his belief in their rational basis. He had read in Foresti's *Supplementum* that "various persons such as St. Peter, St. James, and others have written Gospels, which justice has suppressed." Here, too, the corrosive influence of analogy had worked on Menocchio's mind. If some of the Gospels are apocryphal, human and not divine, why aren't they all? This brought to light all the implications of what he had maintained fifteen years before, namely that Scripture could be reduced to "four words." In all that time, evidently, he had continued to pursue the thread of his old ideas. And now, once more, he had the opportunity of expressing them to those (so he thought) who were in a position to understand them. He blindly cast aside all prudence and caution: "I believe that God made all things, that is earth, water, and air." "But what about fire?" interjected the vicar of the Bishop of Concordia with ironic superiority, "who made that?" "Fire is everywhere, just as God is, but the other three elements are the three persons: the Father is air, the Son is earth, and the Holy Spirit is water." And then Menocchio added: "This is how it seems to me; but I don't know if it is the truth; and I believe that those spirits that are in the air fight among themselves, and that the lightning flashes are their anger."

Thus, in his laborious journey backwards into time, Menocchio had unwittingly rediscovered, beyond the Christian image of the universe, the universe of the ancient Greek philosophers. This peasant Heraclitus had recognized the primordial element in fire, utterly mobile and indestructible. For Menocchio, all of reality was permeated with it ("it is everywhere"): a coherent reality, yet in its many manifestations it was full of spirits, permeated with divinity. For this reason he stated that fire was God. It's true that Menocchio had also devised a captious, detailed correspondence between the other three elements and the persons of the Trinity: "I believe that the Father is air, because air is an element higher than water and earth; next I say that the Son is earth because the Son is produced by the Father; and since water comes from air and earth, so the Holy Spirit comes from the Father and from the Son." But behind these relationships, which he immediately rejected in a belated and useless burst of caution ("but I do not want to believe these things"), Menocchio's most deeply-held conviction emerged: God is one, and he is the world. The inquisitor concentrated his attack on this point: did he believe then that God has a body? "I know that Christ had a body," Menocchio replied evasively. To get the upper hand with someone who argued like this wasn't easy. From his scholastic armory the inquisitor drew forth a syllogism. "You say that the Holy Spirit is water; water is a body; thus, would it not follow that the Holy Spirit is a body?" "I say these things as similitudes," Menocchio replied. Perhaps there was a trace of complacency: he too knew how to reason, how to use the tools of logic and rhetoric.

Then the inquisitor returned to the offensive: "It appears in the records that you said God is nothing other than air." "I do not know that I said this, but I did really say that God is all things." "Do you believe that God is all things?" "My lords, yes indeed I do believe it." But in what sense? The inquisitor couldn't grasp this. "I believe that God is everything that he wants to be," Menocchio explained. "Can God be a stone, a serpent, a devil and such things?" "God can be everything that is good." "Then God could be a creature, since there are good creatures?"

"I do not know what to say," replied Menocchio.

53

Actually, the distinction between creator and creatures, the very idea of a creator God, was totally foreign to him. He knew perfectly well that his ideas were different from those of the inquisitor: but now he found himself without the words to express this difference. Certainly fra Gerolamo Asteo's logical snares couldn't convince him that he was in the wrong, no more than could the judges who had tried him fifteen years before. For that matter, he promptly tried to seize the initiative, actually overturning the mechanism of the interrogation. "I beg you, sir, listen to me. . . . " Through the telling of the legend of the three rings, Menocchio, as we have seen, bolstered that doctrine of tolerance that he had already expounded at his first trial. At that time, however, the argument had been a religious one: all faiths (including heresies) were of equal value since "God has given the Holy Spirit to all." Now, instead, the emphasis was on the equivalence of the various churches inasmuch as they were entities linked to the life of society: "Yes sir, I do believe that every person considers his faith to be right, and we do not know which is the right one. But because my grandfather, my father, and my people have been Christians, I want to remain a Christian and believe that this is the right one." The entreaty to remain within the sphere of the traditional religions was supported by the appeal to the legend of the three rings: but it is difficult not to see in these words the bitter fruit of Menocchio's experience after the condemnation by the Holy Office. It was better to dissemble, better to observe externally rites that he inwardly recognized as "merchandise." This withdrawal was leading Menocchio to give less importance to the question of heresy, to the question of the open, conscious break with traditional religion. At the same time, however, he ended up by considering religion purely as a worldly reality much more than he had in the past. To insist that we are Christians only by chance, because of tradition, involved a critical disjunction of serious proportions—of the sort that in these same years led Montaigne to write: *"Nous sommes Chrestiens à mesme titre que nous sommes ou Perigordins ou Alemans."* Both Montaigne and Menocchio, each in his way, had made the disturbing discovery of the relativity of beliefs and institutions.

But this adherence—conscious and not passive—to the religion of his ancestors was, nonetheless, only external. Menocchio attended Mass, went to confession, and received communion: but inside he kept turning over thoughts that were both old and new. He told the inquisitor that he considered himself "a philosopher, astrologer, and prophet," adding modestly in his own defense that "even the prophets err." And he explained: "I thought I was a prophet, because the evil spirit made me see vanities and dreams and convinced me that I knew the nature of the heavens, and such things: and I believe that the prophets spoke what angels dictated to them."

In the first trial, as we recall, Menocchio had never mentioned supernatural revelations. Now, instead, he was alluding to experiences of a mystical sort, even though he disavowed them vaguely as "vanities" and "dreams." What may have influenced him was a reading of that Koran (the "most beautiful book" identified by the converted Jew Simon), which the archangel Gabriel had dictated to the prophet Mohammed. Menocchio may have thought that he could discover "the nature of the heavens" in the apocryphal dialogue between the rabbi Abdullah ibn Sallam and Mohammed, inserted in book one of the Italian translation of the Koran: "He said, go on, and tell me why the sky is called sky. He answered, because it is created of vapor, vapor from the steam of the sea. He asked, whence comes its green? He replied, from Mount Caf, and Mount Caf received it from the emeralds in paradise. This is the mountain that girdles the circle of the earth and holds up the sky. He asked, does the sky have a door? He replied, it has doors that hang down. He asked, and do the doors have keys? He replied that they have keys that are to God's treasure. He asked, of what are the doors made? He answered, of gold. He asked, you, tell me the truth, but tell me, this sky of ours from what was it created? He replied: the first of green water, the second of clear water, the third of emeralds, the fourth of the purest gold, the fifth of hyacinth, the sixth of a shining cloud, the seventh of the splendor of fire. He said, and in this you speak the truth. But what is there above these seven skies? He replied, a life-giving sea, and above it a nebulous sea, and proceeding in this way in order, there is the aereal sea, and above it the sorrowful sea, and above it the somber sea, and above it the sea of pleasure, and above that the Moon, and above that the Sun, and above that the name of God, and above it supplication . . . " and so forth.

These are merely conjectures. We don't have proof that the "most beautiful book" about which Menocchio had spoken enthusiastically was indeed the Koran; and even if we did, we couldn't reconstruct the way in which Menocchio read it. A text so totally foreign to his experience and culture would have been incomprehensible to him—and would have led him for this very reason to project his own thoughts and fantasies onto the page. But we know nothing about this projection (if it actually occurred). And in general, it's very difficult to penetrate this final phase of Menocchio's intellectual life. Unlike fifteen years before, fear drove him little by little to deny almost everything that the inquisitor brought out against him. But once again, it was an effort for him to lie: only after remaining "briefly lost in thought" did he assert that he had never "doubted that Christ was God." Subsequently he contradicted himself saying that "Christ did not have the power of the Father, since he had a human body." "This is a confusion," the judges protested. To this Menocchio replied, "I do not remember having said this and I am an ignoramus." Humbly he affirmed that when he had said that the Gospels had been written by "priests and monks who had studied," he had the evangelists in mind "whom, I believe, all studied." He tried to tell them everything that he thought they wanted to know: "It is true that inquisitors and our other superiors do not want us to know what they know; and so we should remain silent." But every now and then he couldn't restrain himself: "I did not believe that paradise existed, because I did not know where it was."

At the end of the first interrogation Menocchio submitted a piece of paper on which he had written something about the words of the Pater Noster, *"et ne nos inducas in tentationem, sed libera nos a malo,"* explaining, "with this I ask to be freed from these tribulations of mine." Then, before being led back to prison, he signed it with an old man's trembling hand.

54

This is what he had written:

"In the name of our Lord Jesus Christ and of his mother the Virgin Mary and of all the saints in paradise I appeal for help and counsel.

Oh great, omnipotent, and holy God, creator of heaven and earth, I beg you, in the name of your most saintly goodness and infinite mercy, to enlighten my spirit, and my soul, and my body so that it will think, and say, and do everything that is pleasing to your divine majesty: and so be it in the name of the most holy Trinity, Father, Son and Holy Spirit, and Amen. I the wretched Menego Scandella who have fallen into disgrace with the world and with my superiors resulting in the ruin of my house, of my life, and of my entire poor family, no longer know what to say or do except to speak these few words. First: *'Set libera nos a malo et ne nos inducas in tentazionem et demite nobis debita nostra sicut ne nos dimitimus debitoribus nostris, panem nostrum cotidianum da nobis hodie':* and so I pray our Lord Jesus Christ and my superiors that out of their mercy they give me some help with little harm to themselves. And wherever I Menego Scandella shall go I will beg all faithful Christians to observe everything commanded of them by our Holy Mother Catholic Roman Church and her officials, that is, inquisitors, bishops, vicars, priests, chaplains, and curates of her dioceses, so that they should profit from my experience. I Menego also thought that death would free me from these fears, so I would not bother anyone, but it has done just the opposite, it has taken away a son of mine who was able to keep every trouble and suffering from me; and then it has wanted to take my wife who looked after me; and the sons and daughters who remain to me consider me crazy because I have been their ruination, which is only the truth, and if only I had died when I was fifteen, they would be without the bother of this poor wretch.

And if I have had some evil thought or said some word falsely, I never believed them or ever even acted against the Holy Church, because our Lord God has taught me to believe that everything I thought and said was vanity, not wisdom.

And this I hold to be the truth, because I do not want to think or believe except what the Holy Church believes and to do what my priests and superiors will command of me."

55

At the foot of the page there were a few lines written by the priest of Montereale, Giovan Daniele Melchiori, at Menocchio's request and dated 22 January 1597. They declared that "if the internal can be judged by the external" Menocchio's life was "Christian and orthodox." His caution, as we know (and which perhaps the priest also knew), was well founded. But the willingness to submit expressed in Menocchio's "writing" was certainly sincere. Rejected by his children who considered him a burden, a disgrace in the eyes of the village, a ruin for his family, he passionately longed to be restored to that church that had once separated him from herself, and even had marked him visibly as a reprobate. Because of this he was making a pathetic gesture of homage to his "superiors": "inquisitors" (understandably in first place) and then in succession "bishops, vicars, priests, chaplains, and curates." It was a useless act of submission, in a sense, because when he wrote this, the investigation of Menocchio by the Holy Office hadn't yet resumed. But the uncontrollable yearning "to seek exalted things" tormented him, filled him with "anxiety," made him feel guilty "and in disgrace with the world." And then he desperately cried out for death. But death had bypassed him: "It has done just the opposite, it has taken away a son of mine . . . ; and then it has wanted to take my wife. . . . " At that moment he cursed himself: "if only I had died when I was fifteen"—before growing up and becoming the man he was, to his disgrace and that of his children.

56

After another interrogation (19 July) Menocchio was asked if he wanted a lawyer. He replied, "I do not want to make any other defense, except to ask for mercy; yet, if I could have a lawyer I would accept him, but I am poor." At the time of the first trial Ziannuto had struggled hard for his father and had found a lawyer for him: but Ziannuto was dead and Menocchio's other children hadn't lifted a finger. A court-appointed defender, Agostino Pisensi, was assigned to Menocchio, and on the 22nd of July he presented a long brief to the judges in defense "of the poor Domenico Scandella." In it he declared that the evidence had been secondhand, contradictory, and defective because of its obvious animosity; it clearly demonstrated the "pure simplicity and ignorance" of the accused, whose acquittal was requested.

On 2 August the members of the Holy Office met: unanimously it was decreed that Menocchio was a *relapsus*, a backslider. The trial was over. Nevertheless, it was decided to interrogate the offender under torture to obtain the names of his accomplices. This took place on the 5th of August; the previous day Menocchio's house had been searched. In the presence of witnesses, all his chests had been opened and "his books and writings" confiscated. Unfortunately, we don't know what these "writings" were.

57

They asked him to reveal the names of his accomplices so that torture might be avoided. He replied, "Sir, I do not remember having discussions with anyone." He was undressed and examined to determine—as Holy Office regulations prescribed—whether he was fit to undergo torture. Meanwhile, they continued questioning him. He replied, "I have discussed things with so many people that now I cannot remember who they were." Then they ordered him to be tied, and asked him one more time to state the truth about his accomplices. Again, he repeated, "I do not remember." They conducted him to the torture chamber, continually insisting on the same question. "I have tried to think and imagine," he said, "to try to remember with whom I talked, but have not been able to remember." They prepared him for the strappado. "Oh Lord Jesus Christ, mercy, Jesus mercy, I don't remember having spoken with anyone, may I die if I have either followers or companions, but I have read on my own, oh Jesus mercy." They gave a first jerk on the rope: "Oh Jesus, oh Jesus, oh poor me, oh poor me." "With whom have you had discussions?" they asked him. He replied, "Jesus, Jesus I know nothing." They urged him to tell the truth: "I would say it willingly, let me down and I'll think about it."

Then they ordered him to be lowered. He thought for a moment and then said, "I don't remember having talked with anyone, nor do I know that anyone shares my ideas, and I certainly know nothing." They ordered that he be given another pull with the cord. While they were raising him, he cried out, "Alas, alas martyr, oh Lord Jesus Christ." And then, "Sir, let me be and I'll say something." When he was on the ground once more, he said, "I spoke to signor Zuan Francesco Montareale and told him we don't know what the true faith is." (The next day he specified: "The aforesaid lord Gio. Francesco reproached me for my lunacies".) That's all they could get out of him. Then he was unbound and led back to his cell. The notary recorded that the torture had been applied "with moderation." It had lasted half an hour.

We can only imagine the judges' state of mind resulting from the monotonous repetition of the same question. They may have felt the same combination of annoyance and disgust that the nuncio Alberto Bolognetti had written about in these very years. On the subject of the Holy Office he complained of "the nuisance, for anyone who isn't a model of patience, of having to listen to the inanities uttered by so many, especially during torture, that have to be written down word for word." The obstinate silence of the old miller must have been incomprehensible to them.

Thus, not even physical pain had succeeded in bending Menocchio. He hadn't named names, or, more precisely, he had named only one—that of the lord of Montereale—which seems to have been done intentionally to deter the judges from probing too deeply. Doubtless, he had something to hide: but probably he wasn't too far from the truth when he declared that he had "read on [his] own."

58

By his silence Menocchio had wanted to underscore for his judges, to the very end, that his ideas had been conceived in isolation, strictly through contact with books. But as we saw, he projected onto the written page, elements taken from oral tradition.

It is this tradition, deeply rooted in the European countryside, that explains the tenacious persistence of a peasant religion intolerant of dogma and ritual, tied to the cycles of nature, and fundamentally pre-Christian. In many cases, it was a matter of actual estrangement from Christianity, as with those herdsmen in the rural areas around Eboli who in mid-seventeenth century appeared to some astonished Jesuits as "men who had nothing human about them except their form, not very different in their capacities and knowledge from the beasts that they tended: totally ignorant not only of prayers, or of the other special mysteries of the holy faith, but also of the very knowledge of God." But one can discover traces of this peasant religion, which had assimilated and reshaped elements—not the least of which were Christian elements—from without even in situations of lesser geographical and cultural isolation. The old English peasant who thought of God as "a kindly old man," of Christ as "a handsome youth," of the soul as "a big bone stuck in the body," and of the hereafter as "a beautiful green field" where he would go if he had behaved well, certainly wasn't ignorant of Christian doctrines: he simply translated them into images that corresponded to his experiences, to his aspirations, to his fantasies.

We witness a similar process in Menocchio's confessions. Of course, his case is much more complicated. It involves both the mediation of the printed page and the disintegration of much of traditional religion under the blows dealt by the more radical currents within the Reformation. But the pattern is the same, and it isn't an exceptional case.

Some twenty years before Menocchio's trial, an unknown rustic in the Lucchese countryside who hid behind the pseudonym Scolio spoke of his visions in a long, still unpublished poem, the *Settennario,* rich in religious and moral overtones, here and there punctuated with Dantean echoes. It hammers away at its central argument that the various religions have a common base in the Ten Commandments. Appearing in a cloud of gold God explains to Scolio:

> Many prophets have I already sent
> Diverse, because varied were those,
> To whom I directed my prophets
> And I also gave them different laws
> Just as various were the customs I found,
> Just as the physician various purgatives
> Prescribes according to the nature of one's constitution.
> The emperor sends out three captains
> Into Africa, into Asia, and into Europe:
> To the Jews, to the Turks, and to Christians
> Each one makes a copy of his law,
> And depending on the variety and strangeness of the customs
> Dispenses to each people a different and appropriate version of it:
> But gives Ten Commandments to each of them
> The same, but which they comment on separately.
> But God is one, and only one is his faith...

Thus, among the "captains" sent out by the "emperor" there is also Mohammed, "Reputed by criminals to be wicked amidst the good/Yet he was a prophet and a great warrior of God," named at the end of a list that includes Moses, Elias, David, Solomon, Christ, Joshua, Abraham, and Noah. Turks and Christians are exhorted to stop their fighting and become reconciled:

> You Turk and you Christian by my decree
> Do not go on as you have in the past:
> Turk take a step forward
> And you Christian take a step backward.

All this is attainable since the Ten Commandments are the basis not only of the three great Mediterranean religions (we recall the tradition of the fable of the three rings) but also of religions that have appeared and that are yet to come: the fourth, not specifically named; the fifth, which "God gave to us in our time" and which is identified with Scolio's prophecy; and the two in the future that will complete the prophetic number seven.

As we see, Scolio's religious message is very simple. It suffices to obey the Ten Commandments, "nature's great precepts." Dogmas, beginning with the Trinitarian one, are rejected:

> Do not adore or believe but in one God
> Who has neither companion, friend nor son:
> Everyone is his son, servant, and friend

> Who obeys his precepts and what has been said and I say.
> Neither worship others nor a Holy Spirit
> If I am indeed God, God is everywhere.

Baptism and the Eucharist are the only sacraments mentioned. The former is reserved for adults:

> Let everyone be circumcised on the eighth day
> And then be baptized near thirty years of age,
> As God and the prophets commanded
> And as was done to Christ by St. John.

The Eucharist is substantially devalued: "And if I told you," Christ declares

> That the blessed bread
> Was my body, and the wine my blood,
> I said it to you because it was pleasing to me
> And it was a pious food and sacrifice,
> But I did not command it as a precept
> But because the bread and wine resemble God.
> Now of what importance are your disputes
> So long as you observe the Ten Commandments.

This is not simply impatience with theological discussions about the real presence; through the mouth of Christ, Scolio reaches the point of denying any sacramental value to baptism and the Eucharist:

> My baptism with sacrifice,
> My death and the host and my communion,
> Was not a commandment, but an office
> To perform sometimes in memory of me.

What counts for the purposes of salvation, once again, is the literal observance of the Ten Commandments, without "gloss or comment of any kind," without interpretations dictated by "syllogisms or strange logic." Religious ceremonies are considered useless; the cult must be very simple:

> Let there be neither columns nor figures,
> Neither organs, music, nor instruments,
> Neither bell towers, bells, nor pictures,
> Neither reliefs, friezes, nor ornaments:
> Let all things be simple and pure
> So that only the Ten Commandments may be heard...

The Word of God is extremely simple, God who asked Scolio to write his book in a language that was not "Puffed up, obscure, pedantic, or affected/But rather open and plain."

Despite certain similarities (probably independent of direct connections; at any rate they are undocumented) with Anabaptist doctrines, Scolio's statements seem to spring rather from that underground current of peasant radicalism to which we have also traced Menocchio. For Scolio, the pope isn't the Antichrist (even if, as we shall see momentarily, his figure is destined to disappear in the future); the exercise of authority is not, as it was for Anabaptists, inherently to be condemned. Of course, those in power must govern paternally:

> If my Lord made you his steward
> And handed administration over to you,
> If he made you duke, pope, or emperor,
> Endowed you with humanity and discretion,
> If he gave you strength, intelligence, good will, honor,
> You must be a father and defender to us,
> What you have is not yours, it belongs to others and is mine,
> Everything beyond your just due is of God.

The society imagined by Scolio was, in fact, the pious and austere one of the peasant utopias: rid of the useless professions ("Let there be no shops or manual trades/Except the most important and principal ones;/Esteem as vanities all the knowledge/Of physicians and do without doctors"), based on farmers and warriors, governed by a single ruler, who will be Scolio himself.

> let gambling, whores, and the inn,
> The drunkard and the buffoon be swept away,
> And let him who plies the farmer's art
> Surpass every art in utility and honor;
> And those who fight for the faith
> Be worthy of great praise and great reward;
> Pride, pomp, debauchery with ostentation,
> Superstition and vainglory, let them be swept away...
> Let great dinners and great suppers be prohibited
> Because they are full of drunkenness and guzzling,
> Music and dancing, perfumes, baths, and games;
> Dressing and footwear, let them be poor and few;
> Let a single carnal man be sole sovereign,
> Over the temporal and the spiritual,
> Let one man be sole monarch and sole lord
> And let there be a single fold and a single pastor.

In this future society injustices will disappear: "the age of gold" will return. The law, "brief, clear, and common to all" shall be:

> In everybody's hands
> Because through it they will produce good fruits;

And let it be in the vernacular, thus understood by all,
So that they may flee from evil and pursue the good.

A rigid egalitarianism will abolish economic differences:

Man or woman, suffice that it be a mouth
And entitled to its share in life.
It is not fitting for anyone to have more
Than an honest portion of food and clothing,
Or to eat better, dress better, or dwell better.
For, whoever wants to command must first obey.
It is impious and inhuman that you should have a surfeit,
Or that others or I should be made to suffer for you;
God has made us rich and not servants as before:
Why then do you want someone to fatten you up and serve you?
...and whether one is born in city, villa, or castle
And is low or high in birth,
Let there be no difference between one and another
And let no one have the least advantage.

But this sober and pious society is only one aspect—the terrestrial one—of Scolio's peasant utopia. The otherworldly one is very different: "It is only permitted in heaven, not in this world/To be full of abundance and joy." The life of the hereafter revealed to Scolio in one of his first visions is, in fact, a domain of abundance and of pleasure:

God led me on the following Saturday
To such a mountain where the whole world can be seen,
Where there was a paradise, and so beautiful a place
Surrounded by a wall of ice and fire.
Beautiful palaces and beautiful gardens
And orchards and woods, fields, rivers, and ponds,
Celestial foods and precious wines
There were, and dinners and feasts and great wealth;
The rooms of gold, of silk, and linens,
Choice maidens and pages and beds, and great
Trees, and grasses and animals, and all
Renew their fruits ten times each day.

This is an echo of the paradise in the Koran—joined here to a peasant dream of material opulence, characteristically expressed immediately after with features reminiscent of a myth we have previously encountered. The God that appears to Scolio is an androgynous divinity, a *"donnhoma"* with "its hands open and fingers raised." From every finger, symbolizing one of the Ten Commandments, a river gushes forth from which living beings will drink:

The first river is full of sweet honey,
Hard and liquid sugar the second,
Of ambrosia the third, and nectar the fourth,

The fifth manna, the sixth bread that in this world
Has never been seen, the whitest and least heavy
That causes the dead to return joyous.
It was well said by a man of a holy place
That the face of bread represents God.
The seventh is of precious waters,
The eighth is fresh and pure butter,
Partridges the ninth, fat and tasty,
No wonder, as they came out of Paradise,
Milk is the tenth; and precious stones
Are their beds where I always wish to be,
The banks of lilies and roses, gold and violet,
Silver and flowers and splendor of the sun.

This paradise (and Scolio was well aware of it) greatly resembled the land of Cockaigne.

59

The similarities between Scolio's prophecies and Menocchio's discourses are evident. They can't be explained, obviously, by the existence of common sources—the *Divine Comedy*, the Koran—that were certainly known to Scolio and probably to Menocchio. The crucial element is a common store of traditions, myths, and aspirations handed down orally over generations. In both cases, it was contact with written culture through their schooling, that permitted this deeply rooted deposit of oral culture to emerge. Menocchio must have attended an elementary school; about his own experiences Scolio wrote:

I was made a shepherd and later a student,
Then made an artisan and later a shepherd
Over all sorts of beasts, and then a student,
And later an artisan and then shepherd again,
I learned the seven mechanical arts
And then became shepherd and later a student again.

"Philosopher, astrologer, and prophet," Menocchio described himself; Scolio calls himself "astrologer, philosopher, and poet," as well as "prophet of prophets." Still, there are some obvious differences. Scolio gives the impression of being confined to a rural environment, without, or virtually without, contacts with the city; Menocchio traveled; he made several trips to Venice. Scolio denies any possible value to books that are not the four sacred books, namely the Old and New Testaments, the Koran and his own *Settennario:*

By obeying God you can make yourself wise
And not through books and study.
And let us forbid and remove every doctor,
Who would compose or study,
Every reader, author, and printer
Who would write or print a book,
Every logician, debater, preacher
Who would dispute or preach
On anything but the three holy books I have named,
And this book of mine, that is, of God.

Menocchio purchased the *Fioretto della Bibbia* but was loaned the *Decameron* and Mandeville's *Travels;* he declared that Scripture could be contained in four words, but also felt the need to acquire the inherited knowledge of his adversaries, the inquisitors. In the case of Menocchio, in short, we perceive a free and aggressive spirit intent on squaring things with the culture of the dominant classes; in the case of Scolio, we find a more reserved position, which expends its polemical charge in a moralizing condemnation of urban culture and in the longing for an egalitarian and patriarchal society. Even if the outlines of Menocchio's "new world" elude us, we are tempted to suppose that it differs, at least partly, from the one described in Scolio's desperately anachronistic utopia.

Another miller, Pellegrino Baroni, called Pighino, "the fat," who lived in a village in the Modenese Appennines, Savignano sul Panaro, seems to resemble Menocchio more closely. In 1570 he was tried by the Holy Office in Ferrara; but already nine years before he had been compelled to abjure certain of his errors in matters of the faith. His fellow villagers considered him "a poor Christian," "a heretic," "a Lutheran"; some described him as "an eccentric and weak-minded," or actually "more a fool than anything else." As a matter of fact, Pighino was anything but stupid: during the trial he succeeded in matching wits with the inquisitors showing besides great strength of will, a subtle, almost cunning, intelligence. But it's not hard to imagine the confusion of the villagers or the indignation of the parish priest when faced by Pighino's ideas. He denied the intercession of the saints, confession, the fasting prescribed by the Church—if we stopped here we'd be within the realm of a generic sort of "Lutheranism." He also insisted, however, that all the sacraments, including the Eucharist (but not baptism, apparently), had been instituted by the Church, rather than by Christ, and that they were unnecessary for salvation. He affirmed, moreover, that in paradise "we will all be equal, and grace will be had by the great and the humble alike"; that the Virgin Mary "was born of a serving maid"; that "there is neither hell nor purgatory; they were invented by priests and monks for the sake of money"; that "if Christ had been a worthy man, he would not have been crucified"; that "when the body dies the soul perishes with it"; and finally that "all religions were good for those who observed them inviolably." Although he was tortured on more than one occasion, Pighino obstinately denied having accomplices and asserted that his opinions were the result of illumination received while reading the Gospels in the vernacular—one of the four books he had read. The other three were the Psalter, the grammar by Aelius Donatus, and the *Fioretto della Bibbia.*

Pighino's fate differed from Menocchio's. Condemned to reside for life in the village of Savignano, he fled to escape the hostility of the other villagers; but almost at once he reappeared before the Holy Office of Ferrara, his torturers, to plead for forgiveness. He was a beaten man. The inquisitor, charitably, ended by finding a position for him as a servant with the bishop of Modena. These two millers ended differently; but the similarities in their lives are surprising, probably something more than an extraordinary coincidence.

The primitive state of communications in preindustrial Europe caused even the smallest centers of habitation to have at least one mill powered by water or wind. The occupation of miller, consequently, was one of the most widespread, and their prominence in medieval heretical sects and, in even greater measure, among Anabaptists is not surprising. All the same, when in mid-sixteenth century such a satirical poet as the previously mentioned Andrea da Bergamo asserted that "a true miller is half-Lutheran," he seemed to be alluding to something more specific.

The age-old hostility between peasants and millers had solidified an image of the miller—shrewd, thieving, cheating, destined by definition for the fires of hell. It's a negative stereotype that is widely corroborated in popular traditions, legends, proverbs, fables, and stories. "I descended into hell and saw the Antichrist," so went a Tuscan popular song

> And he had a miller by the beard,
> And a German under his feet,
> Here and there an innkeeper and a butcher:
> I asked him which was the most wicked,
> And he said to me: "Listen and now I'll tell you.
> Look who is grabbing with his hands,
> It's the miller of the white flour.
> Look who is stealing with his hands,
> It's the miller of the white flour.
> He passes the quarter off as a full bushel;
> The biggest thief of all is the miller."

The charge of heresy was wholly consistent with a stereotype such as this. Contributing to it was the fact that the mill was a place of meeting, of social relations, in a world that was predominantly closed and static. Like the inn and the shop it was a place for the exchange of ideas. The peasants who jostled before the gates of the mill, on "the soft ground muddied by the piss of the village mules" (still Andrea da Bergamo speaking) waiting to have their grain ground, must have talked about many things. And the miller, too, must have had his say. It isn't difficult to imagine scenes such as one that took place a certain day at Pighino's mill. Turning to a group of peasants, Pighino had begun to grumble "about priests and monks" until one of the villagers, Domenico de Masafiis, came back and convinced the bystanders to go on their way, saying "Look, boys, you'd better leave the recitation of the Office to priests and monks, and not speak badly about them, and ignore Pelegrino di Grassi" (namely Pighino). Their working conditions made millers—like innkeepers, tavern keepers, and itinerant artisans—an occupational group especially receptive to new ideas and inclined to propagate them. Moreover, mills, generally located on the peripheries of settled areas and far from prying eyes, were well suited to shelter clandestine gatherings. The case in Modena where, in 1192, the persecution of the Cathari led to the devastation of the mills of the Patarines *(molendina paterinorum)* must not have been exceptional.

Finally, the particular social position of the millers tended to isolate them from the communities in which they lived. We've already mentioned the traditional hostility of the peasants. To this should be added the bond of direct dependence that tied millers to the local feudal lords who, for centuries, had retained possession over the milling privilege. We don't know if this was the situation also in Montereale: the mill to full cloth rented by Menocchio and his son, for example, was privately owned. Nevertheless, an attempt, such as the one to convince the lord of the village, Giovan Francesco, count of Montereale, that "we do not know which is the true faith," on the basis of the story of the three rings, probably had been made possible by the atypical nature of Menocchio's social position. His occupation as miller set him apart at once from the anonymous mass of peasants with whom Giovan Francesco di Montereale would never have dreamed of discussing questions of religion. But Menocchio was also a peasant who worked the land—"a peasant dressed in white," as he was described by the ex-lawyer Alessandro Policreto who had met him briefly before the trial. All this may help us to understand the complicated relationship between Menocchio and the community of Montereale. Even if no one, except Melchiorre Gerbas, had ever approved of his ideas (but it's difficult to estimate possible reticence in the testimony before the inquisitors), a great deal of time passed, perhaps as much as thirty years, before Menocchio had first been denounced to the religious authorities. And it was the priest of the village, put up to it by another cleric, who finally accused him. To the peasants of

Montereale, Menocchio's statements, despite their peculiarity, must not have seemed so alien to their existence, to their beliefs and hopes.

60

In the case of the miller of Savignano sul Panaro, the connections with cultivated and socially prominent circles had been even closer. In 1565 fra Gerolamo da Montalcino, on a visit of the diocese for the bishop of Modena, met Pighino who was pointed out to him as a "concubine-keeping Lutheran." In his account of the visit, the monk described him as "a poor, ailing peasant, ugly as sin, and short in stature" and he added: "while speaking with him he astounded me, saying things that were false but ingenious, which led me to suppose that he learned them in some gentleman's home." Five years later, when he was tried by the Holy Office in Ferrara, Pighino affirmed that he had been a servant in the homes of several Bolognese gentlemen: Natale Cavazzoni, Giacomo Mondino, Antonio Bonasone, Vincenzo Bolognetti, and Giovanni d'Avolio. When he was asked if religious discussions had taken place in the homes of any of them, he denied it emphatically, even under the threat of torture. He was then confronted with the monk who had met him in Savignano years before. Fra Gerolamo declared that at that time Pighino had said he had learned those "false but ingenious" things in the home of a Bolognese gentleman, from a person who gave certain unspecified "readings" there. The monk's memory had faded: too much time had passed. He had forgotten both the name of the gentleman in question, as well as that of the person—a priest, he thought—who had given the "readings." But Pighino denied everything: "Father, I don't remember at all." Not even the torture of fire to which he was subjected (he was spared the strappado because he had a hernia) induced him to confess.

But there can be no doubt that he was holding back information. There may be a way to see through his reticence, however. The day after his encounter with the monk (11 September 1570) the inquisitors again asked Pighino to name the Bolognese gentlemen in whose homes he had served. He repeated the list, with a variation that went unnoticed: he named Vincenzo Bonini in the place of Vincenzo Bolognetti. This makes us suspect that Bolognetti may indeed have been the gentleman whom Pighino was trying to protect by his silence. If this is so (there's no proof of it) who then had given the "readings" that had made such a strong impression on Pighino?

One possibility is the famous heretic Paolo Ricci, better known as Camillo Renato. After arriving in Bologna in 1538, Ricci (who was then going by the humanistic name of Lisia Fileno) remained for two years as tutor to the children of various noble families: the Danesi, Lambertini, Manzoli, and Bolognetti. It was to the Bolognetti that he alluded in a passage of the *Apologia,* which he wrote in 1540 in his own defense before the Holy Office. In it, Fileno, taking as his point of departure the ingenuously anthropomorphic beliefs of the peasants and the masses who attributed to the Madonna power equal or superior to Christ's, proposed a Christocentric religion, free of superstitions: "Again, I have heard with my own ears that most of the peasants and all the masses firmly believe that the blessed Mary is equal to Jesus Christ in power and in bestowing grace, and some even believe that she is greater. This is the reason that they give: the earthly mother may not only ask but even compell her son to do something; and so the law of motherhood demands that the mother is greater than the son. They say, we believe it is the same in heaven between the blessed Virgin Mary and her son Jesus Christ." In the margin he noted, "Heard in Bologna 1540 in the home of the knight Bolognetti." This is a specific recollection, as we see. Could Pighino have been one of the "peasants" encountered by Fileno in Bolognetti's house? If this is the case, we would have in the reticent confessions made to the Ferrarese inquisitors by the miller of Savignano, an echo of discussions heard from Fileno thirty years before. It's true that Pighino traced his heretical opinions to a more recent date—first eleven, then twenty or twenty-two years before—coinciding with the first time he read the Gospels in the vernacular. But his uncertainty over this date may have been concealing a deliberate plan to confuse the inquisitors. The fact that Paolo Ricci-Lisia Fileno was a defrocked monk, rather than a priest as fra Gerolamo da Montalcino had stated, doesn't pose a problem since the latter was simply making a conjecture.

Indeed, even the possibility of an encounter and of a discussion between the sophisticated humanist Lisia Fileno and the miller Pighino Baroni, "the fat," is also a conjecture, however fascinating. What is certain, at least, is that in October 1540 Fileno was arrested "in the Modenese countryside, where he was subverting the peasants," as Giovanni Domenico Sigibaldi wrote to cardinal Morone. There was another person with Fileno "performing the same Lutheranizing office": "his name was Turchetto, son of a Turcho or Turcha." In all probability he was Giorgio Filaletto, nicknamed Turca, author of that mysterious Italian translation of Servetus's *De Trinitatis erroribus,* which Menocchio may have seen at one time. In so many different ways we keep running into those delicate threads that in this period tie heretics of humanistic background to the world of the peasants.

But after everything that has been said thus far we shouldn't have to insist on the impossibility of ascribing manifestations of peasant religious radicalism to influences from outside—and above. Pighino's ideas also testify to the fact that he was not just passively receiving motifs that were then current in heretical circles. His most original statements—on Mary's humble birth, on the equality of the "great" and the "small" in paradise—clearly reflect the peasant egalitarianism being voiced in these very years by Scolio's *Settennario.* Thus, the notion that "when the body dies the soul also dies" has the appearance of being inspired by an instinctive peasant materialism. In this instance, however, the course followed by Pighino was more complicated. First of all, his belief in the mortality of the soul seemed to clash with that of the equality of the blessed in paradise. To the inquisitor who pointed out this contradiction to him, Pighino explained: "I believed that the souls of the saved have to remain in paradise for a long time, but that finally, when it shall please God, they will have to vanish into nothing, and not feel any pain." A little earlier he had admitted believing "that the soul finally has to come to an end and be resolved into nothing: and I thought this was because of our Lord's words, where he said 'Heaven and earth will pass, but my Word will not pass.' So I concluded that if heaven had to end some time, so much more should our soul." All this recalls the doctrine of the sleep of souls after death, which had been taught by Fileno in Bologna, as we know from his *Apologia* of 1540. This could constitute one more element in favor of identifying Pighino's unknown "teacher" as Fileno. But it's noteworthy that Pighino's position was much more radically materialistic than the doctrines circulating among the heretical groups of the time. In fact, he asserted the final annihilation of the souls of the *blessed*—and not just of the *damned,* as did the Venetian Anabaptists, who reserved resurrection for the souls of the just on Judgment Day. It's possible that Pighino misconstrued, especially after such a long interval, the significance of the discussions, undoubtedly packed with recondite philosophical terms, which he had heard in Bologna. But in any case it was a noteworthy distortion, just as was the type of Scriptural argument that he used. Fileno wrote in his *Apologia* that he had seen with his own eyes references to the doctrine of the sleep of souls not only in patristic writings, but also in Scripture itself, without specifying where. Pighino, instead, didn't appeal to a passage such as the one in which St. Paul comforts the brethren of the church of Thessalonica by speaking to them of the final resurrection of those sleeping in Christ. He cited a much less obvious passage, one in which the soul wasn't even mentioned. Why deduce the final annihilation of the soul from the annihilation of the world? Most likely Pighino had reflected on passages in the *Fioretto della Bibbia*—one of the very few books that he had read, as we recall (even if he had said earlier, perhaps out of prudence, that although he owned it, he "hadn't read it").

"And all the things that God created out of nothing," the *Fioretto* declared, "are eternal and will endure forever. And these are the eternal things, angels, light, world, man, soul." Slightly before, however, a different thesis had been offered: "there are some things that have a beginning and an end: and these are the world, and created things that are visible. There are other things that have a beginning and will not have an end, and these are the angels and our souls that will never have an end." Later on, among the "great errors" held by "many philosophers" regarding the creation of souls, the following were mentioned: "that all souls are one and that the elements are five, the four mentioned above, and in addition one other, which is called *orbis:* and they say that out of this *orbis* God made the soul of Adam and all the others. And for this reason they say that the world will never end, because when man dies he returns to his elements." The Averroist philosophers refuted by the *Fioretto* taught that if the soul is immortal, the world is eternal; if the world is to perish (as the *Fioretto* asserted at one point) the soul is mortal, Pighino "concluded." This radical reversal implies a reading of the *Fioretto* that, at least in part, resembled Menocchio's: "I believe that the whole world, that is air, earth, and all the beauties of this world are God . . . : because we say that man is made in the image and likeness of God, and in man there is air, fire, earth, and water, and it follows from this that air, earth, fire, and water are God." From the identity of man with the world, based on the four elements, Menocchio had deduced ("and it follows from this") the oneness of the world and of God. Pighino's deduction ("I concluded") of the final mortality of the soul from the finiteness of the world implied an identity between man and the world. Pighino, more cautious than Menocchio, didn't mention the relationship between God and the world.

To suggest that Pighino and Menocchio read the *Fioretto* in a similar manner may seem arbitrary. But it is significant that both should have fallen into the same contradiction, one immediately pounced upon by the inquisitors in both the Friuli and in Ferrara. What sense does it make to speak of paradise if the immortality of the soul is denied, they asked? We've seen how this objection drew Menocchio into an inextricable tangle of new contradictions. Pighino resolved the dilemma by speaking of a temporary paradise followed by the final annihilation of souls.

Truly these two millers, who had lived hundreds of kilometers apart and died without ever meeting, spoke the same language and shared the same culture. Pighino said: "I have not read any books except those I mentioned above, nor did I learn these errors from anybody; they came from my own imaginings or else the devil put these things into my head, as I believe: because many times he pursued me and I fought him in certain apparitions and visions, night and day, fighting him as if he were a man. In the end I began to realize that he was a spirit." As for Menocchio: "I have never associated with anyone who was a heretic, but I have an artful mind, and I wanted to seek out higher things about which I did not know. . . . I uttered those words because I was tempted. . . . It was the evil spirit who made me believe those things. . . . The devil or something tempted me. . . . The false spirit was always after me to make me think what was false and not true. . . . I thought I was a prophet, because the evil spirit made me see vanities and dreams. . . . May I die if I have either followers or companions, but I have read on my own. . . . " And Pighino, again: "I wanted to infer that every man is obliged to remain under his own religion, meaning the Hebrew, the Turkish, and every other faith. . . ." And Menocchio: "It would be as if four soldiers were fighting, two on each side; and if one from one side went over to the other, wouldn't he be a traitor? So I thought that if a Turk abandoned his law and made himself a Christian, he would be doing wrong, and so I also thought that a Jew was wrong to make himself a Turk or a Christian, and all those who left their own faith. . . . " According to a witness, Pighino had maintained "that there is neither hell nor purgatory, and they were invented by priests and monks for the sake of money. . . . " He explained to the inquisitors: "I have never rejected paradise, although I said: 'Oh, God where can hell and purgatory be?' since it seemed to me that underground is packed with earth and water and there can be no hell or purgatory there, but that both are on earth while we live. . . . " As for Menocchio, he said: "Preaching that men should live in peace pleases me, but preaching about hell, Paul says one thing, Peter says another, so that I think it is a business, an invention of men who know more than others. . . . I did not believe that paradise existed, because I did not know where it was."

61

We have seen cropping up repeatedly, from beneath a very profound difference in language, surprising similarities between basic currents in the peasant culture we have endeavored to reconstruct and those in the most progressive circles of sixteenth-century culture. To explain these similarities simply on the basis of movement from high to low involves clinging to the unacceptable notion that ideas originate exclusively among the dominant classes. On the other hand, rejection of this simplistic explanation implies a much more complicated hypothesis about relationships in this period between the culture of the dominant classes and the culture of the subordinate classes.

It's more complicated and also, to some extent, indemonstrable. The state of the documentation reflects, obviously, the state of the relationship of power between the classes. An almost exclusively oral culture such as that of the subordinate classes of preindustrial Europe tends not to leave traces, or, at least, the traces left are distorted. Thus, there is a symptomatic value in a limited case such as Menocchio's. It forcefully poses a problem the significance of which is only now beginning to be recognized: that of the popular roots of a considerable part of high European culture, both medieval and postmedieval. Such figures as Rabelais and Brueghel probably weren't unusual exceptions. All the same, they closed an era characterized by hidden but fruitful exchanges, moving in both directions between high and popular cultures. The subsequent period was marked, instead, by an increasingly rigid distinction between the culture of the dominant classes and artisan and peasant cultures, as well as by the indoctrination of the masses from above. We can place the break between these two periods in the second half of the sixteenth century, basically coinciding with the intensification of social differentiation under the impulse of the price revolution. But the decisive crisis had occurred a few decades before, with the Peasants' War and the reign of the Anabaptists in Münster. At that time, while maintaining and even emphasizing the distance between the classes, the necessity of reconquering, ideologically as well as physically, the masses threatening to break loose from every sort of control from above was dramatically brought home to the dominant classes.

This renewed effort to achieve hegemony took various forms in different parts of Europe, but the evangelization of the countryside by the Jesuits and the capillary religious organization based on the family, achieved by the Protestant churches, can be traced to a single current. In terms of repression, the intensification of witchcraft trials and the rigid control over such marginal groups as vagabonds and gypsies corresponded to it. Menocchio's case should be seen against this background of repression and effacement of popular culture.

62

Despite the conclusion of the trial, Menocchio's case was not yet closed; in a certain sense, the most extraordinary part was about to begin. When evidence had begun to accumulate against Menocchio for the second time, the inquisitor of Aquileia and Concordia had written to Rome, to the Congregation of the Holy Office, to inform them of the new developments. On 5 June 1599 the cardinal of Santa Severina, a senior member of the Congregation, replied urging the earliest possible incarceration of "that person from the diocese of Concordia who *had* denied the divinity of Christ, our Lord," "his case is extremely serious, especially since he has been condemned as a heretic on another occasion." Moreover, he ordered that his books and "writings" be confiscated. The confiscation took place; as we saw, "writings"—we don't know of what sort—also were found. In view of Rome's interest in the case, the Friulian inquisitor sent a copy of three accusations against Menocchio to the Congregation. On 14 August another letter was received from the cardinal of Santa Severina: "that recidivist . . . has revealed himself to be an atheist in his examinations," it was thus necessary to proceed "according to the prescribed terms of the law also to discover the accomplices"; the case "is extremely serious," therefore "Your Reverence must send a copy of his trial or at least a summary of it." The month following, the news reached Rome that Menocchio had been condemned to death, but the sentence had not yet been carried out. The inquisitor in the Friuli was hesitating, perhaps out of a belated impulse toward leniency. On 5 September he wrote a letter (which hasn't survived) communicating his doubts to the Congregation of the Holy Office. The reply of the cardinal of Santa Severina, dated 30 October, written in the name of the entire Congregation, was peremptory: "I inform you by order of His Holiness, Our Lord, that you must not fail to proceed with that diligence required by the gravity of the case, so that he may not go unpunished for his horrible and execrable excesses, but that he may serve as an example to others in those parts by receiving a just and severe punishment. Therefore do not fail to carry it out with all the promptness and rigor of mind demanded by the importance of the case. And this is the express desire of His Holiness."

The supreme head of Catholicism, the pope himself, Clement VIII, was bending toward Menocchio, who had become a rotten member of Christ's body, to demand his death. In these very months in Rome the trial against the former monk Giordano Bruno was drawing to a close. It's a coincidence that seems to symbolize the twofold battle being fought against both high and low in this period by the Catholic hierarchy in an effort to impose doctrines promulgated by the Council of Trent. This explains the persistence of the proceedings, which are otherwise incomprehensible, against the old miller. A short time later (13 November) the cardinal of Santa Severina renewed his insistence: "Your Reverence must not fail to proceed in the case of that peasant of the diocese of Concordia, suspected of having denied the virginity of the forever blessed Virgin Mary, the divinity of Christ our lord, and the providence of God, in accordance with what I already wrote to you at the express order of His Holiness. The jurisdiction of the Holy Office over a case of such importance can in no way be doubted. Therefore, manfully perform everything that is required, according to the terms of the law."

It was impossible to resist such powerful pressure: and, shortly after, Menocchio was put to death. We know this with certainty from the depositions of a certain Donato Serotino who told the commissioner of the inquisitor of the Friuli on 6 July 1601 that being in Pordenone not long after "Scandella . . . had been executed by order of the Holy Office," he had met an innkeeper who told him that "in that town . . . there was a certain man named Marcato, or perhaps Marco, who believed that when the body died the soul also died with it."

About Menocchio we know many things. About this Marcato, or Marco—and so many others like him who lived and died without leaving a trace—we know nothing.

NOTES

ABBREVIATIONS USED IN THE NOTES

ACAU	Archivio della Curia Arcivescovile, Udine
ACVP	Archivio della Curia Vescovile, Pordenone
ASM	Archivio di Stato, Modena
ASP	Archivio di Stato, Pordenone
ASVat	Archivio Segreto Vaticano
ASVen	Archivio di Stato, Venice
BCU	Biblioteca Comunale, Udine
BGL	Biblioteca Governativa, Lucca

PREFACE

1

xv. The common man, according to Vicens Vives, "se ha convertido en el principal protagonista de la Historia," (cited from P. Chaunu, "Une histoire religieuse sérielle," *Revue d'histoire moderne et contemporaine* 12 [1965]: 9, n. 2). The quote from Brecht is found in "Fragen eines lesenden Arbeiters," *Hundert Gedichte, 1918–1950* (Berlin, 1951), pp. 107–8. I see now that the same poem has also been used by J. Kaplow, *The Names of Kings: The Parisian Laboring Poor in the Eighteenth Century* (New York, 1973). See also H. M. Enzensberger, "Letteratura come storiografia," *Il Menabò*, no. 9 (1966): 13.

2

I use A. Gramsci's term "subordinate classes" because it is broad enough in scope without having the more or less deliberately paternalistic connotations of "inferior classes." On the themes elicited by the publication of Gramsci's notes on folklore and subordinate classes, see the discussion among E. De Martino, C. Luporini, F. Fortini, and others (the list of participants is in L. M. Lombardi Satriani, *Antropologia culturale e analisi della cultura subalterna* [Rimini, 1974], p. 74, n. 34). For the modern dimensions of the question, many of which were efficaciously anticipated by E. J. Hobsbawm ("Per lo studio delle classi subalterne," *Società* 16 [1960]: 436–49), see below.

The trials against Menocchio are preserved in the Archivio della Curia Arcivescovile, Udine (henceforth cited as ACAU), *Sant'Uffizio, Anno integro 1583 a n. 107 usque ad 128 incl.*, Trial no. 126 and *Anno integro 1596 a n. 281 usque ad 306 incl.*, Trial no. 285. The only scholar to mention them (although without having seen them) is A. Battistella, *Il S. Officio e la riforma religiosa in Friuli: Appunti storici documentati* (Udine, 1895), p. 65, who mistakenly states that Menocchio was not executed.

3

xvi. The literature on these issues is obviously vast. For an easily accessible introduction, see A. M. Cirese, "Alterità e dislivelli interni di cultura nelle società superiori," in *Folklore e antropologia tra storicismo e marxismo*, ed. A. M. Cirese (Palermo, 1972), pp. 11–42; L. M. Lombardi Satriani, *Antropologia culturale e analisi della cultura subalterna* (Rimini, 1974); P. Rossi, ed., *Il concetto di cultura: I fondamenti teorici della scienza antropologica* (Turin, 1970). The concept of folklore as "an incoherent fragmentary mass of theories" etc., was adopted, with some variation, even by A. Gramsci: see *Letteratura e vita nazionale* (Turin, 1950), pp. 215 ff. Cf. Lombardi Satriani, *Antropologia culturale*, pp. 16 ff.

xvii. *Largely* oral: See, in this regard, C. Bermani, "Dieci anni di lavoro con le fonti orali," *Primo Maggio* 5 (spring, 1975): 35–50.

R. Mandrou, *De la culture populaire aux 17e et 18e siècles: La Bibliothèque bleue de Troyes* (Paris, 1964) emphasizes that "culture populaire" and "culture de masse" are not synonymous. (It may be noted that "culture de masse" and the corresponding Italian term are equivalent rather to the Anglo-American expression "popular culture"—a source of great confusion.) "Culture populaire," which is an older term, designates in a "populist" perspective, "la culture qui est l'oeuvre du peuple." Mandrou uses the same term with a "broader" (actually different) meaning: "la culture des milieux populaires dans la France de l'Ancien Régime, nous l'entendons . . . , ici, comme la culture acceptée, digérée, assimilée, par ces milieux pendant des siècles" (pp. 9–10). In this way, popular culture almost ends up being identified with mass culture. This is anachronistic since mass culture in the modern sense presupposes a cultural industry that certainly did not exist in the France of the Ancien Régime (see also p. 174). Even the term "superstructure" (p. 11) is equivocal. From Mandrou's point of view it would have been better to speak of a false consciousness. For the literature of *colportage* as escapist literature, and simultaneously as a reflection of a view of the world held by the popular classes, see pp. 162–63. In any case Mandrou is well aware of the limitations of his pioneering study, which, as such, is indeed praiseworthy. See by G. Bollème, "Littérature populaire et littérature de colportage au XVIIIe siècle," in *Livre et société dans la France du XVIIIe siècle*, 2 vols. (Paris and The Hague, 1965) 1:61–92; idem, *Les Almanachs populaires aux XVIIe et XVIIIe siècle, essai d'histoire sociale* (Paris and The Hague, 1969); an anthology, idem, *La Bibliothèque bleue: La littérature populaire en France du XVIIe au XIXe siècle* (Paris, 1971); "Représentation religieuse et thèmes d'espérance dans la 'Bibliothèque bleue:' Littérature populaire en France du XVIIe au XIXe siècle," in *La società religiosa nell'età moderna. Atti del convegno di studi di storia sociale e religiosa, Capaccio—Paestum, 18–21 maggio 1972* (Naples, 1973), pp. 219–43. The studies contained in this volume are of uneven quality. The best is the one introducing the anthology of the *Bibliothèque bleue* (at pp. 22–23 are remarks on the type of use that was probably made of these texts), which, however, contains statements such as these: "à la limite, l'histoire qu'entend ou lit le lecteur n'est que celle qu'il veut qu'on lui raconte.... En ce sens on peut dire que l'écriture, au même titre que la lecture, est collective, faite par et pour tous, diffuse, diffusée, sue, dite, échangée, non gardée, et qu'elle est en quelque sorte spontanée. . . . "(ibid.). The unacceptable distortions in a populistic-Christian direction contained, for example, in the essay "Représentation religieuse," are based on sophistry of this kind. Impossible as it seems, A. Dupront has criticized Bollème for having attempted to characterize "l'historique dans ce qui est peut-être l'anhistorique, manière de fonds commun quasi 'indatable' de traditions.... ("Livre et culture dans la société Française du 18e siècle," in *Livre et société* 1:203–4).

xviii. On "popular literature" see the important essay by N. Z. Davis, "Printing and the People," in her *Society and Culture in Early Modern France* (Stanford, 1975), pp. 189–206, which is based on premises in part similar to those in this book.

Among the works that deal with the period after the industrial revolution, see L. James, *Fiction for the Working Man, 1830–1850* (1963; reprint ed., London, 1974); R. Schenda, *Volk ohne Buch: Studien zur Sozialgeschichte der populären Lesestoffe (1770–1910)* (Frankfort, 1970) (in a series devoted to *Triviallitteratur)*; J. J. Darmon, *Le colportage de librairie en France sous le second Empire: Grands colporteurs et culture populaire* (Paris, 1972).

4

See Mikhail Bakhtin, *Rabelais and His World,* trans. Helene Iswolsky (Cambridge, Mass., 1968). In a similar vein, see the comment by A. Berelovič in the symposium volume *Niveaux de culture et groupes sociaux* (Paris, 1967), pp. 144–45.

5

xix. See E. Le Roy Ladurie, *Les paysans de Languedoc,* 2 vols. (Paris, 1966) 1:394 ff. (English translation, *The Peasants of Languedoc,* trans. John Day [Urbana, 1974], pp. 192 ff.). See also by E. Le Roy Ladurie, *Le carnaval de Romans: De la Chandeleur au mercredi des Cendres (1579–1580)* (Paris, 1979); and the English translation, *Carnival in Romans,* trans. Mary Feeney (New York, 1979); N. Z. Davis, "The Reasons of Misrule: Youth Groups and Charivaris in Sixteenth-Century France," *Past and Present,* no. 50 (1971): 41–75; E. P. Thompson, " 'Rough Music:' Le Charivari anglais," *Annales: ESC* 27 (1972): 285–312 (and now, on the same subject, C. Gauvard and A. Gokalp, "Les conduites de bruit et leur signification à la fin du Moyen Age: Le Charivari," *Annales: ESC* 29 [1974]: 693—704). These works are cited simply as illustrations. On the somewhat different question of the persistence of preindustrial cultural models among the industrial proletariat, see E. P. Thompson, "Time, Work-Discipline, and Industrial Capitalism," *Past and Present,* no. 38 (1967): 56–97, and idem, *The Making of the English Working Class* (2nd enlarged ed., London, 1968); by E. J. Hobsbawm see especially *Primitive Rebels: Studies in Archaic Forms of Social Movement in the Nineteenth and Twentieth Centuries* (Manchester, 1959) and "Les classes ouvrières anglaises et la culture depuis les débuts de la révolution industrielle," in *Niveaux de culture et groupes sociaux* (Paris, 1967), pp. 189–99.

a number of scholars: See M. De Certeau, D. Julia, and J. Revel, "La beauté du mort: Le concept de 'culture populaire,' " *Politique aujourd'hui* (December 1970), pp. 3–23 (the phrase quoted is on p. 21).

In *Folie et déraison: Histoire de la folie à l'age classique* (Paris, 1961), p. vii, M. Foucault states that: "faire l'histoire de la folie, voudra donc dire: faire une étude structurale de l'ensemble historique—notions, institutions, mesures juridiques et policières, concepts scientifiques—qui tient captive une folie dont l'état sauvage ne peut jamais être restitué en lui-même; mais à défaut de cette inaccessible pureté primitive, l'étude structurale doit rémonter vers la décision qui lie et sépare à la fois raison et folie." All this explains the absence of madmen from the pages of his book—an absence that isn't due solely, or even primarily, to the difficulty of access to the necessary sources. The deliria, recorded over thousands of pages and preserved in the Bibliothèque de l'Arsenal, of a servant living at the end of the seventeenth century who was semi-literate and "dément furieux" don't have, according to Foucault, a place in "the universe of our discourse," and are something "irreparably less than history" (p. v). It's difficult to say if evidence such as this could throw light on the "pureté primitive" of madness—which, after all, is perhaps not totally "inaccessible." In any case, Foucault's logic in this frequently irritating but brilliant book is undoubted (despite an occasional contradiction: see, for example, pp. 475–76). For an opinion concerning Foucault's regression from the *Histoire de la Folie* (1961) to *Les mots et les choses* (1966) and *L'archéologie du savoir* (1969), see P. Vilar, "Histoire marxiste, histoire en construction," in *Faire de l'histoire,* 3 vols., ed. J. Le Goff and P. Nora (Paris, 1974) 1:188–89. On Derrida's objections, see D. Julia, "La religion-histoire religieuse," in ibid., 2:145–46. See now, M. Foucault et al., eds., *Moi, Pierre Rivière, ayant égorgé ma mère, ma soeur, et mon frère* (Paris, 1973). On the "stupor," "the silence," the refusal to interpret, see pp. 11, 14, 243, 314, 348 n. 2. For Rivière's readings, see pp. 40, 42, 125. The passage about wandering through the forest is at p. 260, the suggestion of cannibalism at p. 249. As for the populist distortion, see especially Foucault's "Les meurtres qu'on raconte," pp. 265–75. In general, see G. Huppert, "Divinatio et Eruditio: Thoughts on Foucault," *History and Theory* 13 (1974): 191–207.

6

xxi. By J. Le Goff see "Culture clericale et traditions folkloriques dans la civilisation mérovingienne," *Annales: ESC* 22 (1967): 780–91; idem, "Culture ecclésiastique et culture folklorique au Moyen Age: Saint Marcel de Paris et le dragon," in *Ricerche storiche ed economiche in memoria di Corrado Barbagallo,* 3 vols., ed. L. De Rosa (Naples, 1970) 2:53–94.

acculturation: See V. Lanternari, *Antropologia e imperialismo* (Turin, 1974), pp. 5 ff. and N. Wachtel, "L'acculturation," in *Faire de l'histoire,* 3 vols., ed J. Le Goff and P. Nora (Paris, 1974) 1: 124–46.

research on witchcraft trials: See C. Ginzburg, *I benandanti: Stregoneria e culti agrari tra '500 e '600* (1966; reprint ed., Turin, 1979).

7

xxii. quantitative *history of ideas or* . . . serialized *religious history:* For the first, see *Livre et société;* for the second, P. Chaunu, "Une histoire religieuse sérielle," *Revue d'histoire moderne et contemporaine* 12 (1965), and now also M. Vovelle, *Piété baroque et déchristianisation en Provence au XVIIIe siècle* (Paris, 1973). In general, see F. Furet, "L'histoire quantitative et la construction du fait historique," *Annales: ESC* 26 (1971): 63–75, who, among other things, properly notes the ideological implications of a method that tends to reabsorb the discontinuities (and revolutions) over a long period and in the equilibrium of the system. In this regard, see Chaunu's work and the essay by A. Dupront, "Livre et culture dans la société Française du 18e siècle," in *Livre et société dans la France du XVIIIe siècle,* 2 vols. (Paris and The Hague, 1965) 1:185 ff.), which, after several hazy digressions on "the collective spirit," concludes by boasting of the virtues of a method that allows one to study the French eighteenth century and ignore its revolutionary outcome—which would be equivalent to freeing oneself "from the eschatology of history" (p. 231).

those who, like François Furet, have maintained: See F. Furet "Pour une définition des classes inférieures à l'époque moderne," *Annales: ESC* 18 (1963): 459–74, esp. p. 459.

Histoire événementielle *(which is not only . . . political history):* See R. Romano, "À propos de l'édition italienne du livre de F. Braudel . . . " *Cahiers Vilfredo Pareto* 15 (1968): 104–6.

the Austrian nobility or the lower clergy: I'm referring to O. Brunner, *Adeliges Landleben und europäischer Geist* (Salzburg, 1949); (cf. C. Schorske, "New Trends in History," *Daedalus*, no. 98 [1969]: 963); A. Macfarlane, *The Family Life of Ralph Josselin, a Seventeenth-Century Clergyman: An Essay in Historical Anthropology* (Cambridge, 1970) (but see the critical remarks by E. P. Thompson, "Anthropology and the Discipline of Historical Context," *Midland History* 1, no. 3 [1972]: 41–45).

As with language, culture: See the observations by P. Bogatyrëv and R. Jakobson, "Il folclore come forma di creazione autonoma," *Strumenti critici* 1 (1976): 223–40. The celebrated pages by G. Lukács on a possible consciousness (see his *History and Class Consciousness* [London, 1971], p. 79) although originating in a totally different context, are applicable here.

xxiii. *In conclusion, even a limited case:* See D. Cantimori, *Prospettive di storia ereticale italiana del Cinquecento* (Bari, 1960), p. 14.

"archives of the repression": See D. Julia, "La religion-histoire religieuse," in *Faire de l'Histoire,* 3 vols., ed. J. Le Goff and P. Nora (Paris, 1974) 2:147.

On the connection between quantitative and qualitative research, see the remarks by E. Le Roy Ladurie, "La révolution quantitative et les historiens français: Bilan d'une génération (1932–1968)," in his *Le territoire de l'historien* (Paris, 1973), p. 22. Among the disciplines "pionnières et prometteuses" that remain steadfastly and quite properly qualitative, Le Roy Ladurie cites "psychologie historique." The quotation from E. P. Thompson is in "Anthropology and the Discipline of Historical Context," *Midland History* 1, no. 3 (1972):50.

An Italian scholar: See F. Diaz, "Le stanchezze di Clio," *Rivista storica italiana* 84 (1972): esp. 733–34, and also by the same author, "Metodo quantitativo e storia delle idee," *Rivista storica italiana* 78 (1966): 932–47 (on Bollème's work, pp. 939–41). See also the critical observations by F. Venturi, *Utopia e riforma nell'illuminismo* (Turin, 1970), pp. 24–25. On the question of reading, see the literature cited below at p. 149.

8

xxv. On the history of mentalities, see J. Le Goff, "Les mentalités: Une histoire ambiguë," in *Faire de l'histoire,* 3 vols., ed. J. Le Goff and P. Nora (Paris, 1974), 3:76–94. The passage quoted is at p. 80. Le Goff observes characteristically: "Eminemment collective, la mentalité semble soustraite aux vicissitudes des luttes sociales. Ce serait pourtant une grossière erreur que de la détacher des structures et de la dynamique sociale. . . . Il y a des mentalités de classes, à côté de mentalités communes. Leur jeu reste a étudier" (pp. 89–90).

In a fascinating but mistaken book: See L. Febvre, *Le problème de l'incroyance au XVIe siècle: La religion de Rabelais* (1942; reprint ed., Paris, 1968). As is well known, Febvre's argument, from a circumscribed theme—the confutation of A. Le Franc's thesis that Rabelais proved himself a champion of atheism in *Pantagruel* (1532)—expands in ever-widening circles. The third part of his work, on the limits of sixteenth-century incredulity, is certainly the newest from the methodological point of view, but also the most general and inconsistent, as Febvre himself seemed to have been aware (p. 19). The unjustified inferences about the collective mentalities of "sixteenth-century men" owe too much to the theories about primitive mentalities of Lévy-Bruhl ("notre maître," p. 17). It's curious that Febvre should be ironic concerning such a phrase as "les gens du Moyen Age," and yet himself speak, perhaps only a few pages later, of "hommes du XVIe siècle," and of "hommes de la Renaissance," although adding in the second instance that this is a formula "clichée, mais commode": cf. pp. 153–54, 142, 382, 344. The allusion to the peasants is at p. 253. Bakhtin had already noted (*Rabelais and His World,* trans. Helene Iswolsky [Cambridge, Mass., 1968], p. 132) that Febvre's analysis is based exclusively on circles representing official culture. For the comparison with Descartes, see pp. 393, 425, and passim. On this last point, see also G. Schneider, *Der Libertin: Zur Geistes-und Sozialgeschichte des Bürgertums im 16. und 17. Jahrhundert* (Stuttgart, 1970); Italian translation, *Il libertino: Per una storia sociale della cultura borghese nel XVI e XVII secolo* (Bologna, 1974), and the (not entirely acceptable) remarks at pp. 7 ff. (Italian ed.). On the danger, in Febvre's historical writings, of falling into subtle forms of tautology, see D. Cantimori, *Storici e storia* (Turin, 1971), pp. 223–25.

xxvi. *marginal groups:* See B. Geremek, "Il pauperismo nell'età preindustriale (secoli XIV–XVIII)," in *Storia d'Italia,* vol. 5, *I documenti,* ed. R. Romano and C. Vivanti (Turin, 1973), pt. 1, pp. 669–98; P. Camporesi, ed., *Il libro dei vagabondi* (Turin, 1973).

specific analyses: The publication of Valerio Marchetti's important research on artisans in Siena during the sixteenth century is eagerly awaited.

9

For what has been said in this section, see below pp. 58–60.

10

xxvii. *taking note of a historical mutilation:* Obviously, this shouldn't be confused either with a reactionary nostalgia for the past, or with an equally reactionary rhetoric about an assumed immobile and ahistorical "peasant civilization."

The quotation from Benjamin is found in his *Angelus novus: Saggi e frammenti,* which appears in *Tesi di filosofia della storia,* ed. R. Solmi (Turin, 1962), p. 73.

TEXT

1

1. *Menocchio:* This is the name that recurs in the inquisitorial documents. Elsewhere he is also called "Menoch" and "Menochi." Today, the Italian transcription of his name's pronunciation would be "Menocio."

at his first trial: See ACAU, *Sant'Uffizio,* Trial no. 126, fol. 15 v.

Montereale: Today known as Montereale Cellina, a hill town (317 meters above sea level) located at the mouth of the Val Cellina. In 1584 the parish had a population of 650. See ACVP, "Sacrarum Visitationum Nores ab anno 1582 usque ad annum 1584," fol. 168 v.

following a brawl: See ACAU, *Sant'Uffizio,* Trial no. 126, fol. 20 r.

the traditional miller's costume: "indutus vestena quadam et desuper tabaro ac pileo aliisque vestimentis de lana omnibus albo colore" (Ibid., fol. 15 v.). This manner of dress was still used by Italian millers in the nineteenth century. See C. Cantú, *Portafoglio d'un operaio* (Milan, 1871), p. 68.

A couple of years later: See ACAU, "Sententiarum contra reos S. Officii liber II," fol. 16 v.

two fields in perpetual lease: On perpetual leases in this period, see G. Giorgetti, *Contadini e proprietari nell'Italia moderna: Rapporti di produzione e contratti agrari dal secolo XVI a oggi* (Turin, 1974), pp. 97 ff. We don't know if they were "perpetual" leases or for shorter periods (for example, twenty-nine or, more probably, nine years). On the lack of precision in the terminology surrounding contracts in this period, which makes it difficult at times to distinguish among emphyteusis, perpetual lease, and lease, see the observations by G. Chittolini, "Un problema aperto: la crisi della proprietà ecclesiastica fra Quattro e Cinquecento," *Rivista storica italiana* 85 (1973): 370. The probable location of these two fields appears in a later document: an assessment prepared in 1596 at the request of the provincial Venetian governor (see ASP, *Notarile*, b. 488, no. 3785, fols. 17 r.–22 r.). Among the 255 parcels of land located in Montereale and Grizzo (a neighboring village) there appear (fol. 18 r.): "9. Aliam petiam terrae arativae positam in pertinentis Monteregalis in loco dicto alla via del'homo dictam la Longona, unius iug. in circa, tentam per Bartholomeum Andreae: a mane dicta via, a meridie terrenum ser Dominici Scandellae, a sero via de sotto et a montibus terrenum tentum per heredes q. Stephani de Lombarda"; (fol. 19 v.): "Aliam petiam terrae unius iug. in circa in loco dicto . . . il campo del legno: a mane dicta laguna, a meridie terrenum M. d. Horatii Montis Regalis tentum per ser Jacomum Margnanum, a sero terrenum tentum per ser Dominicum Scandelle et a montibus suprascriptus ser Daniel Capola." It hasn't been possible to verify the place names with any great degree of precision. The identification of these two parcels of land with "the two fields in perpetual lease" mentioned by Menocchio twelve years before (1584) is not absolutely certain. Moreover, only the second plot is specifically described as "terrenum *tentum*," meaning, presumably, in perpetual lease. It should be noted that in a 1578 assessment (ASP, *Notarile*, b. 40, no. 332, fols. 115 r. ff.) Domenico Scandella's name doesn't appear, while that of a Bernardo Scandella (we don't know if they were related; Menocchio's father was called Giovanni) is mentioned several times. The name Scandella, incidentally, is still common today in Montereale.

rent (probably in produce): See A. Tagliaferri, *Struttura e politica sociale in una comunità veneta del '500 (Udine)* (Milan, 1969), p. 78 (rent of a mill with dwelling in Udine in 1571, for example, amounted to sixty-one bushels of wheat and two hams). See also the contract for the rent of a new mill to which Menocchio bound himself in 1596 (see at p. 97).

banished to Arba: See ACAU, *Sant'Uffizio,* Trial no. 126, interrogation of 28 April 1584 (unnumbered leaves).

2. *When his daughter Giovanna:* See ASP, *Notarile,* b. 488, no. 3786, fols. 27 r.—27 v., 26 January 1600. The groom's name was Daniele Colussi. For a comparison with other dowries, see Ibid., b. 40, no. 331, fols. 2 v. ff.: 390 lire and 10 soldi; Ibid., fols. 9 r. ff.: c. 340 lire; Ibid., b. 488, no. 3786, fols. 11 r.–11 v.: 300 lire; Ibid., fols. 20 v.–21 v.: 247 lire and 2 soldi; Ibid., fols. 23 v.–24 r.: 182 lire and 15 soldi. The modesty of the last dowry must certainly have been due to the fact that the bride, Maddalena Gastaldione of Grizzo, was marrying a second time. Unfortunately, we are in the dark about the social standing or the occupations of the persons named in the contracts. Giovanna Scandella's dowry consisted of the following items:

One bed with a new mattress with a pair of linen sheets of half-length, and new pillow cases, pillows and cushions; with a bed cover, which the aforesaid ser Stefano promises to buy her new	l. 69 s.	4
A new undershirt	5	10

An embroidered shawl, with folds	l. 4	s. —
A gray dress	11	—
A new linsey-woolsey with the bodice of reddish cloth	12	—
Another linsey-woolsey similar to the above	12	—
A gray dress of half-length	10	—
A white linsey-woolsey, bordered with white cotton and linen, with fringes at the feet	12	10
A blouse of half wool	8	10
A pair of cloth sleeves, light orange in color, with silk ribbons	4	10
A pair of sleeves of silver colored cloth	1	10
A pair of lined sleeves of heavy cloth	1	—
Three new sheets of flax	15	—
A light sheet of half-length	5	—
Three new pillow cases	6	—
Six shawls	4	—
Four shawls	6	—
Three new scarfs	4	10
Four scarfs of half-length	3	—
One embroidered apron	4	—
Three shawls	5	10
One drape of heavy cloth	1	10
One old apron, one shawl, one of heavy cloth	3	—
One new embroidered kerchief	3	10
Five handkerchiefs	6	—
One mantle for the head of half-length	3	—
Two new bonnets	1	10
Five new undershirts	15	—
Three shirts of half-length	6	—
Nine silken ribbons of every color	4	10
Four belts of various colors	2	—
One new apron of thick cloth	—	15
A chest without lock	5	—
	256	9

I haven't been able to consult L. D'Orlandi and G. Perusini, *Antichi costumi friulani—Zona di Maniago* (Udine, 1940).

Menocchio's place: M. Berengo's observations *(Nobili e mercanti nella Lucca del Cinquecento* [Turin, 1965]) concerning the Lucchese countryside should be borne in mind: in the smallest villages "every actual social distinction is eliminated since all earn their livelihood through the exploitation of collectively held land. And even if here, as elsewhere, people will continue to speak of rich and poor . . . there will indeed not be anyone who couldn't be suitably described as a rustic or even as a peasant." The miller's case was a special one: "They could be found in any place of some importance . . . frequently creditors of both the town and of private individuals, not participating in the cultivation of land, richer than most. . . . " (Ibid., pp. 322,327). On the social position of the miller see pp. 119–21.

In 1581 he had been mayor: See ASP, *Notarile,* b. 40, no. 333, fol. 89 v.: an order issued by Andrea Cossio, a nobleman of Udine, "potestati, iuratis, communi, hominibus Montisregalis" requiring payment for rents owed to him for certain lands. On 1 June the order is transmitted "Dominico Scandellae vocato Menochio de Monteregali . . . potestati ipsius villae." In a letter of Ziannuto, a son of Menocchio (see above, p. 7), the latter is referred to as having been "mayor and warden *(rector)* in the five hamlets" (for their names, see *Leggi per la Patria e Contadinanza del Friuli* (Udine, 1686), Introduction, fol. d 2 r.) and "administrator" *("camararo")* of the parish.

the old system of rotating offices: See G. Perusini, "Gli statuti di una vicinia rurale friulana del Cinquecento," *Memorie storiche forogiuliesi* 43 (1958–59): 213–19. The *vicinià*, namely the assembly of heads of families, is that of Bueris, a tiny village near Tricesimo. Six family heads belonged to it in 1578.

"read": See ACAU, *Sant'Uffizio,* Trial no. 126, fol. 15 v.

Administrators: See G. Marchetti, "I quaderni dei camerari di S. Michele a Gemona," *Ce Fastu?* 38 (1962): 11–38. Marchetti observes (p. 13) that the *camerari* didn't belong to the clergy or to the notariate, namely to the "literate" class; usually they were "bourgeois or plebeians who had frequented the public school of the town" and he cites the probably exceptional case of an illiterate blacksmith who had served as *cameraro* in 1489 (p. 14).

Schools of this type: See G. Chiuppani, "Storia di una scuola di grammatica dal Medio Evo fino al Seicento (Bassano)," *Nuovo archivio veneto* 29 (1915): 79. The humanist Leonardo Fosco, who was originally from Montereale, is thought to have taught at Aviano. See F. Fattorello, "La cultura del Friuli nel Rinascimento," *Atti dell'Accademia di Udine* 6th series, 1 (1934–35): 160. But this information doesn't appear in the biographical sketch of Fosco by A. Benedetti in *Il Popolo,* a weekly published by the diocese of Concordia-Pordenone, in the issue for 8 June 1974. Study on the municipal schools of this period would be extremely useful. They existed even in very small towns. See, for example, A. Rustici, "Una scuola rurale della fine del secolo XVI," *La Romagna* n.s. 1 (1927): 334–38. On the spread of education in the Lucchese countryside, see Berengo, *Nobili e mercanti,* p. 322.

denounced: See ACAU, *Sant'Uffizio,* Trial no. 126, unpaginated: "fama publica deferente et clamorosa insinuatione producente, non quidem a malevolis orta sed a probis et honestis viris catolicaeque fidei zelatoribus, ac fere per modum notorii devenerit quod quidam Dominicus Scandella. . . . " (this is the usual formula).

"Preaching and dogmatizing shamelessly": "praedicare et dogmatizare non erubescit."

"He is always arguing"' See ACAU, *Sant'Uffizio,* Trial no. 126, fol. 2 r.

"He will argue": Ibid., fol. 10 r.

"he knew": Ibid., fol. 2 r.

the village priest: Ibid., fols. 13 v., 12 r.

In the public square: Ibid., fols. 6 v., 7 v., unnumbered leaf (interrogation of Domenico Melchiori), fol. 11 r., etc.

3. *"he usually:* Ibid., fol. 8 r.

2

"Menocchio, please": See ACAU, *Sant'Uffizio,* Trial no. 126, fol. 10 r.

Giuliano Stefanut: Ibid., fol. 8 r.

The priest Andrea Bionima: Ibid., fol. 11 v.

Giovanni Povoledo: Ibid., fol. 5 r. It's well known that in this period the term "Lutheran" was employed in a very general way.

some for thirty or forty years: Ibid., fol. 4 v. (Giovanni Povoledo); fol. 6 v. (Giovanni Antonio Melchiori, not to be confused with Giovanni Daniele Melchiori, vicar of Polcenigo); fol. 2 v. (Francesco Fasseta).

Daniele Fasseta: Ibid., fol. 3 r.

"many years": Ibid., fol. 13 r. (Antonio Fasseta); fol. 5 v. (Giovanni Povoledo, who first said that he had known Menocchio for forty years, and later changed this to twenty-five or thirty.) The only recollection that can be dated precisely is the following,

pertaining to Antonio Fasseta (fol. 13 r.): "Coming down from the mountain one day with Menocchio at the time that the empress was passing through, speaking about her, he said: 'This empress is greater than the virgin Mary.' " Now, the empress Mary of Austria entered the Friuli in 1581. See G. F. Palladio degli Olivi, *Historie della Provincia del Friuli,* vol. 2 (Udine, 1660), p. 208.

people repeated it: See ACAU, *Sant'Uffizio,* Trial no. 126, fol. 6 r.

"I see him having dealings'" Ibid., Trial no. 285, interrogation of the priest Curzio Cellina, 17 December 1598, unnumbered leaf.

4. *For four years Menocchio:* Ibid., Trial no. 126, fol. 18 v.

   "I don't remember": Ibid., fol. 14 r.

   it had been Vorai: He himself recalled this to the Holy Office during the interrogation of 1 June 1584 (Ibid., Trial no. 136), regretful that he hadn't done so sooner.

   by another priest, don Ottavio: Ibid., Trial no. 284, unnumbered leaf (session of 11 November 1598).

   "What popes": Ibid., Trial no. 126, fol. 10 r.

   practically setting himself up against: See a similar Friulian case cited by G. Miccoli, "La storia religiosa," in *Storia d'Italia,* vol. 2, *Dalla caduta dell'Impero romano al secolo XVIII,* ed. R. Romano and C. Vivanti (Turin 1974), pt. 1, p. 994.

   "beyond measure": See ACAU, *Sant'Uffizio,* Trial no. 126, fol. 10 r.

   "Everybody has his calling": Ibid., fol. 7 v.

   "The air is God": Ibid., fol. 3 r. (Daniele Fasseta); fol. 8 r. (Giuliano Stefanut); fol. 2 r. (Francesco Fasseta); fol. 5 r. (Giovanni Povoledo); fol. 3 v. (Daniele Fasseta).

   "He is always arguing": Ibid., fol. 11 v. (the priest Andrea Bionima).

5. *Giovanni Daniele Melchiori:* Ibid., Trial no. 134, interrogation of 7 May 1584. On the trial held earlier against Melchiori, and on his relationship to Menocchio, see above p. 73. Both Melchiori and Policreto were tried by the Holy Office (in March and May 1584, respectively) after having been accused of attempting through their suggestions to influence the outcome of Menocchio's case. See Ibid., Trials nos. 134 and 137. Both claimed they were innocent. Melchiori was ordered to remain at the disposal of the court, and the case ended there; Policreto was made to undergo canonical purgation. The mayor of Pordenone, Gerolamo de'Gregori, and such members of the local nobility as Gerolamo Popaiti testified in behalf of Policreto. It appears that Policreto was attached to the Mantica-Montereale family, to which the lords of Montereale also belonged. In 1583 he was appointed arbiter (succeeding his father, Antonio, in this function) in a lawsuit between Giacomo and Giovan Battista Mantica on one side, and Antonio Mantica on the other (see BCU, ms. 1042).

   "conducted in handcuffs": See ACAU, *Sant'Uffizio,* Trial no. 126, fol. 15 v.

3

"It is true that": See ACAU, *Sant'Uffizio,* Trial no. 126, fols. 16 r.–v.

"I have said": Ibid., fols. 17 r.–v.

6. *"he might have said:* Ibid., fol. 6 r. (Giovanni Povoledo).

4

"in earnest": See ACAU, *Sant'Uffizio,* Trial no. 126, fols. 2 v.–3 r. Manifestations of heresy by the uneducated frequently were interpreted as the fruit of madness. See,

for example, G. Miccoli, "La vita religiosa," in *Storia d'Italia,* vol. 2, *Dalla caduta dell'Impero romano al secolo XVIII,* ed. R. Romano and C. Vivanti (Turin, 1974), pt. 1, pp. 994–95.

"sane": See ACAU, *Sant'Uffizio,* Trial no. 126, fol. 6 v.

Ziannuto: Ibid., Trial no. 136, interrogations of 14 May 1584, unnumbered leaves.

A century or so later: See M. Foucault, *Folie et déraison: Histoire de la folie à l'age classique* (Paris, 1961), pp. 121–22 (case of Bonaventure Forcroy); p. 469 (in 1733 a man was confined as a madman in the hospital Saint Lazare because he was affected by "sentiments extraordinaires").

5

7. The letter from Ziannuto to the lawyer Trappola and the letter written by the priest at Ziannuto's suggestion are both contained in the dossier of Menocchio's first trial (ACAU, *Sant'Uffizio,* Trial no. 126). The explanations of the circumstances in which the letter to Menocchio was written, furnished by Ziannuto and the priest (foreseeably different but not contradictory), instead are among the records of the trial against the priest himself (Trial no. 136). The charges against Vorai, besides the one of having written to Menocchio suggesting a line of defense, were the following: having waited ten years to denounce Menocchio to the Holy Office, although he considered him a heretic; stating, while conversing with Nicolò and Sebastiano, counts of Montereale, that the church militant, even though governed by the Holy Spirit, may err. The very brief trial ended with the canonical purgation of the defendant. During the interrogation of 19 May 1584 the priest had declared, among other things: "I was moved to write this letter because I feared for my life. The sons of this Scandella used to pass near me and showed themselves to be angry. They didn't greet me as they had been accustomed to do. In fact, friends warned me to be on my guard because it was rumored that I had denounced the aforesaid ser Domenego and they could have done me some harm. . . . " Among those who had accused Vorai of being an informer was that Sebastiano Sebenico who had advised Ziannuto to spread the word that Menocchio was mad or possessed (see above p. 6).

   Instead he attributed them to a Domenego Femenussa: The attribution had been suggested, it appears, by Ziannuto. See ACAU, *Sant'Uffizio,* Trial no. 126, fol. 38 v.

   "Sir": Ibid., fol. 19 r.

8. *"It would appear from the trial records":* Ibid.

   According to Giuliano Stefanut: Ibid., fol. 8 r.

   "I meant": Ibid., fol. 19 r.

   "Do not try to talk too much": Ibid., Trial no. 134, proceedings of 7 May 1584.

   Fra Felice da Montefalco: See C. Ginzburg, *I benandanti: Stregoneria e culti agrari tra '500 e '600* (1966; reprint ed., Turin, 1979), index.

   The conflict between the two jurisdictions: See P. Paschini, *Venezia e l'Inquisizione Romana da Giulio III a Pio IV* (Padua, 1959), pp. 51 ff; A. Stella, *Chiesa e stato nelle relazioni dei nunzi pontifici a Venezia* (Vatican City, 1964), esp. pp. 290–91.

   "He said to me": See ACAU, *Sant'Uffizio,* Trial no. 126, fol. 3 r.

   "Domenego said": Ibid., fol. 4 r.

9. *"It's true I said":* Ibid., fol. 27 v.

6

"I think": See ACAU, *Sant'Uffizio,* Trial no. 126, fols. 27 v.–28 v.

10. *"you want to become gods on earth":* See Psalm 81:6.

About marriage: Here Menocchio shows his impatience with the matrimonial regulations introduced by the Council of Trent. See A. C. Jemolo, "Riforma tridentina nell'ambito matrimoniale,"in *Contributi alla storia del Concilio di Trento e della Controriforma* (Florence, 1948), pp. 45 ff. *(Quaderni di Belfagor,* 1).

About confession: See ACAU, *Sant'Uffizio,* Trial no. 126, fol. 11 v.

"If that tree": Ibid., fol. 38 r.

"By the Virgin Mary": Ibid., fol. 6 v.

"I do not see anything": Ibid., fol. 11 v.

11. *"I did say":* Ibid., fol. 18 r.

"I like this about the sacrament": Ibid., fols. 28 r.–v.

"I believe that sacred Scripture": Ibid., fols. 28 v.–29 r.

12. *"[Menocchio] also told me":* Ibid., fol. 2 v.

"I believe that saints": Ibid., fol. 29 r.

"He has been beneficial": Ibid., fol. 33 r. (I have corrected a slip: "Christ" rather than "God.")

"of the very same nature": Ibid., fol. 17 v.

"If a person has sinned": Ibid. fol. 33 r.

"I would say enough": Ibid. fol. 4 r.

"I have never associated": Ibid. fols. 26 v.–27 r.

"to speak out": Ibid., fol. 3 r.

"My lords, I beg you": Ibid., fols. 29 v.–30 r.

13. *"In the previous examination":* Ibid., fol. 30 r.

7

On the Friuli in this period, besides P. Paschini *(Storia del Friuli,* 2 vols. [Udine, 1953–54] vol. 2, 2nd rev. ed.), who concerns himself exclusively with political events, see especially the numerous studies by P. S. Leicht: "Un programma di parte democratica in Friuli nel Cinquecento," in *Studi e frammenti* (Udine, 1903), pp. 107–21; "La rappresentanza dei contadini presso il veneto Luogotenente della Patria del Friuli," in *Studi e frammenti,* pp. 125–44; "Un movimento agrario nel Cinquecento," in *Scritti vari di storia del diritto italiano* 2 vols. (Milan, 1943), 1:73–91; "Il parlamento friulano nel primo secolo della dominazione veneziana," *Rivista di storia del diritto italiano* 21 (1948): 5–50; "I contadini ed i Parlamenti dell'età intermedia," *IXe Congrès International des Sciences Historiques . . . Etudes présentées à la Commission Internationale pour l'histoire des assemblées d'états* (Louvain, 1952), pp. 125–28. Among more recent works, see above all A. Ventura, *Nobiltà e popolo nella società veneta del '400 e '500* (Bari, 1964), especially pp. 187–214. See also A. Tagliaferri, *Struttura e politica sociale in una comunità veneta del '500 (Udine)* (Milan, 1969).

the masnada *form of serfdom:* See A. Battistella, "La servitú di masnada in Friuli," *Nuovo archivio veneto* 11 (1906), pt. 2, pp. 5–62; 12 (1906), pt. 1, pp. 169–91, pt. 2, pp. 320–31; 13 (1907), pt. 1, pp. 171–84, pt. 2, pp. 142–57; 14 (1907), pt. 1, pp. 193–208; 15 (1908), pp. 225–37. The last traces of this institution disappeared about 1460. But in Friulian statutes of a century later such provisions remained as *De nato ex libero ventre pro libero reputando* (with the corresponding declaration "Quicumque vero natus ex muliere serva censeatur et sit servus cuius est mulier ex qua natus est, etiam si pater eius sit liber") or *De servo communi manumissio.* See also G. Sassoli De Bianchi, "La scomparsa della servitú di masnada in Friuli," *Ce Fastu?* 32 (1956): 145–50.

in the hands of Venetian officials: See *Relazioni dei rettori veneti in Terraferma,* vol. 1 *La patria del Friuli (luogotenenza di Udine)* (Milan, 1973). (About this edition see the review by M. Berengo in *Rivista storica italiana* 86 [1974]: 586–90.)

As early as 1508: See G. Perusini, *Vita di popolo in Friuli: Patti agrari e consuetudini tradizionali* (Florence, 1961), pp. xxi–xxii *(Biblioteca di "Lares,"* 8).

14. On the events of 1511, see Leicht, "Un movimento agrario" and Ventura, *Nobiltà e popolo.*

the Contadinanza: See Leicht, "La rappresentanza dei contadini." We lack a modern study on this subject.

the statutes of the Patria: See *Constitutiones Patrie Foriulii cum additionibus noviter impresse* (Venice, 1524), fols. lx v., lxviii v. The same provisions reappear in the 1565 edition.

the legal fiction: See Leicht, "I contadini ed i Parlamenti" who emphasizes the exceptional quality of the Friulian case. In no other part of Europe, in fact, did a representative body of the peasantry stand alongside a parliament or assembly of the states.

The list of measures: See *Leggi per la Patria,* pp. 638 ff., 642 ff., 207 ff.

15. *attempted to transform the long-term leases:* See Perusini, *Vita di popolo,* p. xxvi, and, in general, G. Giorgetti, *Contadini e proprietari nell'Italia moderna: Rapporti di produzione e contratti agrari dal secolo XVI a oggi* (Turin, 1974), pp. 97 ff.

the total population . . . declined: See Tagliaferri, *Struttura,* pp. 25 ff. (with bibliography).

The reports of the Venetian officials: Relazioni, pp. 84, 108, 115.

the decline of Venice: See *Aspetti e cause della decadenza economica veneziana nel secolo XVII* (Venice and Rome, 1961); B. Pullan, ed., *Crisis and Change in the Venetian Economy in the Sixteenth and Seventeenth Centuries* (London, 1968).

8

16. *a totally dichotomous view:* See the translation of the important book by S. Ossowski, *Class Structure in the Social Consciousness,* trans. Sheila Patterson (New York, 1963).

"It also seems to me": See ACAU, *Sant'Uffizio,* Trial no. 126, fols. 27 v.–28 r.

"Everything belongs to the Church": Ibid., fol. 27 v.

From an assessment made in 1596: See ASP, *Notarile,* b. 488, no. 3785, fols. 17 r. ff., especially fol. 19 v. Unfortunately, for this period we lack an inventory of ecclesiastical property in the Friuli such as the extremely detailed one compiled in 1530 by order of the governor, Giovanni Basadona (see BCU ms. 995). At fols. 62 v.–64 v. of this manuscript there is a listing of the lessees of the church of Santa Maria di Montereale, among which the name Scandella doesn't appear.

17. *At the end of the sixteenth century:* See A. Stella, "La proprietà ecclesiastica nella Repubblica di Venezia dal secolo XV al XVII," *Nuova rivista storica* 42 (1958): 50–77; A. Ventura, "Considerazioni sull'agricoltura veneta e sull'accumulazione originaria del capitale nei secoli XVI e XVII," *Studi storici* 9 (1968): 674–722; and now, in general, the important essay by G. Chittolini, "Un problema aperto: la crisi della proprietà ecclesiastica fra Quattro e Cinquecento," *Rivista storica italiana* 85 (1973): 353–93.

18. *"I believe a Lutheran":* See ACAU, *Sant'Uffizio,* Trial no. 126, fol. 27 r.

    "some Lutherans will learn of it": Ibid., Trial no. 285, unnumbered leaves.

    In the complex religious picture: Obviously, the bibliography on the subject is endless. On radical tendencies in general, see G. H. Williams, *The Radical Reformation* (Philadelphia, 1962). On Anabaptism, see C.-P. Clasen, *Anabaptism, a Social History (1525–1618): Switzerland, Austria, Moravia, South and Central Germany* (Ithaca and London, 1972). For Italy, see the rich documentation gathered by A. Stella, *Dall'Anabattismo al socinianesimo nel Cinquecento veneto* (Padua, 1967) and *Anabattismo e antitrinitarismo in Italia nel XVI secolo* (Padua, 1969).

    "I believe that as soon as we are born": See ACAU, *Sant'Uffizio,* Trial no. 126, fol. 28 v.

    broken in mid-sixteenth century: See Stella, *Dall'Anabattismo,* pp. 87 ff.; idem, *Anabattismo e antitrinitarismo,* pp. 64 ff. See also C. Ginzburg, *I costituti di don Pietro Manelfi,* Corpus Reformatorum Italicorum: Biblioteca (De Kalb and Chicago, 1972).

19. *But a few dispersed conventicles:* On the religious situation in the Friuli in the sixteenth century, see P. Paschini, *Eresia e Riforma cattolica al confine orientale d'Italia,* Lateranum, n.s. 17, nos. 1–4 (Rome, 1951); L. De Biasio, "L'eresia protestante in Friuli nella seconda metà del secolo XVI," *Memorie storiche Forogiuliesi* 52 (1972): 71–154. On the artisans of Porcía, see Stella, *Anabattismo e antitrinitarismo,* pp. 153–54.

    an Anabaptist . . . could never have spoken: See, for example, what Marco, a dyer, a repentant Anabaptist, wrote in 1552: "and they [the Anabaptists] preached to me that we shouldn't have faith in the forgiveness of the pope because they say that they are lies. . . . " (ASVen, *Sant'Uffizio,* b. 10).

    "I believe that they are good": See ACAU, *Sant'Uffizio,* Trial no. 126, fol. 29 r.

    "aside from this": See Stella, *Anabattismo e antitrinitarismo,* p. 154. See also the statement made by Ventura Bonicello, a vendor of rags, who was tried as an Anabaptist: "any other books besides the Holy Scriptures are an abomination to me" (ASVen, *Sant'Uffizio,* b. 158, "libro secondo" fol. 81 r.).

    a typical exchange: See ACAU, *Sant'Uffizio,* Trial no. 126, fols. 37 v.–38 r.

20. *The porter:* See Andrea da Bergamo (P. Nelli), *Il primo libro delle satire alla carlona* (Venice, 1566), fol. 31 r.

    Neapolitan tanners: See P. Tacchi Venturi, *Storia della Compagnia di Gesù in Italia,* 2 vols. (Rome, 1910–51), 1: 455–56.

    in a prostitute's appeal: See F. Chabod, "Per la storia religiosa dello stato di Milano" in Chabod's *Lo stato e la vita religiosa a Milano nell'epoca di Carlo V* (Turin, 1971), pp. 335–36.

    almost all have an urban setting: Evidence such as the following, contained in a letter from the Venetian ambassador in Rome, M. Dandolo (14 June 1550) is quite rare: "some monkish inquisitors . . . here are relating fantastic happenings in Brescia and perhaps even stranger ones in Bergamo, including about some artisans who during holy days go about in the villages and climb trees from which they preach the Lutheran sect to the people and to the peasants. . . . " (P. Paschini, *Venezia e l'Inquisizione Romana da Giulio III a Pio IV* [Padua, 1959] p. 42).

    The religious conquest: This is a theme that I touched upon in an earlier study ("Folklore, magia, religione," in *Storia d'Italia,* vol. 1, *I caratteri originali,* ed. R. Romano and C. Vivanti [Turin, 1972], pp. 645 ff., 656 ff.) and that I intend to develop further elsewhere.

    This doesn't mean: What follows is an attempt to define more closely and, in part to correct, what I wrote in "Folklore," p. 645.

21. *an autonomous current:* Although I distrust disquisitions on terminology, I think I should explain why I have preferred the expression "peasant radicalism" to "popular rationalism," "popular Reformation," or "Anabaptism." 1) the term "popular rationalism" has been used by M. Berengo (*Nobili e mercanti nella Lucca del Cinquecento* [Turin, 1965], pp. 435 ff.) to describe phenomena basically similar to those studied here. Nevertheless, it doesn't appear to be wholly appropriate for attitudes that only in part are traceable to our concept of "Reason"—beginning with the visions of Scolio (see pp. 112 ff). 2) The peasant radicalism that I am trying to reconstruct is certainly one of the basic elements in the "popular Reformation" described by Macek ("*autonomous* movements that accompany European history of the fifteenth and sixteenth centuries and that may be understood as a popular or radical Reformation": J. Macek, *La Riforma popolare* [Florence, 1973], p. 2; my italics). It should be remembered, however, that it predates the fifteenth century (see the following note) and that it can't be reduced to a popular equivalent of the official Reformation. 3) The term "Anabaptism" as a comprehensive label for all manifestations of sixteenth-century religious radicalism was proposed by D. Cantimori *(Eretici italiani del Cinquecento* [Florence, 1939], pp. 31 ff) and abandoned by him in the face of G. Ritter's criticism. It has been newly proposed by A. Rotondò to designate "the mixture of prophetism, anticlerical radicalism, antitrinitarianism, and social egalitarianism diffused among notaries, physicians, and teachers of grammar, among monks and merchants, among artisans in the city, and peasants in the country in sixteenth-century Italy" ("I movimenti ereticali nell'Europa del Cinquecento," *Rivista storica italiana* 78 [1966]: 138–39). This extension of the term seems inappropriate because it tends to minimize the deep-seated differences that existed between popular religion and the religion of the educated classes as well as between the radicalism of the countryside and the radicalism of the cities. Certainly, vague "typologies" and "sensibilities" such as those suggested by A. Olivieri ("Sensibilità religiosa urbana e sensibilità religiosa contadina nel Cinquecento veneto: suggestioni e problemi," *Critica storica,* n.s. 9 [1972]: 631–50) are not very helpful, subsuming under the banner of Anabaptism phenomena that are totally extraneous to it—including processions in honor of the Madonna. Research should have as its object, instead, the reconstruction of the still obscure connections that existed between the various components of the "popular Reformation," giving due consideration especially to the religious and cultural substratum not only of the Italian but also of the European countryside of the sixteenth century—that substratum that comes through in Menocchio's confessions. In defining it, I have spoken of "peasant radicalism," not so much with Williams's *Radical Reformation* in mind (on which see Macek's critical comments) as with Marx's phrase, according to which radicalism "grasps things at the roots," an image that, after all, is singularly appropriate in the present context.

but which was much older: See the important essay by W. L. Wakefield, "Some Unorthodox Popular Ideas of the Thirteenth Century," *Medievalia et humanistica,* n.s. 4 (1973): 25–35, based on inquisitorial documents from the area of Toulouse that contain "statements often tinged with rationalism, skepticism, and revealing something of a materialistic attitude. There are assertions about a terrestrial paradise for souls after death and about the salvation of unbaptized children; the denial that God made human faculties; the derisory quip about the consumption of the host; the identification of the soul as blood; and the attribution of natural growth to the qualities of seed and soil alone" (pp. 29–30). These statements are convincingly traced, not to the direct influence of Cathar propaganda, but rather to a current of autonomous ideas and beliefs. (If anything Catharism may have contributed to bringing them to light, directly or indirectly, by provoking the inquisitors' investigations.) It's significant, for example, that a proposition attributed to a Cathar notary at the end of the fourteenth century, "quod Deus de celo non facit crescere fructus, fruges et herbas et alia, quae de terra nascuntur, sed solummodo humor terre," should have been echoed almost to the letter by a peasant of the Friuli three centuries later: "that the blessings that priests lay over fields, and the holy water that they sprinkle over them on the day of Epiphany, in no way help vines and trees to bear fruit, but only manure, and man's industry" (see respectively A. Serena, "Fra gli eretici trevigiani," *Archivio veneto-tridentino* 3 [1923]: 173 and C. Ginzburg, *I benandanti: Stregoneria e culti agrari tra '500 e '600* [1966; reprint ed., Turin, 1979], pp. 38–39, to be corrected in the above sense). Obviously, Catharism isn't an issue here. Instead, we are faced with statements that "may well have arisen spontaneously from the cogitation of men and women searching for explanations that accorded with the realities of the life in which they were enmeshed" (Wakefield, "Some Unorthodox," p. 33). Other examples similar to those cited here could be found. It is to this cultural tradition, which reemerges centuries later, that we alluded with the expression "peasant (or "popular") radicalism." To the elements listed by Wakefield—rationalism, skepticism, materialism—one should add egalitarian utopianism and religious naturalism. The joining together of all, or almost all, of these elements produces the recurrent phenomena of peasant "syncretism"—which could be defined more precisely as latent phenomena. See, for example, the archeological material collected by J. Bordenave and M. Vialelle, *Aux racines du mouvement cathare: La mentalité religieuse des paysans de l'Albigeois medieval* (Toulouse, 1973).

10

"had spoken sincerely": ACAU, *Sant'Uffizio,* Trial no. 126, fols. 2 v.—3 r.

"Sir": Ibid., fol. 21 v.

don Ottavio Montereale: Ibid., Trial no. 285, unnumbered leaves (11 November 1598).

had emerged even during the first trial: Ibid., Trial no. 126, fol. 23 v. No Nicola da Porcía is mentioned in the studies of sixteenth-century Friulian painting that are known to me. Antonio Forniz, who is conducting research on painters born in Porcía, kindly informed me with a letter dated 5 June 1972 that he had not turned up any trace of either a "Nicola da Porcía" or of a "Nicola de Melchiori" (see below). It should be noted that the meeting between the painter and the miller could have been connected to relations that were professional, as well as religious. In fact, in the registers of Venetian patents it isn't unusual to find painters, sculptors, and architects applying for licenses to construct mills. Occasionally, such prominent names are encountered as those of the sculptor Antonio Riccio and of the architect Giorgio Amadeo, or of Jacopo Bassano, who obtained licenses for certain mills in 1492 (the first two) and in 1544 (the third) respectively: See G. Mandich, "Le privative industriali veneziane (1450–1550)," *Rivista del diritto commerciale* 34 (1936): 1, 538, 545. But see also p. 541. I have been able to discover similar cases for a later period on the basis of photocopies of documents in ASVen, *Senato Terra,* graciously put at my disposal by Carlo Poni.

22. *"It may be"*: See ACAU, *Sant'Uffizio,* Trial no. 285, unnumbered leaves (interrogation of 19 July 1599).

    a couple of weeks later: Ibid., unnumbered leaves (interrogation of 5 August 1599).

    We don't know: No Nicola appears in the trial against the group of Porcía (see ASVen, *Sant'Uffizio,* b. 13 and b. 14, dossier *Antonio Deloio).*

    "a great heretic": See ASVen, *Sant'Uffizio,* b. 34, dossier *Alessandro Mantica,* interrogation of 17 October 1571. Nicola had gone to Rorario's house "to take some headboards for painting."

    "I know": See ACAU, *Sant'Uffizio,* Trial no. 126, fol. 23 v.

23. *Il sogno dil Caravia:* Colophon: "In Vinegia, nelle case di Giovanni Antonio di Nicolini

da Sabbio, ne gli anni del Signore, MDXLI, dil mese di maggio." There is no study specifically devoted to this work, but see V. Rossi, "Un aneddoto della storia della Riforma a Venezia," in *Scritti di critica letteraria*, vol. 3, *Dal Rinascimento al Risorgimento* (Florence, 1930), pp. 191–222, and the Introduction to *Novelle dell'altro mondo: Poemetto buffonesco del 1513*, Nuova scelta di curiosità letterarie inedite o rare, vol. 2 (Bologna, 1929) which illustrate in an exemplary manner the person of Caravia and the literary current to which the *Sogno*, at least in part, belongs. On journeys into hell by buffoons and other popular comic figures, see M. Bakhtin, *Rabelais and His World* (Cambridge, Mass., 1968), ch. 6.

"You appear to me to be melancholia": See *Il sogno*, fol. A iii r. The iconography on the title page is the customary one for "the melanchonic": but its dependence on Dürer's engraving, which was well-known in Venetian circles, seems certain. See R. Klibansky, F. Saxl, and E. Panofsky, *Saturn and Melancholy: Studies in the History of Natural Philosophy, Religion, and Art* (London, 1964).

"Oh how dearly": See *Il sogno*, fol. B ii v.

"I know that Farfarel": Ibid., fols. G v.–G ii r.

24. "sgnieffi": Ibid., fol. G iii r.

"showing him": Ibid., fol. G ii v.

"A certain Martin Luther": Ibid., fols. F iv r.–v. (here and below the italics are mine).

25. *"The first cause":* Ibid., fol. B v.

"Many fools": Ibid., fol. B iii v.

26. *"They make a business":* Ibid., fol. B iv r.

There's an implicit denial: Zanpolo doesn't describe Purgatory. At one point there's an ambiguous allusion to "the punishment of hell down there, or purgatory" (Ibid., fol. iv r.).

"Purposefully": Ibid., fol. C ii v.

"sumptuous churches": Ibid., fol. E r. Caravia stresses this point in particular, criticizing, among other things, the grandiosity of the School of San Rocco.

"Saints should be honored": Ibid., fol. D iii v.

"Every faithful Christian": Ibid., fol. E r.

"the papists": Ibid., fol. B iv v.

For men like Caravia: On his productivity after the *Sogno*, see Rossi, *Un aneddoto*. In 1557 Caravia underwent an inquisitorial trial, in the course of which the *Sogno* was also brought out against him, inasmuch as it had been composed "in derision of religion." Ibid., p. 220; Caravia's characteristic testament, dated 1 May 1563, is reprinted in part on pp. 216–17.

27. *Long before the date:* It's impossible, as we've seen, to date the onset of Menocchio's heresy. At any rate, it should be noted that he once declared he hadn't observed Lent for twenty years (ACAU, *Sant'Uffizio*, Trial no. 126, fol. 27 r.)—a date that coincides approximately with his banishment from Montereale. Menocchio could have had contacts with Lutheran groups during his sojourn in Carnia—a border area where penetration by the Reformation was particularly successful.

11

"Would you like me to teach you": See ACAU, *Sant'Uffizio*, Trial no. 126, fols. 16 r.–v.

"What I said": Ibid., fol. 19 r.

"The devil": Ibid., fol. 21 v.

28. *from the prophets:* See F. Chabod, "Per la storia religiosa dello stato di Milano" in *Lo*

stato e la vita religiosa a Milano nell'epoca di Carlo V (Turin, 1971), pp. 299 ff.; D. Cantimori, *Eretici italiani del Cinquecento* (Florence, 1939), pp. 10 ff; M. Reeves, *The Influence of Prophecy in the Later Middle Ages: A Study in Joachimism* (Oxford, 1969); and now G. Tognetti, "Note sul profetismo nel Rinascimento e la letteratura relativa," *Bullettino dell'Istituto storico italiano per il Medio Evo,* no. 82 (1970), pp. 129–57. On Giorgio Siculo, see Cantimori, *Eretici,* pp. 57 ff.; C. Ginzburg, "Due note sul profetismo cinquecentesco," *Rivista storica italiana* 78 (1966): 184 ff.

"On confessing": See ACAU, *Sant'Uffizio,* Trial no. 126, fol. 16 r.

12

At the moment of his arrest: See ACAU, *Sant'Uffizio,* fol. 14 v., 2 February 1584: "inveni [the notary is speaking] quosdam libros qui non erant suspecti neque prohibiti, ideo R. P. inquisitor mandavit sibi restitui."

29. *The Bible:* Judging from G. Spini's bibliography, this would not appear to be Antonio Brucioli's translation (see *La Bibliofilia* 42 [1940]: 138 ff.).

Il fioretto della Bibbia: See H. Suchier, ed., *Denkmäler Provenzalischer Literatur und Sprache* (Halle, 1883), 1: 495 ff.; P. Rohde, "Die Quellen der Romanische Weltchronik," in Suchier, ed., *Denkmäler,* pp. 589–638; F. Zambrini, *Le opere volgari a stampa dei secoli XIII e XIV* (Bologna, 1884), col. 408. As has been noted, editions vary in scope: some stop with the birth, others with the infancy or passion of Christ. Those known to me (and I haven't made a systematic search) date from 1473 to 1552, and almost all are Venetian. We don't know when precisely Menocchio purchased the *Fioretto.* The work long continued to circulate: the *Index* of 1569 lists a *Flores Bibliorum et doctorum* (see F. H. Reusch, *Die Indices librorum prohibitorum des sechszehnten Jahrhunderts* [Tübingen, 1886], p. 333). In 1576 the Commissioner of the Sacred Palace, fra Damiano Rubeo, replying to certain questions raised by the inquisitor of Bologna, ordered him to remove the *Fioretti della Bibbia* from circulation (see A. Rotondò, "Nuovi documenti per la storia dell' 'Indice dei libri proibiti' (1572–1638)," *Rinascimento,* 14 [1963]: 157).

Il Lucidario: Menocchio first spoke of a *Lucidario della Madonna;* later he corrected himself: "I do not remember exactly whether that book was called *Rosario* or *Lucidario,* but it was printed" (see ACAU, *Sant'Uffizio,* Trial no. 126, fols. 18 r., 20 r.). I have found at least fifteen editions of the *Rosario* by Alberto da Castello printed between 1521 and 1573. In this case, as in the preceding, I haven't made a systematic search. If the book read by Menocchio really was the *Rosario* (as we shall state below, the identification isn't certain), the "Lucidario" would still have to be explained. Was it an unwitting recollection of a *Lucidario* derived in some way from that of Honorius of Autun? On this literature, see Y. Lefèvre, *L'Elucidarium et les lucidaires* (Paris, 1954).

Il Lucendario: Even in this *lapsus* we should probably see the echo of the reading of a *Lucidarius* (see above). There are endless editions of the *Legenda aurea* in the vernacular. Menocchio, for example, could have seen a copy of the edition published in Venice, 1565.

Historia del giudicio: See A Cioni, ed., *La poesia religiosa: I cantari agiografici e le rime di argomento sacro,* Biblioteca bibliografica italica, vol. 30 (Florence, 1963), pp. 253 ff. The text read by Menocchio was part of the group in which the *cantare* (songster) on the story about the Judgment is preceded by a briefer one on the coming of the Antichrist (which begins: "To you I appeal eternal Creator"). I know of four copies, of which three are preserved in the Biblioteca Trivulziana, Milan (See M. Sander, *Le livre à figures italien depuis 1467 jusqu'à 1530,* vol. 2 (Milan, 1942), nos. 3178, 3180, 3181); the fourth is in the Biblioteca Universitaria, Bologna (*Opera nuova del giudicio generale, qual tratta della fine del mondo,* printed in Parma, and reprinted in Bologna, by Alexandro Benacci, with permission of the Holy Inquisition, 1575; about this copy, see below p.

149). These four imprints contain the passage, paraphrased from the Gospel of Matthew, remembered by Menocchio (see pp. 38 ff.); it's lacking instead in the briefer versions preserved in the Biblioteca Marciana, Venice (see A. Segarizzi, *Bibliografia delle stampe popolari italiane della R. Biblioteca nazionale di S. Marco di Venezia,* 1 [Bergamo, 1913], nos. 134, 330).

Il cavallier: There is a vast literature on this work. See the most recent edition known to me (M. C. Seymour, ed., *Mandeville's Travels* [Oxford, 1967]) and the opposing interpretations by M.H.I. Letts (*Sir John Mandeville: The Man and His Book* [London, 1949]) and of J. W. Bennett *(The Rediscovery of Sir John Mandeville* [New York, 1954]) who seek to demonstrate with unpersuasive arguments that Mandeville existed historically. The *Travels,* which was translated into Latin and into all the European vernaculars, circulated widely in both manuscript and printed form. In the British Library alone there are twenty editions of the Italian version, which appeared between 1480 and 1567.

Zampollo: On the *Sogno dil Caravia,* see the studies by V. Rossi cited above, p. 145.

Il Supplimento: I know of at least fifteen vernacular editions of Foresti's chronicle printed between 1488 and 1581. On the author, see E. Pianetti, "Fra Iacopo Filippo Foresti e la sua opera nel quadro della cultura bergamasca," *Bergomum* 33 (1939): 100–09, 147–74; A. Azzoni, "I libri del Foresti e la biblioteca conventuale di S. Agostino," *Bergomum* 53 (1959): 37–44; P. Lachat, "Une ambassade éthiopienne auprès de Clement V, à Avignon, en 1310," *Annali del pontificio museo missionario etnologico già lateranensi* 31 (1967): 9, n. 2.

Lunario: Sander *(Le livre à figures,* vol. 2 nos. 3936–43) lists eight editions issued between 1509 and 1533.

the Decameron: On the fact that Menocchio read a copy free of Counter-Reformation censorship, see above, pp. 50 ff. On this question see F. H. Reusch, *Der Index der verbotenen Bücher* (Bonn, 1883), 1: 389–91; A Rotondò, "Nuovi documenti," pp. 152–53; C. De Frede, "Tipografi, editori, librai italiani del Cinquecento coinvolti in processi d'eresia," *Rivista di storia della Chiesa in Italia* 23 (1969): 41; P. Brown, "Aims and Methods of the Second *Rassettatura* of the Decameron," *Studi secenteschi* 8 (1967): 3–40. In general, see A. Rotondò, "La censura ecclesiastica e la cultura," in *Storia d'Italia,* vol. 5, *I documenti,* ed. R. Romano and C. Vivanti (Turin, 1973), pt. 2, pp. 1399–1492.

30. *The Koran:* See C. De Frede, *La prima traduzione italiana del Corano sullo sfondo dei rapporti tra Cristianità e Islam nel Cinquecento* (Naples, 1967).

13

"which . . . I bought": See ACAU, *Sant'Uffizio,* Trial no. 126, fol. 20 r.

Supplementum: Ibid., Trial no. 285, unnumbered leaves (interrogation of 12 July 1599).

Lucidario: Ibid., Trial no. 126, fols. 18 r., 20 r.

Her son, Giorgio Capel: Ibid., unnumbered leaves (interrogation of 28 April 1584).

The Bible: Ibid., fol 21 v.

The Mandeville: Ibid., fols. 22 r., 25 v.

The Sogno dil Caravia: Ibid., fol. 23 v.

Nicola de Melchiori: Ibid., Trial no. 285, unnumbered leaves (interrogation of 5 August 1599).

Menocchio . . . had loaned: Ibid., Trial no. 126, unnumbered leaves (interrogation of 28 April 1584).

31. *We know that in Udine:* See reference to A. Battistella, in A. Tagliaferri, *Struttura e politica sociale in una comunità veneta del '500 (Udine)* (Milan, 1969), p. 89.

Elementary schools: See G. Chiuppani, "Storia di una scuola di grammatica dal Medio Evo fino al Seicento (Bassano)," *Nuovo archivio veneto* 29 (1915): 79. On these questions, given the lack of modern studies, still useful is the old work by G. Manacorda: *Storia della scuola in Italia,* vol. 1, *Il Medioevo* (Milan, Palermo, Naples, 1914).

it's astonishing: We should remember, however, that the history of literacy is in its infancy. The rapid general survey by C. Cipolla *(Literacy and Development in the West* [London, 1969]) is already outdated. Among the recent studies, see L. Stone, "The Educational Revolution in England, 1560–1640," *Past and Present,* no. 28 (1964), pp. 41–80; idem, "Literacy and Education in England, 1640–1900," ibid., no. 42 (1969), pp. 69–139; A. Wyczanski, "Alphabétisation et structure sociale en Pologne au XVIe siècle," *Annales: ESC* 29 (1974): 705–13; F. Furet and W. Sachs, "La croissance de l'alphabétisation en France—XVIIIe–XIXe siècle," ibid., pp. 714–37. Wyczanski's study is especially appropriate for comparison with the case we are presently examining. From the analysis of a series of financial documents from the region about Cracow during the biennium 1564–65, it appears that 22 percent of the peasants mentioned knew how to write their own signatures. The author warns that the figure must be accepted with caution, since it deals with a very small sample (eighteen persons), consisting, moreover, of peasants who were well off and who frequently held offices in the village (as was precisely Menocchio's case). He concludes, nevertheless, that "instruction at an elementary level existed among peasants" ("Alphabétisation," p. 710). We await with interest the results of research by B. Bonnin ("Le livre et les paysans en Dauphiné au XVIIe siècle") and J. Meyer ("Alphabétisation, lecture et écriture: Essai sur l'instruction populaire en Bretagne du XVIe siècle au XIXe siècle").

14

32. *Menocchio knew little more Latin:* See ACAU, *Sant'Uffizio,* Trial no. 126, fol. 16 r.: "He replied: 'I know how to say the Credo, and also I have heard the Credo that is recited in the Mass, and I have helped sing it in the church of Monte Reale.' Interrogated: 'Since you know the Credo, what do you have to say about that article, 'et in Iesum Christum filium eius unicum dominum nostrum qui conceptus est de Spiritu santo, natus ex Maria virgine,' what did you say and believe about it in the past, and what do you believe now?' And when it was said to him: 'Do you even understand these words, "qui conceptus est de Spiritu santo, natus ex Maria virgine"?' he replied: 'Yes sir I understand.' " The course of the dialogue recorded by the notary of the Holy Office seems to indicate that Menocchio comprehends only when the words of the Credo are being repeated to him, perhaps more slowly. The fact that he also knew the Pater Noster (ibid., Trial no. 285, unnumbered leaves, interrogation of 12 July 1599) doesn't contradict what we've suggested. Less obvious, instead, are the words of Christ to the thief which Menocchio cites ("hodie mecum eris in paradiso": see Trial no. 126, fol. 33 r.). But to conclude on this basis alone that he knew Latin well would be hazardous indeed.

various social levels: Unfortunately, systematic research doesn't exist on books that circulated among the lower classes in sixteenth-century Italy—more precisely, among the minority of the members of these classes able to read. An investigation carried out on wills, *post mortem* inventories (such as those pursued by Bec especially on mercantile circles), and inquisitorial trials would be very useful. See also the evidence gathered by H.-J. Martin, *Livre, pouvoirs et société à Paris au XVIIe siècle (1598–1701),* 2 vols. (Geneva, 1969), 1: 516–18 and, for a later period, J. Solé, "Lecture et classes populaires à Grenoble au dix-huitième siècle: Le témoignage des inventaires après décès," *Images du peuple au XVIIIe siècle—Colloque d'Aix-en-Provence, 25 et 26 Octobre 1969* (Paris, 1973), pp. 95–102.

The Foresti and the Mandeville: For Foresti, see Leonardo da Vinci, *Scritti letterari,* ed. A. Marinoni, new enlarged ed., (Milan, 1974), p. 254 (it's a conjecture, but plausibly founded). For Mandeville, see E. Solmi, *Le fonti dei manoscritti di Leonardo da Vinci* (Turin, 1908), p. 205, supplement, nos. 10–11 of the *Giornale storico della letteratura italiana.* On Leonardo's reaction to Mandeville, see esp. p. 54. In general, besides the Marinoni edition just cited, pp. 239 ff., see E. Garin, "Il problema delle fonti del pensiero di Leonardo," in *La cultura filosofica del Rinascimento italiano* (Florence, 1961), pp. 388 ff., and C. Dionisotti, "Leonardo uomo di lettere," *Italia medioevale e umanistica* 5 (1962): 183 ff. (which we have tried to keep in mind, especially in terms of methodology).

Historia del Giudicio: This is the copy of the *Opera nuova del giudicio generale* preserved in the Biblioteca Universitaria, Bologna (Aula V, Tab. I, JI, vol. 51.2). On the title page there is a note: "Ulyssis Aldrovandi et amicorum." Other notes on the title and on the last leaf don't appear to be in Aldrovandi's hand. On the latter's encounters with the Inquisition, see A. Rotondò, "Per la storia dell'eresia a Bologna nel secolo XVI," *Rinascimento* 13 (1962): 150 f., with bibliography.

"fantastic opinions": See ACAU, *Sant'Uffizio,* Trial no. 126, fol. 12 v.

15

33. *how did he read them:* On the question of reading—almost always surprisingly neglected by students of these questions, see the legitimate observations by U. Eco ("Il problema della ricezione," in A. Ceccaroni and G. Pagliano Ungari, eds., *La critica tra Marx e Freud* [Rimini, 1973], pp. 19–27), which in large part agree with what has been said here. Some very interesting material emerges from the investigation by A. Rossi and S. Piccone Stella, *La fatica di leggere* (Rome, 1963). On "error" as a methodologically crucial experience (which is demonstrated even in the case of Menocchio's readings) see C. Ginzburg, "A proposito della raccolta dei saggi storici di Marc Bloch," *Studi medievali,* ser. 3, 6 (1965), pp. 340 ff.

"opinions": ACAU, *Sant'Uffizio,* Trial no. 126, fol. 21 v.

16

34. *"was called a Virgin":* See ACAU, *Sant'Uffizio,* Trial no. 126, fols. 17 v.–18 r.

"Contemplate": I quote from the 1575 Venetian edition ("appresso Dominico de'Franceschi, in Frezzaria al segno della Regina"), fol. 42 r.

Calderari: See J. Furlan, "Il Calderari nel quarto centenario della morte," *Il Noncello,* no. 21 (1963), pp. 3–30. The painter's real name was Giovanni Maria Zaffoni. I don't know if it has been noticed that the feminine group on the right, in the scene of Joseph with the pretenders, resembles a similar group painted by Lotto at Trescore, in the fresco that depicts Saint Clare taking the veil.

17

"I believe": See ACAU, *Sant'Uffizio,* Trial no. 126, fol. 29 v.

35. *"Yes sir":* Ibid.

"And the angels": I quote from the Venice edition of 1566 ("appresso Girolamo Scotto"), p. 262. Incidentally, it should be noted that among the scenes painted by Calderari at San Rocco there is also one of Mary's death.

18

36. *"because many men":* ACAU, *Sant'Uffizio,* Trial no. 126, fol. 16 r.

    in chapter 166 of the Fioretto: I quote from the 1517 Venetian edition ("per Zorzi di Rusconi milanese ad instantia de Nicolo dicto Zopino et Vincentio compagni"), fol. Ov v.

    "Christ was born a man": ACAU, *Sant'Uffizio,* Trial no. 126, fol. 9 r.

    "if he was God": Ibid., fol. 16 v.

19

37. *"he is always arguing":* ACAU, *Sant'Uffizio,* Trial no. 126, fol. 11 v.

    "I say": Ibid., fols. 22 v.–23 r.

    "Oh, you who have": I quote, in the process correcting a couple of material errors, from the *Iudizio universal overo finale* "in Firenze, appresso alle scale di Badia," n.d. (but 1570–80), a copy preserved in the Biblioteca Trivulziana. The 1575 Bologna edition (see above p. 146) has minor variants.

38. *Even the Anabaptist Bishop:* See A. Stella, *Anabattismo e antitrinitarismo in Italia nel XVI secolo* (Padua, 1969), p. 75.

39. *"because it only hurts":* ACAU, *Sant'Uffizio,* Trial no. 126, fol. 21 v.

    "I teach you": Ibid., fol. 9 r.

    But during the interrogation: Ibid., fols. 33 v.–34 r.

40. Alcune ragioni del perdonare: "In Vinegia per Stephano da Sabbio, 1537." On Crispoldi, see A. Prosperi, *Tra evangelismo e Controriforma: G. M. Giberti (1495–1543)* (Rome, 1969), index. On the booklet, see C. Ginzburg and A. Prosperi, *Giochi di pazienza: Un seminario sul 'Beneficio di Cristo'* (Turin, 1975).

    "The prescription ": [Crispoldi] *Alcune ragioni,* fols. 34 r.–v.

    He is familiar with: Ibid., fols. 29 ff., especially fols. 30 v.–31 r.: "And to be sure they [soldiers and men of rank] and every state and condition of person and each and every republic and reign deserve perpetual war and never to enjoy peace, where there are so many who hate forgiving, or speak badly and have a low esteem of those who pardon. They deserve to have every person take the law into his own hands and have a private accounting, and that there should be neither judge nor public official, so that with a multitude of ills they may see how great an evil it is when everyone takes the law into his own hands; how vendettas, for the sake of the common good, are entrusted to public officials even by the laws of the pagans, and that even among them to pardon was the correct thing to do, especially when this was done for the good of the republic or even of some private person, as in the case where a father was pardoned so that his little children might not be deprived of his support. And think how much more important it is to do it because God wishes it so. This question of the common good is discussed at length elsewhere and by many." Cf. chapters 11–15 of book 1 of the *Discorsi* (first published in 1531).

    not the Machiavelli diminished: See the Introduction by G. Procacci to N. Machiavelli, *Il Principe e Discorsi sopra la prima deca di Tito Livio* (Milan, 1960), pp. lix–lx.

20

41. *all his accomplices":* See ACAU, *Sant'Uffizio,* Trial no. 126, fol. 27 r.

42. *in a letter to his judges:* See p. 89.

The Travels, *probably . . . written:* See the essential bibliography cited above, p. 147.

It's well known: See G. Atkinson, *Les nouveaux horizons de la Renaissance française* (Paris, 1935), pp. 10–12.

"the different manners of Christians": I quote from the 1534 Venice edition (Joanne de Mandavilla, *Qual tratta delle più maravigliose cose)*, fol. 45 v.

"They say that a man": Ibid., fol. 46 r.–v.

43. *"If that tree":* See ACAU, *Sant'Uffizio,* Trial no. 126, fol. 38 r.

"among all the prophets": Mandavilla, *Qual tratta,* fol. 51 v.

"I doubted that": See ACAU, *Sant'Uffizio,* Trial no. 126, fol. 16 v.

"but he was never crucified": Mandavilla, *Qual tratta,* fol. 52 r.

"it is not true that Christ": See ACAU, *Sant'Uffizio,* Trial no. 126, fol. 13 r.

"it seemed a strange thing": Ibid., fol. 16 v.

44. *"they [the Christians]":* Mandavilla, *Qual tratta,* fols. 53 r.–v.

21

"the peoples": Joanne de Mandavilla, *Qual tratta delle più maravigliose cose* (Venice, 1534), fol. 63 r. "Channe" is Thana, a place located on the island of Salsette, northeast of Bombay (for the identification of geographical names in Mandeville, I've used Seymour's commentary to the edition [M. C. Seymour, ed., *Mandeville's Travels* (Oxford, 1967)]).

45. *"they are people short in stature":* Mandavilla, *Qual tratta,* fol. 79 v. On the possibility that this passage served as a source for Swift, see J. W. Bennett, *The Rediscovery of Sir John Mandeville* (New York, 1954), p. 255–56.

"So many kinds": See ACAU, *Sant'Uffizio,* Trial no. 126, unnumbered leaves; Mandavilla, *Qual tratta,* fol. 22 r.

Michel de Montaigne: On the limits of Montaigne's relativism, see S. Landucci, *I filosofi e i selvaggi, 1580–1780* (Bari, 1972), pp. 363–64 and passim.

"In this island": Mandavilla, *Qual tratta,* fols. 76 v.–77 r. Dondina (Dondun) may be one of the Andaman islands. Chapter 148 of the Italian edition of Mandeville corresponds to chapter 22 of the English version (translators' note).

46. *as it had Leonardo:* See E. Solmi, *Le fonti dei manoscritti di Leonardo da Vinci* (Turin, 1908), p. 205, supplement, nos. 10–11 of the *Giornale storico della letteratura italiana.*

"Tell me": See ACAU, *Sant'Uffizio,* Trial no. 126, fols. 21 v.–22 r.

22

47. *"And you should know":* Joanne de Mandavilla, *Qual tratta delle più maravigliose cose* (Venice, 1534), fol. 63 v.

48. *"the holiest beast":* Ibid. fols. 63 v.–64 r.

"the heads of dogs": Ibid., fol. 75 r. The description of the Cynocephales is taken from the *Speculum historiale* of Vincent of Beauvais.

"you should know that in all that country": Mandavilla, *Qual tratta,* fols. 118 v.–19 r. "Et metuent": Ps. 66:8; "Omnes gentes": Ps. 71:11.

"although": Mandavilla, *Qual tratta,* fols. 110 r.–v. For the Scriptural citations, see Hos. 8:12; Song. of Sol. 8:14; John, 10:16.

Mesidarata and Genosaffa: These are two places mentioned in the classical tradition, Oxydraces and Gymnosophistae. To these passages from Mandeville one can compare the depictions of men with large ears or enormous feet who are among the saved on the portal of the church of the Madeleine in Vezelay (see E. Mâle, *L'art religieux du XIIe siècle en France* [Paris, 1947], p. 330 and see also the iconography of St. Christopher dog-faced in L. Réau, *L'iconographie de l'art chrétien* [Paris, 1958], vol. 3, pt. 1, 307–8; these references have been graciously communicated to me by Chiara Settis Frugoni), where the emphasis, however, is on the diffusion of Christ's Word even among distant and monstrous peoples.

49. *a popular current . . . favoring toleration:* See, for example, C. Vivanti, *Lotta politica e pace religiosa in Francia fra Cinque e Seicento* (Turin, 1963), p. 42.

legend of the three rings: Besides M. Penna, *La parabola dei tre anelli e la tolleranza nel Medio Evo* (Turin, 1953), which is unsatisfactory, see U. Fischer, "La storia dei tre anelli: Dal mito all'utopia," *Annali della Scuola Normale Superiore di Pisa-Classe di Lettere e Filosofia* ser. 3, 3 (1973): 955–98.

23

Gerolamo Asteo: See C. Ginzburg, *I benandanti: Stregoneria e culti agrari tra '500 e '600* (1966; reprint ed., Turin, 1979), index.

"I beg you, sir": See ACAU, *Sant'Uffizio,* Trial no. 285, interrogations of 12 July, 19 July, 5 August 1599.

50. *fallen under the scissors:* See above p. 147. The novella ("Melchizedek the Jew, with a story of three rings, escapes the great danger set for him by Saladin," the third of the first day) lacks any reference to the three rings in the Giunti edition corrected by Leonardo Salviati (Florence, 1573, pp. 28–30; Venice, 1582, etc.). In the edition "riformata da Luigi Groto cieco d'Adria" (Venice, 1590, pp. 30–32) not only has the most explosive passage disappeared ("And so I say to you, my lord, of the three Laws to the three peoples given by God the Father, about which you question me: each one believes to have directly received and need carry forward His inheritance, His very Law and His commandments; but who actually has them, even as with the rings, the question is still pending": G. Boccaccio, *Il Decamerone,* ed. V. Branca [Florence, 1951], 1: 78), but the entire novella has been rewritten beginning with the title "The youthful Polifilo with a story of three rings escapes a great danger set for him by three women."

51. *Castellio:* See D. Cantimori, "Castellioniana (et Servetiana)," *Rivista storica italiana* 67 (1955): 82.

24

that possible relations with one heretical group: In general, see the methodological suggestions regarding "contracts" and "influences" in L. Febvre, "Une question mal posée: les origines de la Réforme française et le problème des causes de la Réforme," in *Au coeur religieux du XVIe siècle* (Paris, 1957).

25

52. *"I have said that":* See ACAU, *Sant'Uffizio,* Trial no. 126, fol. 17 r.

"if this book": Ibid., fol. 22 r.

"As it is said, in the beginning God made a great substance": Fioretto della Bibbia, fol. A iiii r.

"and it is said in the beginning God made heaven and earth": See Foresti, *Supplementum,* fol. I v. (of the Venice 1553 ed.).

53. *"I heard him say"*: ACAU, *Sant'Uffizio,* Trial no. 126, fol. 6 r.

"I have said that": Ibid., fol. 17 r. The italics, here and below, are mine.

54. *"What was this"*: Ibid., fol. 20 r.

"that most holy majesty": Ibid., fol. 23 r.

"I believe that the eternal God": Ibid., fols. 30 r.–v.

"This God": Ibid., fol. 31 v.

26

"It appears that": ACAU, *Sant'Uffizio,* Trial no. 126, fols. 36 v.–37 v. The transcription is complete. I have only substituted the names of the two interlocutors for the formula "Interrogatus . . . respondit."

27

57. *"Angelic, that is to say divine"*: See *Dante con l'espositioni di Christoforo Landino et d'Alessandro Vellutello* (Venice, 1578), fol. 201 r. *Paradiso* 30, 134 ff. also alludes to the thesis of the creation of man as reparation for the fall of the angels. On this question see, B. Nardi, *Dante e la cultura medievale: Nuovi saggi di filosofia dantesca* (Bari, 1949), pp. 316–19.

"And this God": See ACAU, *Sant'Uffizio,* Trial no. 126, fol. 17 v.

had read Dante: For an example of the reading of Dante in a popular (but urban and, moreover, Florentine) environment, see V. Rossi, "Le lettere di un matto," in *Scritti di critica letteraria,* vol. 2, *Studi sul Petrarca e sul Rinascimento* (Florence, 1930), pp. 401 ff., especially pp. 406 ff. Even closer to Menocchio's case is that of the commoner of the Lucchese countryside who called himself Scolio. For echoes of Dante in his poem, see below p. 168.

Actually, Menocchio: There's no evidence that Menocchio had read any of the contemporary vernacular translations of Diodoro Siculo's *Biblioteca storica.* In the opening chapter of this work, at any rate, there is no mention of cheese, even if there is a reference to the generation of living beings from putrefaction. I shall return in another essay to the history of this passage. On the other hand, we know with certainty that Menocchio had had Foresti's *Supplementum* in his hands. Here he could have encountered, in a hasty summary, certain cosmological doctrines traceable to antiquity or the Middle Ages: "Briefly then all these things have been taken from the book of Genesis, so that by means of them any one of the faithful may come to understand that the theology of pagans is totally useless; in fact by comparing it (with Genesis) he may understand that it is impiety rather than theology. Of these pagans some said there was no God; others believed and said that the stars fixed in the sky were fire, or actually fire that girated and was moved about, and they adored it in the place of God; others said that the world was governed not by any divine providence, but by a rational nature; some say that the world never had a beginning but was from eternity, that in no way was it begun by God, but rather was ordained by chance and fortune; some finally, that it was composed of atoms and sparks and minute animated bodies. . . . " (*Supplementum,* fol. II r.). This allusion to "the world ordained by chance" recurs (unless it's an echo of *Inferno* IV, 136, which is unlikely) in a conversation mentioned by the priest of Polcenigo, Giovan Daniele Melchiori, when he went to testify before the Holy Office of Concordia (16 March). Fifteen years before, a friend—most likely the priest himself—had exclaimed, walking in the country: "Great is the goodness of God in having created these mountains, these plains, and this beautiful machine that is the world." And Menocchio who was with him had asked: "Who do you believe created this world?" "God." "You're fooling yourself, because this world was made by chance, and if I could talk I would, but I don't want to talk." (ACAU, *Sant'Uffizio,* Trial no. 126, fols. 24 v.–25 r.).

"From the most perfect": Ibid., fol. 37 r.

Francesco Redi's experiments: Redi demonstrated in 1688 that in organic substances removed from contact with air, putrefaction did not occur, and thus not even "spontaneous generation."

Walter Raleigh: Quoted from H. Haydn, *The Counter-Renaissance* (New York, 1960), p. 209.

58. *ancient and distant myths:* U. Harva, *Les représentations religieuses des peuples altaïques* (Paris, 1959), pp. 63 ff.

"In the beginning": See ACAU, *Sant'Uffizio,* Trial no. 126, fol. 6 r. (and see pp. 52 ff.).

It can't be excluded: See G. De Santillana and H. von Dechend, *Hamlet's Mill* (London, 1970), pp. 382–83, who declare that an exhaustive study of this cosmogonic tradition would require a book in itself. Who knows if, after having written a fascinating one on the mill wheel as the image of the heavenly vault, they might not perceive more than a casual occurrence in the restatement of this ancient cosmogony by a miller. Unfortunately, I lack the competence to judge such a work as *Hamlet's Mill.* Its presuppositions, as well as the audacity of some of its passages, obviously inspire suspicion. But only by daring to question certainties that have been lazily acquired does the study of such persistent cultural continuities become possible.

Paola Zambelli has recently argued against "the concept of the absolute autonomy of peasant culture," which I am supposed to have maintained in *The Cheese and the Worms* (see "Uno, due, tre, mille Menocchio?" *Archivio storico italiano* 137 (1979): 59, 51–90 passim). It seems to me that the hypothesis around which this book is constructed, one that moreover has been frequently explicitly confirmed—that of the "circularity" between dominant and subordinate cultures—signifies exactly the opposite. But, according to Zambelli, the notion of circularity doesn't correspond to the thesis of the book (p. 61, n. 19). The phrase "complex relationship, made up of *reciprocal exchanges* [Zambelli's italics], in addition to repression operating in one direction only," which I have used elsewhere, appears to her endowed with "notably different nuances," and more acceptable (even if, however, they don't correspond to my research)—without noticing that in a passage from the introduction to this book, which she herself cited (p. 63), I had already spoken of "a *reciprocal influence* (my italics) between the cultures of subordinate and ruling classes." Undoubtedly more carefully written, and more useful, are Zambelli's observations on the diffusion of the notion of spontaneous generation in Italian philosophical (Neoplatonic and Aristotelian) circles in the fifteenth and sixteenth centuries. Still, it doesn't seem to me that the references cited by Zambelli furnish convincing precedents with which to explain the origins of Menocchio's ideas. It should be noted first of all that either they talk of the putrefaction of cheese (Pomponazzi, p. 74, n. 24), but without connecting this to the origin of the cosmos; or they talk of the origins of angels and of men from chaos, but without mentioning the putrefaction of cheese or putrefaction in general (Tiberio Russilliano Sesto, and the vernacular translation of *Pimander,* pp. 78–79). Now in a culture tied to daily experience, as was Menocchio's, the separation of the "image" (better: of the "experience") from the "idea" of the fermentation (p. 74) was neither taken for granted nor obvious. The repeated appearance, in Menocchio's cosmological talk, of the allusion to the putrefied cheese in an analogical-explicative key persuades us decisively to exclude the bookish mediation hypothesized (and not proven) by Zambelli. Actually, an argument in favor of her thesis presupposes an extreme permeability, which would have to be demonstrated, between upper class culture and peasant culture. (To avoid misunderstandings I'd like to emphasize that here too I'm not proposing the "concept of the absolute autonomy of peasant culture.") It is absurd to suppose that for a miller in contact with heretical circles "acquaintance, mediated of direct," with Ficino's writings was "infinitely easier" than with Servetian texts, "since they [Ficino's] were extremely widespread" (p. 69). As we've already said, a Mantuan goldsmith could try to read Servetus (without understanding a thing); but the hypothesis that Ficino's writings were among Menocchio's books recalls C. Dionisotti's quip about the "truly marvelous identification," confuted by Garin, of a *De immortalità d'anima,* mentioned in the list of books owned by Leonardo (who, after all, was Leonardo) with Ficino's *Theologia platonica:* "thinking about it always gave me the impression of a giraffe in a hen house" (C. Dionisotti, "Leonardo uomo di lettere," *Italia medioevale e umanistica* 5 (1962): 185). Really surprising is Zambelli's observation (pp. 79–80) regarding the term *terrigenae* used by Ficino, and later by Pomponazzi's disciple, Tiberio Russilliano Sesto—"indeed when a theme is so familiar as to cause a special word to be coined in their Latin, it isn't necessary to have to suppose a direct and purely oral descent from India." That Latin would have been incomprehensible to Menocchio, in the highly unlikely assumption that those texts has actually fallen into his hands. In short, we are in the presence of two cultures, linked, however—and this is the point—by circular (reciprocal) relationships that will have to be analytically demonstrated, case by case. However, if we accept the assumption of circularity, we have to admit that it imposes on the historian standards of proof different from the usual. This is due to the fact that dominant culture and subordinate culture are matched in an unequal struggle, where the dice are loaded. Given the fact that the documentation reflects the relationship of power between the classes of a given society, the possibility that the culture of the subordinate classes should leave a trace, even a distorted one, in a period in which illiteracy was still so common, was indeed slim. At this point, to accept the usual standards of proof entails exaggerating the importance of the dominant culture. In the present instance, for example, to assume that every scrap of written evidence—even a still unpublished lecture of Pomponazzi's or a text of Tiberio Russilliano Sesto published clandestinely and destined to remain virtually unknown—is of greater validity in the reconstruction of Menocchio's ideas than a "purely" oral tradition (the tell-tale adverb is Zambelli's) means deciding the issue in advance in favor of one (the more privileged) of the contenders on the field. In this way we inevitably finish by "demonstrating" the traditional thesis that ideas by definition originate *always and only* in educated circles (perhaps out of radical positions: but that doesn't concern us here)—in the heads of monks and university professors, certainly not of millers or of peasants. An absurd example of this type of distortion, oblivious even to the most basic chronological precautions, is furnished by G. Spini, "Noterelle libertine," *Rivista storica italiana* 88 [1976]: 792–802: see Zambelli's remarks, pp. 66–67.) It's legitimate to object that the hypothesis that traces Menocchio's ideas about the cosmos to a remote oral tradition is also unproven—and perhaps destined to remain so (see G. C. Lepschy, "Oral Literature," *The Cambridge Quarterly* 8 [1979]: 186–87) even if, as I've stated above, I intend in the future to demonstrate its possibility with additional evidence. In any case, it would be advisable to develop new criteria of proof specifically suited to a line of research based on so thoroughly a heterogeneous, in fact unbalanced, documentation. That a new field of investigation alters not only the methods but the very criteria of proofs in a given discipline is shown, for example, in the history of physics: the acceptance of atomic theory has necessitated a change in the standards of evidence that had developed within the sphere of classical physics.

the English theologian Thomas Burnet: "Tellurem genitam esse atque ortum olim traxisse ex Chao, ut testatur antiquitas tam sacra quam profana, supponamus: per Chaos autem nihil aliud intelligo quam massam materiae exolutam indiscretam et fluidam . . . Et cum notissimum sit liquores pingues et macros commixtos, data occasione vel libero aëri expositos, secedere ab invicem et separari, pinguesque innatare tenuibus; uti videmus in mistione aquae et olei, et *in separatione floris lactis a lacte tenui,* aliisque plurimis exemplis: aequum erit credere, hanc massam liquidorum se partitam esse in duas massas, parte ipsius pinguiore supernatante reliquae . . . " (T. Burnet, *Telluris theoria sacra, originem et mutationes generales orbis nostri, quas aut jam subiit, aut olim subiturus est, complectens* [Amsterdam, 1699], pp. 17, 22; I heartily thank Nicola Badaloni for bringing this passage to my attention.) For the reference to Indian cosmology, see ibid., pp. 344–47, 541–44.

a cult with shamanistic undercurrents: See C. Ginzburg, *I benandanti: Stregoneria e culti agrari tra '500 e '600* (1966; reprint ed., Turin, 1979), p. xiii. I shall deal with this theme more fully in a future work.

28

59. *The Reformation and the diffusion of printing:* On the relationship between the two phenomena see E. L. Eisenstein, "L'avènement de l'imprimerie et la Réforme," *Annales: ESC* 26 (1971): 1355–82 and most recently, idem, *The Printing Press as an Agent of Change,* 2 vols. (Cambridge, 1979), esp. pp. 367 ff.

the historic leap: On all this see the fundamental essay by J. Goody and J. Watt, "The Consequences of Literacy," *Comparative Studies in Society and History* 5 (1962–63): 304–45, which, however, curiously ignores the break constituted by the invention of printing. E. L. Eisenstein ("The Advent of Printing and the Problem of the Renaissance," *Past and Present,* no. 45 [1969]: 66–68) quite properly insists on the possibilities for self-education that it offered.

"a betrayal of the poor": See ACAU, *Sant'Uffizio,* Trial no. 126, fol. 27 v. It should be noted that in 1610 the provincial Venetian governor, A. Grimani, ordered that all Friulian trials involving peasants should be written in the vernacular: *Leggi per la Patria e Contadinanza del Friuli* (Udine, 1686), p. 166.

"Can't you understand": See ACAU, *Sant'Uffizio,* Trial no. 285, unnumbered leaves (6 July 1599).

"to seek exalted things": Ibid., Trial no. 126, fol. 26 v.

29

60. *"How God cannot":* See *Fioretto della Bibbia,* fols. A iii v.–A iv r.

61. *"Now many philosophers":* Ibid., fols. C r.–v.

But the linguistic and conceptual tools: Here I'm making use (although with a different perspective, as I indicated in the preface) of L. Febvre's concept of "outillage mental": *Le problème de l'incroyance au XVIe siècle: La religion de Rabelais* (1942; reprint ed., Paris, 1968), pp. 328 ff.

30

62. *the images that adorn the* Fioretto: See, for example, pp. 69–70.

31

"We are all children": See ACAU, *Sant'Uffizio,* Trial no. 126, fol. 17 v.

"they are all dear to him": Ibid., fol. 28 r.

"He claims all": Ibid., fol. 37 v.

"only hurts oneself": Ibid., fol. 21 v.

63. *But besides being a father:* The two images were traditional. See K. Thomas, *Religion and the Decline of Magic* (London, 1971), p. 152.

"most high majesty": See ACAU, *Sant'Uffizio,* Trial no. 126, fol. 20 r.

"Great captain": Ibid., fol. 6 r.

"he who will sit": Ibid., fol. 35 v.

"I said that if Jesus Christ": Ibid., fol. 16 v.

"as for indulgences": Ibid., fol. 29 r.

"is like a steward of God": Ibid., fol. 30 v.

by "the Holy Spirit": Ibid., fol. 34 r.

"by means of the angels": Ibid.

"Just as someone": Ibid., fol. 37 r.

64. *"where there is will"*: Ibid.

"carpenter": Ibid., fol. 15 v.

"I believe": Ibid., fol. 37 r.

"Has this God": Ibid., fol. 31 v.

"God alone": Ibid., fol. 29 r.

As for the angels: It should be noted that if Menocchio had had in his hands, as we've supposed (see above p. 57), *Dante con l'espositioni di Christoforo Landino et d'Alessandro Vellutello,* he could have read among Landino's glosses to canto 9 of the *Inferno:* "Menandrians take their name from Menander *magus,* disciple of Simon. They say the world was not made by God, but by the angels" (fol. 58 v.). A confused and distorted echo of this passage seems to recur in these words of Menocchio: "In this book by Mandeville it seems to me that I read there was a Simon *magus* who took the form of an angel." Actually, Mandeville doesn't even mention Simon Magus. The slip probably resulted from a moment of confusion for Menocchio. After having said that his ideas originated from a reading of Mandeville's *Travels* that had occurred "five or six years" before, the inquisitor had objected: "It is known that you have held these opinions for about thirty years" (ACAU, *Sant'Uffizio,* Trial no. 126, fol. 26 v.). With his back to the wall Menocchio had tried to get out of his fix by attributing to Mandeville a phrase he had read elsewhere—most likely a long time before—and changing the subject at once. These, however, are simply conjectures.

"they were produced": ACAU, *Sant'Uffizio,* Trial no. 126, fol. 37 r.

"the angels were the first creatures": See *Fioretto della Bibbia,* fol. B viii r.

"And so you see": Ibid., fol. A iii v.

"I believe that the entire world": See ACAU, *Sant'Uffizio,* Trial no. 126, fol. 17 r.

32

65. *"What is this Almighty God"*: See ACAU, *Sant'Uffizio,* Trial no. 126, fol. 11 v.

"what do you imagine": Ibid., fol. 8 r.

"what is this Holy Spirit": Ibid., fol. 12 r.

"You will never find": Ibid., fol. 24 r.

"If I could speak": Ibid., fol. 25 r.

66. *"I said":* Ibid., fol. 27 v.

the now lost Italian translation: See A. Stella, *Anabattismo e antitrinitarismo in Italia nel XVI secolo* (Padua, 1969), pp. 7, 135–36.

At the heart: On Servetus, see D. Cantimori, *Eretici italiani del Cinquecento* (Florence, 1939), pp. 36–49; B. Becker, ed., *Autour de Michel Servet et de Sébastien Castellion* (Haarlem, 1953); R. H. Bainton, *Hunted Heretic: The Life and Death of Michael Servetus, 1511–1553* (Boston, 1953).

"I doubted that": See ACAU, *Sant'Uffizio,* Trial no. 126, fol. 16 v.

"I think that he is a man like us": Ibid., fol. 32 r.

"For by Holy Spirit": M. Servetus, *De Trinitatis erroribus* (1531; reprint ed., Frankfort, 1965), fol. 22 r. The English translation is from *The Two Treatises of Servetus on the Trinity . . . Translated into English by Earl Morse Wilbur,* Harvard Theological Studies, 16 (Cambridge, Mass., 1932), p. 35. "Nam per Spiritum sanctum nunc ipsum Deum, nunc angelum, nunc spiritum hominis, instinctum quendam, seu divinum mentis statum, mentis impetum, sive halitum intelligit, licet aliquando differentia notetur inter flatum et spiritum. Et aliqui per Spiritum sanctum nihil aliud intelligi volunt, quam rectum hominis intellectum et rationem."

"I believe . . . he is God": ACAU, *Sant'Uffizio,* Trial no. 126, fols. 16 v., 29 v., 21 v. For the interpretation of "spirit" in the last quotation, see above at p. 71.

"As though Holy Spirit": Servetus, *De Trinitatis,* fol. 28 v.; *The Two Treatises,* p. 44. "Quasi Spiritus sanctus non rem aliquam separatam, sed Dei agitationem, energiam quandam seu inspirationem virtutis Dei designet."

67. *"In speaking of the Spirit":* Servetus, *De Trinitatis,* fols. 60 r.–v.; *The Two Treatises,* p. 94. "Sufficiebat mihi si tertiam illam rem in quodam angulo esse intelligerem. Sed nunc scio quod ipse dixit: 'Deus de propinquo ego sum, et non Deus de longinquo.' Nunc scio quod amplissimus Dei spiritus replet orbem terrarum, continet omnia, et in singulis operatur virtutes; cum propheta exclamare libet 'Quo ibo Domine a spiritu tuo?' quia nec sursum nec deorsum est locus spiritu Dei vacuus."

"What do you think God is": ACAU, *Sant'Uffizio,* Trial no. 126, fols. 2 r., 5 r.

"Again, all that is made": Servetus, *De Trinitatis,* fols. 66 v.–67 r., 85 v.; *The Two Treatises,* p. 103 (see also Cantimori, *Eretici,* p. 43, n. 3). "Omne quod in virtute a Deo fit, dicitur eius flatu et inspiratione fieri, non enim potest esse prolatio verbi sine flatu spiritus. Sicut nos non possumus proferre sermonem sine respiratione, et propterea dicitur spiritus oris et spiritus labiorum. . . . Dico igitur quod ipsemet Deus est spiritus noster inhabitans in nobis, et hoc esse Spiritum sanctum in nobis. . . . Extra hominem nihil est Spiritus sanctus. . . . "

"What do you imagine": ACAU, *Sant'Uffizio,* Trial no. 126, fols. 8 r., 3 r. (and 10 r., 12 v., etc.), 2 r., 16 v., 12 r.

Servetus's writings: See the pseudo-Melanchthon letter addressed to the Senate of Venice in 1539 discussed by K. Benrath, "Notiz über Melanchtons angeblichen Brief en den venetianischen Senat (1539)," *Zeitschrift f. Kirchengeschichte* 1 (1877): 469–71; the case of the Mantuan goldsmith Ettore Donato who, after having had in his hands the *De Trinitatis erroribus* in the Latin version, declared: "it was in a style so that I didn't understand it" (Stella, *Anabattismo e antitrinitarismo,* p. 135); on the circulation of Servetian writings in the Modenese area see J. A. Tedeschi and J. Von Henneberg, "Contra Petrum Antonium a Cervia relapsum et Bononiae concrematum," in *Italian Reformation Studies in Honor of Laelius Socinus,* ed. J. Tedeschi, (Florence, 1965), p. 252, n. 2.

33

68. *"it's a betrayal":* See ACAU, *Sant'Uffizio,* Trial no. 126, fol. 11 v.

 "I believe that": Ibid., fol. 34 r.

 "the devil": Ibid., fols. 38 r.–v.

 a peasant religion: "And in the peasants' world there is no room for reason, religion, and history. There is no room for religion, because to them everything participates in divinity, everything is actually, not merely symbolically, divine: Christ and the goat; the heavens above, and the beasts of the field below; everything is bound up in natural magic. Even the ceremonies of the church become pagan rites, celebrating the existence of inanimate things, which the peasants endow with a soul, and the innumerable earthy divinities of the village. . . . " (Carlo Levi, *Christ Stopped at Eboli: The Story of a Year,* trans. Frances Frenaye (New York, 1947), p. 117.

34

69. *"We say":* ACAU, *Sant'Uffizio,* Trial no. 126, fol. 17 r.

 "and therefore man": See *Fioretto della Bibbia,* fols. B viii r.–v. The italics are mine.

 "When man dies": ACAU, *Sant'Uffizio,* Trial no. 126, fol. 10 v.

 the verses in Ecclesiastes: See Eccles. 3: 18 ff.: "Dixi in corde meo de filiis hominum, ut probaret eos Deus et ostenderet similes esse bestiis. Idcirco unus interitus est hominum et iumentorum, et aequa utriusque conditio. Sicut moritur homo, sic et illa moriuntur. . . . " In this connection we would do well to remember that among the accusations lodged against the nobleman Alessandro Mantica of Pordenone ten years before (he was condemned later by the Holy Office as "vehemently suspected" of heresy even though nothing very substantial turned up against him) was that of having propounded the thesis of the mortality of the soul on the basis of these verses: "And mindful," one reads in the sentence dated 29 May 1573, "that it was not proper for the aforementioned Alessandro, since he was a man of letters, to say on more than one occasion to ignorant people *'quod iumentorum et hominum par esse interitus,'* suggesting the possibility that the rational soul is mortal. . . . " (ASVen, *Sant'Uffizio,* b. 34, fasc. *Alessandro Mantica,* fols. 21 v.–22 r., and sentence). That Menocchio might have been among those "ignorant people" is an attractive but indemonstrable conjecture—and, at any rate, unnecessary. At this time the Mantica had intermarried with the Montereale family: A. Benedetti, *Documenti inediti riguardanti due matrimoni fra membri dei signori castellani di Spilimbergo e la famiglia Mantica di Pordenone* (n.p. n.d.; reprint ed. Pordenone, 1973).

70. *"What is your belief":* See ACAU, *Sant'Uffizio,* Trial no. 126, fol. 18 v.

35

"You say": See ACAU, *Sant'Uffizio,* Trial no. 126, fols. 20 r.–v. I have made a faithful transcription; only in the following instances has direct discourse been restored: "It being said to him, if the spirit of God . . . and if this spirit of God . . . "; "interrogated if he meant that that spirit of God . . . "; "it being said to him that he should confess the truth and resolve. . . . "

36

71. *pantheistic:* The term "pantheism" was coined by John Toland in 1705 (see P. O. Kristeller, *The Classics and Renaissance Thought* (Cambridge, Mass. 1955), p. 100.

    popular belief: See C. Ginzburg, *I benandanti: Stregoneria e culti agrari tra '500 e '600* (1966; reprint ed., Turin, 1979), p. 92.

    "so, tell the truth": ACAU, *Sant'Uffizio,* Trial no. 126, fol. 21 r.

    "our spirit": Ibid., fol. 20 v.

    "whether he believed": Ibid., fols. 21 r.–v.

72. *"I will tell you":* Ibid., fols. 32 r.–v.

    "is separated from man": Ibid., fol. 34 v.

    Two spirits: In general, on this question, see the important considerations by L. Febvre, *Le problème de l'incroyance au XVIe siècle: La religion de Rabelais* (1942; reprint ed., Paris, 1968), pp. 163–94.

37

"And it is true": See *Fioretto della Bibbia,* fols. B ii v.–B iii r.

The distinction: See also L. Febvre, *Le problème de l'incroyance au XVIe siècle: La religion de Rabelais* (1942; reprint ed., Paris, 1968), p. 178, regarding Postel's distinction between immortal *animus* (in French *anime*) and *anima* (in French *âme*). It should be noted, however, that for Postel the latter is linked to the Spirit, while the *anime* is illuminated by the *mind.*

We must go back: On all this, see G. H. Williams, *The Radical Reformation* (Philadelphia, 1962), in the index *sub voce* "psychopannychism"; idem, "Camillo Renato (c. 1500?—1575)," in *Italian Reformation Studies in Honor of Laelius Socinus,* ed. J. Tedeschi (Florence, 1965), pp. 106 ff, 169–70, passim; A. Stella, *Dall'Anabattismo al socinianesimo nel Cinquecento veneto* (Padua, 1967), pp. 37–44.

73. *Through the direct influence of Renato:* See the trial records of one of Renato's followers in the Valtellina (he declared that he held the "same beliefs" as he), Giovanbattista Tabacchino, a friend of the Vicentine Anabaptist Jacometto "stringaro" (lace maker): A. Stella, *Anabattismo e antitrinitarismo in Italia nel XVI secolo* (Padua, 1969), *sub voce* "Tabacchino." This overthrows the prudent reservation that had been expressed by Rotondò on this question (C. Renato, *Opere, documenti, e testimonianze,* ed. A. Rotondò, Corpus Reformatorum Italicorum (De Kalb and Chicago, 1972), p. 324. It should be noted, however, that the pamphlet "La revelatione," preserved in manuscript among the papers of the Venetian Holy Office and previously attributed to Jacometto "stringaro" (see Stella, *Dall'Anabattismo,* pp. 67–71, who publishes lengthy extracts from it; C. Ginzburg, *I costituti di don Pietro Manelfi,* Biblioteca del Corpus Reformatorum Italicorum [De Kalb and Chicago, 1972], p. 43, n. 22), is actually the work of Tabacchino. See ASVen, *Sant'Uffizio,* b. 158, "liber quartus," fol. 53 v. This writing, which had been intended for members of the sect who had found refuge in Turkey, merits further study in view of the close relationship of its author to Renato. Antitrinitarian ideas had not previously been attributed to the latter (see Renato, *Opere,* p. 328) while Tabacchino's "La revelatione" takes an explicitly antitrinitarian direction.

    "believed that the soul": See Stella, *Anabattismo e antitrinitarismo,* p. 61. The italics are mine.

    "no other hell": See Ginzburg, *I costituti,* p. 35.

the priest of Polcenigo: See ASVen, *Sant'Uffizio,* b. 44 *(De Melchiori don Daniele).*

"we go to paradise": Ibid., fols. 39 v., 23 v., etc.

"I remember": Ibid., fols. 66 r.–v.

74. Discorsi predicabili: I quote from the Venetian edition of 1589, fols. 46 r.–v. The first edition appeared in 1562. On Ammiani, or Amiani, who was secretary of the order and attended the Council of Trent, see the sketch by G. Alberigo in *Dizionario biografico degli italiani* (Rome, 1960), 2: 776–77. The article underlines Ammiani's attitude, hostile to antiprotestant polemic, and favorable, instead, to the recovery of tradition, especially the patristic. This is evident even in these *Discorsi* (which were followed by another two parts in a few years), where an explicit attack on the Lutherans is restricted to the fortieth discourse ("What have the wicked Luther and his disciples done," fols. 51 r.–v.).

"ad perfidam": See ASVen, *Sant'Uffizio,* b. 44, fol. 80 r. The reference to Wyclif in an inquisitorial sentence of this period seems to be quite unusual.

38

75. *"I believe":* See above p. 75.

"What was the Son": See ACAU, *Sant'Uffizio,* Trial no. 126, fols. 31 v.–32 r.

76. *"Yes, my lords":* Ibid., fol. 32 v.

"the seats": Ibid., fol. 33 v.

39

"earlier you affirmed": See above p. 69.

"No sir": ACAU, *Sant'Uffizio,* Trial no. 126, fol. 29 v.

"Preaching": Ibid., fol. 28 v.

"I think they are good": Ibid., fol. 29 r.

77. *"because God":* Ibid., fol. 35 r.

"I believe it is a place": Ibid.

"Intellect": Ibid., fols. 32 r.–v.

"with our bodily eyes": Ibid., fol. 35 v.

"paradise is a gentle place": See Joanne de Mandavilla, *Qual tratta delle piú maravigliose cose,* fol. 51 r.

"do you believe": ACAU, *Sant'Uffizio,* Trial no. 126, fol. 38 v.

40

"my mind": See ACAU, *Sant'Uffizio,* Trial no. 126, fol. 30 r.

In societies: See J. Goody and J. Watt, "The Consequences of Literacy," *Comparative Studies in Society and History* 5 (1962–63): 304–45; F. Graus, "Social Utopias in the Middle Ages," *Past and Present,* no. 38 (1967): 3–19; E. J. Hobsbawm, "The Social Function of the Past: Some Questions," *Past and Present,* no. 55 (1972): 3–17. Still useful is M. Halbwachs, *Les cadres sociaux de la mémoire* (1925; reprint ed., Paris, 1952).

78. *"When Adam":* This famous proverb was already in circulation at the time of the English peasant rebellion in 1381 (see R. Hilton, *Bond Men Made Free: Medieval Peasant Movements and the English Rising of 1381* [London, 1973], pp. 222–23).

primitive Church: See, in general, G. Miccoli, "Ecclesiae primitivae forma," in *Chiesa Gregoriana* (Florence, 1966), pp. 225 ff.

"I wish that": See ACAU, *Sant'Uffizio,* Trial no. 126, fol. 35 r.

The crisis of ethnocentricity; See S. Landucci, *I filosofi e i selvaggi, 1580–1780* (Bari, 1972); W. Kaegi, "Voltaire e la disgregazione della concezione cristiana della storia," in *Meditazioni storiche,* Italian tr. (Bari, 1960), pp. 216–38.

"Martin known as Luther": See Foresti, *Supplementum,* fols. ccclv r.–v. (but there are mistakes in the numbering).

41

80. *"considered":* See ACAU, *Sant'Uffizio,* Trial no. 132, statement by the priest Odorico Vorai, 15 February 1584.

    "in the inns": Ibid., Trial no. 126, fol. 9 r.

    "slandered": Ibid. See also fols. 7 v., 11 r., etc.

    "he provides me": Ibid., Trial no. 132, unnumbered leaves (interrogation of 18 February 1584).

    "working": Ibid., Trial no. 126, fol. 13 v.

81. *"This one":* Ibid., fol. 10 v.

    "he says things": Ibid., fol. 12 v.

    "When you were saying": Ibid., Trial no. 132, unnumbered leaves (interrogation of 25 April 1584).

    "God forbid": Ibid., Trial no. 126, fol. 27 v.

    "That night": Ibid., fols. 23 v.–24 r.

    become an outlaw: See E. J. Hobsbawm, *Bandits* (London, 1969).

    A generation before: See above p. 14.

42

"begins to sin": See ACAU, *Sant'Uffizio,* Trial no. 126, fol. 34 v.

82. *"A few days ago":* *Mundus novus* (n.p. n.d., 1500?), unnumbered leaves. The italics are mine. "Superioribus diebus satis ample tibi scripsi de reditu meo ab novis illis regionibus . . . *quasque novum mundum appellare licet,* quando apud maiores nostros nulla de ipsis fuerit habita cognitio et audientibus omnibus sit novissima res."

    In a letter that Erasmus: See *Opus epistolarum Des. Erasmi* . . . ed. P. S. Allen, 12 vols. (Oxford, 1928), 7: 232–33.

    Capitolo: This writing is found as an appendix to the *Begola contra la Bizaria* (Modena, n.d.). I've used the copy in the Biblioteca Comunale dell'Archiginnasio, Bologna, call no. 8. Lett. it., *Poesie varie,* Caps. XVII, no. 43. I haven't been able to identify the printer. At any rate, see R. Ronchetti Bassi, *Carattere popolare della stampa in Modena nei secoli XV–XVI–XVII* (Modena, 1950).

83. *land of Cockaigne:* See F. Graus, "Social Utopias in the Middle Ages," *Past and Present,* no. 38 (1967): 3–19, especially pp. 7 ff., who, however, seriously underestimates the diffusion of this theme and its popular impact. In general, see M. Bakhtin, *Rabelais and His World,* trans. Helene Iswolsky (Cambridge, Mass., 1968), passim. (It should be noted, incidentally, that in the "nouveau monde" that the author imagines he has discovered in the mouth of Pantagruel, there is an echo of the land of Cockaigne, duly

noted by E. Auerbach, *Mimesis, the Representation of Reality in Western Literature,* trans. W. R. Trask (Princeton, 1953), pp. 262 ff. For Italy still fundamental is V. Rossi, "Il paese di Cuccagna nella letteratura italiana," in appendix to *Le lettere di messer Andrea Calmo,* ed. V. Rossi (Turin, 1888), pp. 398–410. There are some useful references in the essay by G. Cocchiara in the collection, *Il paese di Cuccagna e altri studi di folklore* (Turin, 1956), pp. 159 ff. For France, see A. Huon, " 'Le Roy Sainct Panigon' dans l'imagerie populaire du XVIe siècle," in *François Rabelais: Ouvrage publié pour le quatrième centenaire de sa mort (1553–1953),* ed. M. François (Geneva, Lille, 1953), pp. 210–25. See, in general, E. M. Ackermann, *'Das Schlaraffenland' in German Literature and Folksong . . . with an Inquiry into Its History in European Literature* (Chicago, 1944).

84. *These elements:* Cocchiara's essay, among others, deals with them without connecting them, however, to accounts of the American natives (on the absence of private property, see R. Romeo, *Le scoperte americane nella coscienza italiana del Cinquecento* [Milan, Naples, 1971], pp. 12 ff.). Ackermann touches on this connection briefly: *'Das Schlaraffenland',* pp. 82 and esp. 102.

Not only serious: It may be useful to recall the Freudian category of witticisms directed against "institutions . . . , propositions dealing with morality or religion, conceptions of life so hallowed that any objection leveled against them can only be done in a humorous guise, in fact through a witticism cloaked by a facade" (see the comment by F. Orlando, *Toward a Freudian Theory of Literature with an Analysis of Racine's 'Phèdre',* trans. Charmaine Lee (Baltimore and London, 1978), pp. 153 ff.). Thus, in the course of the seventeenth century More's *Utopia* was included in collections of frivolous or playful paradoxes.

Anton Francesco Doni: See P. F. Grendler, *Critics of the Italian World (1530–1560): Anton Francesco Doni, Nicolò Franco, and Ortensio Lando* (Madison, 1969). I have used the 1562 edition of the *Mondi (Mondi celesti, terrestri et infernali de gli academici pellegrini . . .):* the dialogue on the *Mondo nuovo* is at pp. 172–84.

isn't a peasant utopia: See Graus, "Social Utopias," p. 7, who states that the setting for the land of Cockaigne is never urban. An exception appears to be the *Historia nuova della città di Cuccagna,* printed in Siena toward the end of the fifteenth century, cited by Rossi, ed. (*Le lettere,* p. 399). Unfortunately, I haven't been able to locate this text.

"I enjoy": See Doni, *Mondi,* p. 179.

ancient myth of an age of gold: See A. O. Lovejoy and G. Boas, *Primitivism and Related Ideas in Antiquity* (Baltimore, 1935); H. Levin, *The Myth of the Golden Age in the Renaissance* (London, 1969); H. Kamen, "Golden Age, Iron Age: A Conflict of Concepts in the Renaissance," *The Journal of Medieval and Renaissance Studies,* no. 4 (1974): 135–55.

"a new world different": See Doni, *Mondi,* p. 173.

to project the model: For this distinction, see N. Frye, "Varieties of Literary Utopias," in *Utopias and Utopian Thought,* ed. F. E. Manuel (Cambridge, Mass., 1966), p. 28.

and of property: See Doni, *Mondi,* p. 176: "Everything was in common, and peasants and city dwellers dressed alike, because each carried down the fruit of his labor and took what he needed. There was no need for anyone to have to sell and resell, buy and rebuy."

85. *references in Foresti's* Supplementum: See Foresti, *Supplementum,* fols. cccxxxix v.–cccxl r.

"Because I have read": See ACAU, *Sant'Uffizio,* Trial no. 126, fol. 34 r.

urban, sober "new world": On the significance of Doni's urban utopia, see the rather superficial treatment in G. Simoncini, *Città e società nel Rinascimento,* 2 vols. (Turin, 1974), 1: 271–73 and passim.

religion lacked rites: See Grendler, *Critics,* pp. 175–76 (more generally, pp. 127 ff.). Grendler's statements aren't always convincing. For example, to speak of a more or less explicit "materialism" in regard to Doni seems to be a distortion (besides, see the telling wavering at pp. 135 and 176). In any case, Doni's religious restlessness is unquestionable. A. Tenenti ("L'utopia nel Rinascimento [1450–1550]," *Studi storici* 7 [1966]: 689–707), who speaks of an "ideal theocracy" in connection with the *Mondo nuovo* (p. 697), doesn't seem to have taken it into account.

"know God": See Doni, *Mondi,* p. 184. Grendler (p. 176) speaks of an "orthodox religious coda." Actually these words confirm the simplified religion dear to Doni. See also ACAU, *Sant'Uffizio,* Trial no. 126, fol. 28 r.

"Fasting": See ACAU, *Sant'Uffizio,* Trial no. 126, fol. 35 r.

Lamento: *Lamento de uno poveretto huomo sopra la carestia, con l'universale allegrezza dell'abondantia, dolcissimo intertenimento de spiriti galanti* (n.p. n.d.). I've used the copy in the Biblioteca Comunale dell'Archiginnasio, Bologna, call no. 8. Lett. it., *Poesie varie,* Caps. XVII, no. 40.

86. *Lent and Carnival:* Bakhtin *(Rabelais and His World,* p. 210 and passim) justifiably emphasizes the cyclical vision implicit in popular utopias. At the same time, in contradiction, he sees the carnivalesque Renaissance view of the world as marking an irreversible rupture with the "old" feudal world (pp. 215, 256, 273–74, 392). This superimposition of unilinear and progressive time over cyclical and static time is an indication of an overemphasis of the subversive elements in popular culture—an overemphasis that is the most debatable aspect of a book which, nevertheless, remains fundamental. See also P. Camporesi, "Carnevale, cuccagna e giuochi di villa (Analisi e documenti)," *Studi e problemi di critica testuale,* no. 10 (1975): 57 ff.

popular *origins of the utopias:* See Camporesi, "Carnevale," pp. 17, 20–21, 98–103, and passim (but see the preceding note). The question is raised in the case of Campanella by L. Firpo, "La cité idéale de Campanella et le culte du Soleil," in *Le soleil à la Renaissance: Sciences et mythes* (Brussels, 1965), p. 331.

a core that was ancient: See Bakhtin, *Rabelais and His World,* pp. 80–82.

renaissance: Ibid., pp. 218, 462, and especially G. B. Ladner, "Vegetation Symbolism and the Concept of Renaissance," in *De artibus opuscula XL: Essays in Honor of Erwin Panofsky,* ed. M. Meiss (New York, 1961), 1: 303–22. See also by Ladner, *The Idea of Reform, Its Impact on Christian Thought and Action in the Age of the Fathers* (Cambridge, Mass., 1959). Still important is K. Burdach, *Reformation, Renaissance, Humanismus,* 2nd ed. (Berlin, 1926).

It wasn't the Son of Man: See Dan. 7: 13 ff., one of the basic texts of millenarian literature.

43

a long letter: See ACAU, *Sant'Uffizio,* Trial no. 126, unnumbered leaves.

asked . . . in vain: See above p. 7.

45

89. *"ultramontanes":* See M. Scalzini, *Il secretario* (Venice, 1587), fol. 39.

don Curzio Cellina: There is a fascicle of notarial writings drawn up by him in ASP, *Notarile,* b. 488, no. 3785.

alliteration: See P. Valesio, *Strutture dell'alliterazione: Grammatica, retorica e folklore verbale* (Bologna, 1967), esp. p. 186 on alliteration in religious language.

91. *he stated in his trial:* See ACAU, *Sant'Uffizio,* Trial no. 126, fol. 34 v.

46

to pronounce sentence: See ACAU, *Sant'Uffizio,* "Sententiarum contra reos S. Officii liber II," fols. 1 r.–11 v. The abjuration is at fols. 23 r.–34 r.

"not only a formal heretic": non modo formalem hereticum . . . sed etiam heresiarcam."

"we find you have fallen": "invenimus te . . . in multiplici et fere inexquisita heretica pravitate deprehensum."

"not only with men of religion": "Non tantum cum religiosis viris, sed etiam cum simplicibus et idiotis."

92. *the audacity and obstinacy of the offender:* "ita pertinacem in istis heresibus," "indurato animo permansisti," "audacter negabas," "profanis et nefandis verbis . . . lacerasti," "diabolico animo affirmasti," "intacta non reliquisti sancta ieiunia," "nonne reperimus te etiam contra sanctas conciones latrasse?" "profano tuo iudicio . . . damnasti," "eo te duxit malignus spiritus quod ausus es affirmare," "tandem polluto tuo ore . . . conatus es," "hoc nefandissimum excogitasti," "et ne remaneret aliquod impollutum et quod non esset a te contaminatum . . . negabas," "tua lingua maledica convertendo . . . dicebas," "tandem latrabas," "venenum apposuisti," "et quod non dictu sed omnibus auditu horribile est," "non contentus fuit malignus et perversus animus tuus de his omnibus . . . sed errexit cornua et veluti gigantes contra sanctissimam ineffabilem Trinitatem pugnare cepisti," "expavescit celum, turbantur omnia et contremescunt audientes tam inhumana et horribilia quae de Iesu Christo filio Dei profano ore tuo locutus es."

"You brought again to light": "In lucem redduxisti et firmiter affirmasti vera[m] fuisse alias reprobatam opinionem illam antiqui philosophi, asserentis eternitatem caos a quo omnia prodiere quae huius sunt mundi."

"finally, you resurrected": "tandem opinionem Manicheorum iterum in luce revocasti, de duplici principio boni scilicet et mali . . . "

"You brought again to light Origen's": "heresim Origenis ad lucem revocasti, quod omnes forent salvandi, Iudei, Turci, pagani, christiani et infideles omnes, cum istis omnibus aequaliter detur Spiritus sanctus . . . "

93. *"Regarding the creation of the soul":* "Circa infusionem animae contrariaris non solum Ecclesiae sanctae, sed etiam omnibus philosophantibus . . . . Id quod omnes consentiunt, nec quis negare audet, tu ausus es cum insipiente dicere 'non est Deus' . . . "

In Foresti's Supplementum: See fols. cliii v.–cliv r., clvii r.

"we solemnly condemn you": "te sententialiter condemnamus ut inter duos parietes immurerís, ut ibi semper et toto tempore vitae tuae maneas."

47

"Although I": ACAU, *Sant'Uffizio,* "Sententiarum contra reos S. Officii liber II," fol. 12 r.

94. *the jailer:* Ibid., fols. 15 r.–v.

had Menocchio summoned: Ibid., fols. 16 r.–v.

95. *"And truly":* Et vere cum haec dicebat, aspectu et re ipsa videbatur insipiens, et corpore invalidus, et male affectus."

The bishop of Concordia: Ibid., fols. 16 v.–17 r.

48

in 1590: ACVP, "Visitationum Personalium anni 1593 usque ad annum 1597," pp. 156–57.

96. *There is evidence: ASP, Notarile,* b. 488, no. 3785, fols. 1 r.–2 v.

97. *The same year:* Ibid., fols. 3 r.–v.

In 1595: Ibid., fols. 6 v., 17 v.

following the death of the son: ACAU, *Sant'Uffizio,* Trial no. 285, unnumbered leaves.

49

98. *During the carnival:* See ACAU, *Sant'Uffizio,* Trial no. 285. The leaves of this trial are not numbered.

"Beati qui non viderunt": John 20:29.

99. *It emerged that don Odorico:* See ACAU, *Sant'Uffizio,* Trial no. 285, unnumbered leaves (11 November 1598, deposition of don Ottavio of the counts of Montereale).

questioned the new priest: Ibid. (17 December 1598).

Don Curzio Cellina: Ibid.

50

101. *a certain Simon:* See ACAU, *Sant'Uffizio,* Trial no. 285, unnumbered leaves (3 August 1599).

It may have been Menocchio's rejection: See A. Stella, *Anabattismo e antitrinitarismo in Italia nel XVI secolo* (Padua, 1969), p. 29 and idem "Guido da Fano eretico del secolo XVI al servizio dei re d'Inghilterra," *Rivista di storia della Chiesa in Italia* 13 (1959): 226.

51

102. *An innkeeper of Aviano:* See ACAU, *Sant'Uffizio,* Trial no. 285, unnumbered leaves (6 May 1599).

"if Christ had been God": This was a blasphemous expression in common use, as we see, for example, from testimony in 1599 against Antonio Scudellario, nicknamed Fornasier, who resided near Valvasone (ACAU, "Anno integro 1599, a no. 341 usque ad 404 incl.," Trial no. 361).

the same sally: See A. Bocchi, *Symbolicarum quaestionum . . . libri quinque* (Bologna, 1555), fols. lxxx–lxxxi. I'll return to this emblem on another occasion.

"I believe that he was wrong-headed": ACAU, *Sant'Uffizio,* Trial no. 285, unnumbered leaves (6 July 1599).

52

103. *"After having led"*: See ACAU, *Sant'Uffizio,* Trial no. 285, unnumbered leaves (12 July 1599). "Eductus e carceribus quidam senex . . . "

"I have kept a school": This was the most elementary level of instruction. Unfortunately, there is no other information about this episode in Menocchio's life.

He had read in Foresti's Supplementum: It hasn't been possible to locate the exact page. But see Foresti, *Supplementum,* fols. 180 r.–v.

53

106. *It was better to dissemble:* See C. Ginzburg, *Il nicodemismo. Simulazione e dissimulazione religiosa nell'Europa del'500* (Turin, 1970). But see, for a different interpretation, Carlos M. N. Eire, "Calvin and Nicodemism: a Reappraisal," *Sixteenth Century Journal* 10 (1979) fasc. 1: 45–69.

"Nous sommes Chrestiens": See M. De Montaigne, *Essais,* ed. P. Villey (Paris, 1965), p. 445 (book 2, ch. 12, "Apologie de Raimond Sebond").

107. *He told the inquisitor:* See ACAU, *Sant'Uffizio,* Trial no. 285, unnumbered leaves (19 July 1599).

"He said, go on": See *L'Alcorano di Maometto, nel qual si contiene la dottrina, la vita, i costumi et le leggi sue, tradotto nuovamente dall'arabo in lingua italiana* (Venice, 1547), fol. 19 r.

108. *"briefly lost in thought"*: See ACAU, *Sant'Uffizio,* Trial no. 285, unnumbered leaves (12 July 1599) "aliquantulum cogitabundus."

Subsequently: Ibid. (19 July 1599).

"It is true that inquisitors": Ibid. (12 July 1599).

54

"In the name": See ACAU, *Sant'Uffizio,* Trial no. 285, unnumbered leaves (12 July 1599).

109. *"Consider me crazy"*: In the original, "me trano ne li chochi" (see G. Boerio, *Dizionario del dialetto veneziano* [Venice, 1856], *ad vocem* "cochi").

55

"if the internal": "si interioribus credendum est per exteriora."

110. *"It has done"*: This personification sheds some light on the lower class attitudes toward death in this period—attitudes about which we still know very little. The rare bits of evidence that we do have have almost all been filtered through a distorting stereotype. See, for example, one that is cited in M. Vovelle, ed., *Mourir autrefois* (Paris, 1974), pp. 100–102.

56

"of the poor": "pauperculi Dominici Scandella."

"pure simplicity": "mera simplicitas et ignorantia."

57

111. *torture might be avoided:* See, in general, P. Fiorelli, *La tortura giudiziaria nel diritto comune,* 2 vols. (Milan, 1953–54).

"I do not remember": See ACAU, *Sant'Uffizio,* Trial no. 285, unnumbered leaves (19 July 1599).

"with moderation": "cum moderamine."

"the nuisance": See A. Stella, *Chiesa e Stato nelle relazioni dei nunzi pontifici a Venezia* (Vatican City, 1964), pp. 290–91. Bolognetti's report was written in 1581.

58

112. *"men who had nothing":* See C. Ginzburg, "Folklore, magia, religione," in *Storia d'Italia,* vol. 1, *I caratteri originali,* ed. R. Romano and C. Vivanti (Turin, 1972), p. 658. For similar cases in England, see K. Thomas, *Religion and the Decline of Magic* (London, 1971), pp. 159 ff.

The old English peasant: Thomas, *Religion,* p. 163 and E. P. Thompson's comment in "Anthropology and the Discipline of Historical Context," *Midland History* 1, no. 3 (1972): 43, who is followed here almost to the letter. N. Z. Davis has insisted on the active, in fact creative, role of the popular classes in matters of religion against scholars who study popular religion from the point of view of the upper classes (or even of the clergy) and see it thus simply as a simplification or perversion, in the direction of magical practices, of the official religion. See N. Z. Davis, "Some Tasks and Themes in the Study of Popular Religion," in *The Pursuit of Holiness in Late Medieval and Renaissance Religion,* ed. C. Trinkaus and H. A. Oberman (Leiden, 1974), pp. 307 ff. More generally, see the preface to the present book on the current scholarly discussion over the concept of "popular culture."

Scolio spoke: See the important essay by E. Donadoni, "Di uno sconosciuto poema eretico della seconda metà del Cinquecento di autore lucchese," in *Studi di letteratura italiana* 2 (1900): 1–142. This study is impaired by its attempt to establish precise connections—badly straining the evidence—between Scolio's poem and Anabaptist doctrines. In his discussion of this study M. Berengo (*Nobili e mercanti nella Lucca del Cinquecento* [Turin, 1965], pp. 450 ff.) attenuated its conclusions, without, however, wholly rejecting them. Thus, on the one hand, he stated that "it would be pointless to attempt to insert this text within the context of a precisely defined religious current," and, on the other, he connected Scolio to the stream of "popular rationalism." Apart from reservations about this phrase (see above p. 143), the connection seems correct. On the author, see Donadoni's suggestive hypothesis which proposes to identify "Scolio" with the huntsman, Giovan Pietro di Dezza, who was forced to abjure before the Holy Office in 1559 ("Di uno sconosciuto," pp. 13–14). The writing of the poem, as the author reveals on the last leaf, took seven years (hence the title "Settennario"), beginning in 1563; polishing it required another three.

113. *Dantean echoes:* In addition to the explicit reference to Dante (BGL, ms. 1271, fol. 9 r.) see such verses as "The *alma* Beatrice stands on the stairs" (ibid.) or "they were still on earth in the heat and cold" (see *Paradiso,* 21, 116). See also Donadoni, "Di uno sconosciuto," p. 4.

"Many prophets": BGL, ms. 1271, fol. 10 r.

Mohammed: Ibid., fol. 4 v. (and Donadoni, "Di uno sconosciuto," p. 21). On the last leaf of the poem Scolio inserted an ambiguous disavowal: "because when I was writing it I had been drawn outside of myself, and forced to write, and I was blind, dumb and deaf, and how it really was in fact, I certainly don't remember. . . . " (ibid. p. 2). The corrections and marginal glosses added to most of the passages quoted here are the result of this retraction.

"You Turk": BGL, ms. 1271, fol. 14 r. (and Donadoni, "Di uno sconosciuto," p. 93).

"God gave to us": BGL, ms. 1271, fol. 10 r. (and Donadoni, "Di uno sconosciuto," p. 28).

"nature's great precepts": BGL, ms. 1271, fol. 10 r.

"Do not adore": Ibid., fol. 19 r. (and Donadoni, "Di uno sconosciuto," pp. 130 ff.).

114. *"Let everyone be circumcised":* BGL, ms. 1271, fol. 15 r. (and Donadoni, "Di uno sconosciuto," p. 90).

"And if I told you": BGL, ms. 1271, fol. 2 r. (and Donadoni, "Di uno sconosciuto," p. 120).

"My baptism": BGL, ms. 1271, fol. 2 r.

"gloss": Ibid., fol. 10 r.

"Let there be neither columns": Ibid., fol. 15 r. (in the text "but organs . . . but bell towers." I've followed Donadoni's emendations, "Di uno sconosciuto," pp. 94–95).

"Puffed up": BGL, ms. 1271, fol. 1 r.

115. *"If my Lord":* Ibid., fol. 16 r.

"Let there be no shops": Ibid., fol. 13 r. (and Donadoni, "Di uno sconosciuto," p. 99).

"let gambling": BGL, ms. 1271, fol. 13 r. (and, in part, Donadoni, "Di uno sconosciuto," p. 97).

"the age of gold": See Donadoni, "Di uno sconosciuto," p. 34.

"In everybody's hands": BGL, ms. 1271, fol. 14 r.

116. *"Man or woman":* See Donadoni, "Di uno sconosciuto," pp. 102, 97.

"It is only permitted": BGL, ms. 1271, fol. 19 r.

"God led me": Ibid., fol. 4 r.

"The first river": Ibid., (and, in part, Donadoni, "Di uno sconosciuto," p. 125).

117. *This paradise:* See Donadoni "Di uno sconosciuto," pp. 128–30. Scolio's consciousness transpires from a note added later in the margin of one of these descriptions of paradise: "I, being the prophet and king of the mad was taken to the great paradise of the mad, the foolish, the clumsy, and the dull witted, in the paradise of delights or of donkeys, and it seems to me that I beheld all these things: but about all this I leave it to your judgment." Thus, once again, we have an ambiguous and not wholly sincere retraction, which actually confirms the hold that the myth of the land of Cockaigne had on the peasant imagination. The "paradise of delights" was synonymous with the terrestrial paradise. For the possible connection between the Mohammedan paradise and the land of Cockaigne, see also E. M. Ackermann, *'Das Schlaraffenland' in German Literature and Folksong . . . with an Inquiry into Its History in European Literature* (Chicago, 1944), p. 106. (At any rate the discussion is about asses *(asini)* and not "Urini," as Donadoni has mistakenly read: "Di uno sconosciuto," p. 128).

59

"I was made": See E. Donadoni, "Di uno sconosciuto poema eretico della seconda metà del Cinquecento di autore lucchese," *Studi di letteratura italiana* 2 (1900): 8.

"Philosopher": See above p. 107; BGL, ms. 1271, fol. 30 r. (and Donadoni, "Di uno sconosciuto," p. 40).

118. *"By obeying God"*: BGL, ms. 1271, fol. 12 r.

a more reserved position: I'll pass over those elements that are difficult to interpret, such as the repeated and surprising legitimation of cannibalism, both on earth and in heaven: "To the king for pleasure, to others out of necessity / the eating of human flesh is not impious / the worm eats it and fire devours it / one is earthly, the other is not a little heavenly" (ibid., fol. 13 r.); "If the desire to taste / human flesh as he had it on earth should come to someone / or to try some other food / because frequently here one locks his desire within himself / he immediately sees himself presented with it / and he can eat without strife or battle: / everything is permitted in heaven, everything is well done / because the Law is terminated and the Pact broken" (fol. 17 r.). Unconvincingly Donadoni interprets this last passage as a slangish allusion to sodomy ("Di uno sconosciuto," p. 127).

Pellegrino Baroni: For fuller information on this person, I refer the reader to a forthcoming study promised by A. Rotondò.

In 1570: See ASM, *Inquisizione,* b. 5*b*, fasc. *Pighino Baroni,* only partly paginated. The dossier contains copies of two testimonies pertaining to the Ferrarese trial (1561).

119. *their prominence:* See J. Le Goff, ed., *Hérésies et sociétés dans l'Europe préindustrielle, (11e–18e siècles)* (Paris, 1968), pp. 185–86, 278–80; C.-P. Clasen, *Anabaptism, a Social History (1525–1618): Switzerland, Austria, Moravia, South and Central Germany* (Ithaca and London, 1972), pp. 319–20, 432–35.

a satirical poet: See Andrea da Bergamo [Piero Nelli], *Delle satire alla carlona libro secondo* (Venice, 1566), fol. 36 v.

The age-old hostility: See especially R. Bennett and J. Elton, *History of Corn Milling,* 4 vols., vol. 3, *Feudal Laws and Customs* (London, 1898–1904; reprint ed., New York, 1966), pp. 107 ff. and passim. See also the collection of texts in G. Fenwick Jones, "Chaucer and the Medieval Miller," *Modern Language Quarterly* 16 (1955): 3–15.

"I descended into hell": See A. D'Ancona, *La poesia popolare italiana* (Livorno, 1878), p. 264.

120. *"the soft ground:"* See Andrea da Bergamo [Piero Nelli], *Delle satire,* fol. 35 v.

"about priests and monks": See ASM, *Inquisizione,* b. 5*b*, fasc. *Pighino Baroni,* unnumbered leaves (1 February 1571). As early as the 1561 trial a witness had testified that he had heard Pighino in his mill "speak very badly about the Mass."

Their working conditions: R. Mandrou emphasizes this point in Le Goff, ed., *Hérésies et sociétés,* pp. 279–80.

The case in Modena: See C. Violante, ibid., p. 186.

the bond of direct dependence: See M. Bloch, "Avènement et conquête du moulin à eau," in his *Mélanges historiques,* 2 vols. (Paris, 1963), 2: 800–821.

60

121. *In 1565:* See ASVat., *Concilio Tridentino,* b. 94, fasc. *Visita della diocesi di Modona, 1565,* fol. 90 r. (and see also fol. 162 v. for a visit occurring four years later, and fol. 260 v.).

Natale Cavazzoni: See ASM, *Inquisizione,* b. 5*b*, fasc. *Pighino Baroni,* fols. 18 v.–19 r.

"readings": "lectiones."

"Father": See ASM, *Inquisizione,* b. 5*b*, fasc. *Pighino Baroni,* fol. 24 r.

He repeated the list: Ibid., fol. 25 r.

122. *After arriving in Bologna:* See A. Rotondò, "Per la storia dell'eresia a Bologna nel secolo XVI," *Rinascimento* 13 (1962): 109 ff.

in a passage of the Apologia: See C. Renato, *Opere, documenti, e testimonianze,* ed A. Rotondò, Corpus Reformatorum Italicorum (De Kalb and Chicago, 1972), p. 53.

"Heard in Bologna": "Bononiae audita MDXL in domo equitis Bolognetti."

"in the home of the knight Bolognetti": Rotondò originally identified this individual with Francesco Bolognetti (see "Per la storia," p. 109, n. 3): but the latter became a senator only many years later, in 1555 (see G. Fantuzzi, *Notizie degli scrittori bolognesi* [Bologna, 1782], 2: 244). Thus, Rotondò dropped this identification (see index of names) in his edition of Renato's *Opere.* There is no problem, however, in identifying the person in question with Vincenzo Bolognetti, since he appears after 1534 among the *anziani* and *gonfalonieri:* See G. N. Pasquali Alidosi, *I signori anziani, consoli e gonfalonieri di giustizia della città di Bologna* (Bologna, 1670), p. 79.

first eleven: See ASM, *Inquisizione,* b. 5*b*, fasc. *Pighino Baroni,* fols. 12 v., 30 r.

What is certain . . . is that in October: See Renato, *Opere,* p. 170.

"his name was Turchetto": Ibid., p. 172. His identification with fra Tommaso Paluio d'Apri, nicknamed "il Grechetto," suggested by Rotondò, isn't persuasive. That the person in question may be instead Giorgio Filaletto, known as "Turca" or "Turchetto" was suggested to me by Silvana Seidel Menchi, whom I wish to thank warmly.

123. *"I believed that the souls":* See ASM, *Inquisizione,* b. 5*b*, fasc. *Pighino Baroni,* fol. 33 v.

the doctrine of the sleep of souls: See Renato, *Opere,* pp. 64–65 and Rotondò, "Per la storia," pp. 129 ff.

Venetian Anabaptists: See above p. 73.

a passage such as the one: 1 Thess. 4:13 ff.: "Nolumus autem vos ignorare, fratres, de dormientibus, ut non contristemini sicut et ceteri qui spem non habent. Si enim credimus quod Iesus mortuus est et resurrexit, ita et Deus eos qui dormierunt per Iesum adducet cum eo . . . ." See also G. H. Williams, "Camillo Renato (c. 1500?–1575)" in *Italian Reformation Studies in Honor of Laelius Socinus,* ed. J. Tedeschi (Florence, 1965), p. 107.

124. *he "hadn't read it":* See ASM, *Inquisizione,* b. 5*b*, fasc. *Pighino Baroni,* fol. 2 v.; but cf. fol. 29 v. The *Fioretto* had been placed on the *Index.* See above p. 146.

"And all the things": See *Fioretto,* fol. A vi v.

"there are some things": Ibid., fol. B ii r.

"that all souls": Ibid., fols. C r.–v.

125. *"I have not read":* See ASM, *Inquisizione,* b. 5*b*, fasc. *Pighino Baroni,* fol. 30 r.

"I have never associated": See above pp. 12, 5, etc.

"I wanted to infer": See ASM, *Inquisizione,* b. 5*b*, fasc. *Pighino Baroni,* fol. 20 v.

"It would be as if four soldiers": See ACAU, *Sant'Uffizio,* Trial no. 285, unnumbered leaves (19 July 1599).

Pighino had maintained: See ASM, *Inquisizione,* b. 5*b*, fasc. *Pighino Baroni,* unnumbered leaves (1 February 1571) and fol. 27 r.

"Preaching that men": See above pp. 76, 109.

61

126. *that of the popular roots:* See M. Bakhtin, *Rabelais and His World* (Cambridge, Mass., 1968).

The subsequent period: For a general impression, see J. Delumeau, *Le catholicisme entre Luther et Voltaire* (Paris, 1971), esp. pp. 256 ff. Interesting research possibilities are suggested by J. Bossy, "The Counter-Reformation and the People of Catholic Europe," *Past and Present*, no. 47 (1970): 51–70. I see now that a similar periodization has also been proposed by G. Henningsen, *The European Witch-Persecution* (Copenhagen, 1973), p. 19, who promises to return to this question on another occasion.

with the Peasants' War: It would be very useful to have a comprehensive study of its effects, including those that were indirect and further removed.

the evangelization of the countryside: For this comparison, see Bossy, "The Counter-Reformation."

the rigid control: For vagabonds, see the bibliography cited above at p. 134; for gypsies, see H. Asséo, "Marginalité et exclusion: le traitement administratif des Bohémiens dans la société française du XVIIe siècle," in *Problèmes socio-culturels en France au XVIIe siècle*, ed. H. Asséo and Jean Vittu (Paris, 1974), pp. 11–87.

62

127. *On 5 June 1599:* See ACAU, "*Epistolae Sac. Cong. S. Officii ab anno 1588 usque ad 1613 incl.*," unnumbered leaves. Giulio Antonio Santoro, Cardinal of Santa Severina, barely missed election to the papacy in the conclave that eventually resulted in the elevation of Clement VIII. His reputation for severity was the principal factor that ruined his chances.

    "has revealed himself to be an atheist": Not one, thus, who denied Christ's divinity, but something even worse. On this terminology, see, in general, H. Busson, "Les noms des incrédules au XVIe siècle," *Bibliothèque d'Humanisme et Renaissance* 16 (1954): 273–83.

128. *shortly after:* When, on 26 January 1600, the dowry of Giovanna Scandella was registered with the notary (see above pp. 135–36) the act took place "domi heredum quondam ser Dominici Scandella " (ASP, *Notarile*, b. 488, no. 3786, fol. 27 v.).

    We know this with certainty: See ACAU, "*Ab anno 1601 usque ad annum 1603 incl. a n. 449 usque ad 546 incl.*," Trial no. 497. At any rate, P. Paschini (*Eresia e Riforma cattolica al confine orientale d'Italia*, Lateranum, n.s. 17, nos. 1–4 [Rome, 1951], p. 82), who affirmed on the basis of documents actually examined by him that the only person executed by the Holy Office in the Friuli was a German smith in 1568, should be corrected.

INDEX OF NAMES

This book was composed in Quadritek Palatino text and display type by Brushwood Graphics from a design by Alan Carter. It was printed on 50-lb. Publishers Eggshell Cream and bound in G.S.B. Book Cloth by Universal Lithographers, Inc.